W9-ATW-161

Episode One poster

STAP and Battle Droid
Episode I Toy

G-88 action figure

A MOVIE FAN'S EXTREME GUIDE TO
Collectibles From a
Galaxy Far, Far Away

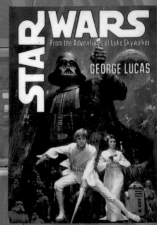

Star Wars poster,
1977

Star Wars Original
Hardcover Novel

Autographed Photo

BY THE STAFF OF
BECKETT HOT TOYS

A Movie Fan's Extreme Guide to Collectibles From a Galaxy Far, Far Away

Presented by Beckett Publications

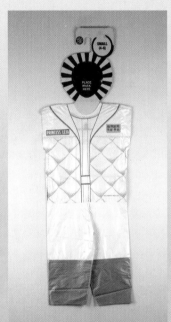

Clockwise from top left: 12-inch IG-88 action figure (1979-80 Star Wars line), Return of the Jedi cap, Princess Leia Halloween costume, Star Wars Insider magazine No. 42, Star Wars Trilogy THX VHS, Pizza Hut Special Edition box.

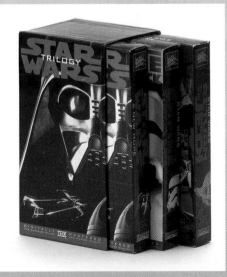

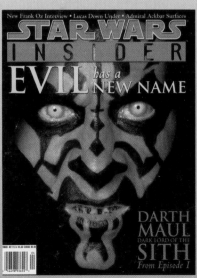

Copyright©1999 by Dr. James Beckett

All rights reserved under International and
Pan-American Copyright Conventions.

Published by: Beckett Publications
15850 Dallas Parkway
Dallas, TX 75248

ISBN: 1-887432-73-6

Beckett® is a registered trademark of
Beckett Publications.

This book is not licensed, authorized or
endorsed by Lucasfilm Ltd. or any company
associated with "Star Wars."

First Edition: April 1999

Beckett Corporate Sales and Information
(972) 991-6657

This reference book is intended to provide an
objective and unbiased representation of values
for the subject collectibles on the secondary market. The independent pricing contained in this
guide reflects current retail rates determined just
prior to printing. They do not reflect for-sale
prices by the author, distributors or any retailers
of collectibles or memorabilia who've contributed
their skills and knowledge to the production of
this guide. All values are in U.S. dollars and are
for informational purposes only.

**Two-Player Collectible Game
cards (clockwise from top
left): AT-AT, C-3PO, Darth
Vader With Lightsaber and
Chewbacca.**

Your Value Guide

When it comes to reporting on values for secondary market collectibles, Beckett Publications is recognized and respected worldwide as the most trusted authority. Founded in 1984 by Dr. James Beckett, the company has sold millions of price guide books and magazines to collectors of sports cards, sports memorabilia, toys and other licensed collectible products.

Presently, Beckett Publications publishes eight popular monthly magazines on collectibles. They are *Beckett Baseball Card Monthly, Beckett Basketball Card Monthly, Beckett Football Card Monthly, Beckett Hockey Collector, Beckett Sports Collectibles and Autographs, Beckett Racing & Motorsports Marketplace, Beckett Hot Toys* and *Beckett Sci-Fi Collector.*

The values published in this guide were compiled in a joint effort by a staff of full-time expert Beckett Publications analysts and independent contributors expert in this field of collecting. The information was gathered from actual buy/sell transactions at collectibles conventions, hobby shops and on-line sites, and, to a lesser extent, from buy/sell advertisements in hobby publications, for-sale prices from collectibles dealers' catalogs and price lists, as well as discussions with leading hobbyists in the U.S. and Canada.

Great care and diligence were taken in determining the prices reported within this book. Our desire to supply independent pricing that is more accurate and reliable than what may be supplied by any other source is paramount to our efforts. It is also a prime reason why the Beckett name is synonymous with collecting and memorabilia. Collectors have come to know Beckett as "the hobby's most reliable and relied upon source."

STAR WARS

Yoda Halloween costume,
Star Wars movie program,
Amanaman action figure
(1985 Power of the Force).

By Matt Brady

Anybody can collect toys. It takes a real fan to collect Star Wars party goods.

Although toys may be what most collectors think about when they think of "Star Wars," toys only make up a tiny portion of the Star Wars collectibles market. There are hundreds of thousands of Star Wars products out there that collectors have been after for years, with more coming out all the time.

While a comprehensive picture of the Star Wars collectibles market would be a book in itself (such as the one you're holding, for example), it's time to take a general look at Star Wars merchandise, old and new, ranging from highly collectible to mildly interesting to stuff someone will give you if you just take it away. With thousands of items to choose from, let's start with the cheap stuff.

Star Wars Freebies and Promotional Goodies

Even today, over 20 years after they came out, food packaging, fast food and promotional giveaways are still excellent entry-level collectibles. For example, the Burger King/Coca-Cola glasses that came out for each of the three original movies are still easy to find, and can be had for under 10 bucks each.

Also included with promotional items are a host of other Star Wars food packages, including Hi-C cans, Kellogg's short-lived C-3PO's cereal, Hershey candy cartons with The Empire Strikes Back pictures, Pepperidge Farm cookies (both the package and the cookies themselves), Pizza Hut boxes, and a host of others, including hundreds of foreign items.

"As other areas of Star Wars collecting start to pick

Lando Calrissian action figure (Power of the Force), Return of the Jedi bed spread, Lando Calrissian Burger King glass.

up activity over the next few years, more and more collectors are going to be looking at these low-end items and realize that they're a real bargain," says Gus Lopez, a Seattle-based Star Wars collector with a 4,000-plus-piece Star Wars collection that includes prototype toys, props and even the coveted Boba Fett cake pan. "Lately, companies were really knocking themselves out to produce some nice-looking products, so they're a pretty cool item from the get go."

The downside of freebie and promotional collectibles, however, is that companies produce a jillion of them, and many more people than your serious Star Wars collector holds on to them for a while, as nearly everyone has heard the urban legend about the grandmother who found Action Comics #1 in her attic, sold it and retired to Florida. Normally, most folks keep Star Wars-themed packaging until spring cleaning, and then they ditch it. With that in mind, Star Wars packaging, whether it's from Pepsi Cubes, Frito-Lay Products, or Mexican cookies, is an area that takes the longest time to show any movement in value. It's just a matter of oversupply and demand.

Along with promotional items and packaging, store displays are another area of Star Wars collecting that has seen increased interest lately. Collectors have been showing interest in displays from the countless Star Wars novels and other Star Wars books, to displays from the Burger King Star Wars drinking glass promotion, cereal displays, Pepsi standees from the Special Edition promotion, and even the in-store display from Wonder Bread's Star Wars card promotion.

The two upsides of display collecting is that, most

often, you can bend the ear of a sympathetic store manager and get the display for free. Also, the art and construction of the displays are normally of very high quality, resulting in a free collectible that's nicer than one you'd pay money for. The downside? Some displays can be huge — requiring lots of dry, cool storage room.

Mid-Range Star Wars — The Stuff Everybody Wants

While any and every established Star Wars collector will tell you there is no science whatsoever to determining which collectible will be the next hot thing, by and large, a good rule of thumb to remember about Star Wars collecting is that the hot, non-toy collectibles tend to be those that intersect with another type of collecting.

For example, Star Wars movie posters are sought after by both Star Wars and movie poster collectors. The story is pretty much the same for lunch boxes, Coca-Cola products, cereal boxes, Ben Cooper Halloween costumes and even cookie jars. If an item crosses into two collectibles markets, you've got twice the demand for that particular item — something that any economist will tell you is a recipe for a higher price.

Additionally, if you look at these other collectible markets, Lopes says you'll get an idea of the potential of Star Wars collectibles. "If you look at old monster movie posters from the '20s, they fetch somewhere in the tens of thousands of dollars," Lopez says. "Some of the more obscure Star Wars posters had a very

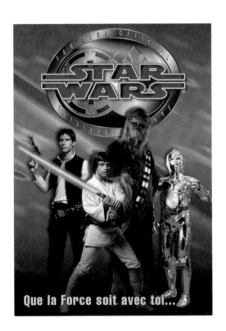

small print run, so it's very easy to see that in a few years, some Star Wars posters, such as the original horizontal Star Wars movie poster, or the subway posters, which have a notorious habit of disappearing, could command major dollars.

"Also, foreign posters are another arena of Star Wars poster collecting which has the added appeal of prospecting, because no one knows exactly what's out there. For many collectors, foreign items have an inherent coolness. The art is usually different than any we've seen here in the States, and everything is in a foreign language. Overall, posters have a long way to go price-wise before they max out."

One last area of mid-range Star Wars collectibles that is still at the entry-level stage are the original Topps Star Wars trading cards.

"You can still find the vintage Topps trading cards for very little money," Lopez says. "In many cases, they're cheaper than some of the recent chase cards, and you can buy full sets of the vintage Star Wars cards for really decent prices, especially if you shop around. There's just an incredible glut of them on the market right now, and not that many people are into collecting them."

**Yoda bubble bath,
Star Wars postcard (France),
Star Wars postcard (Japan),
Walrus Man action figure (1978 Star Wars line).**

Forbidden Fruit: Collecting
What You're Not Supposed to Have

Recently, one of the hottest areas of Star Wars collecting is cast and crew items, such as crew "Blue Harvest" hats (the fake working title for "Return of the Jedi") or cloth patches from the second or third shooting units, such as the Norwegian Unit that filmed many of the Hoth scenes for "The Empire Strikes Back." As such items are in extremely limited supply, they tend to disappear extremely quickly.

Cast and crew item collecting used to be a rather esoteric branch of Star Wars collecting usually left to hard-core "Hollywood insider" collectors. However, over the past decade as the audience has become more savvy of how Hollywood works and what goes on behind the scenes of making movies, interest in crew patches, shooting scripts and other commemorative items has spiked, and the items now demand a pretty penny on the market.

While these are close to the ultimate Star Wars collectible in coolness, cast and crew items are very difficult to find. Many crew members hold on to their memorabilia, and most collectors of these items are apt to lock them up rather than offer them for sale or trade at the next show they attend.

Additionally, no one has a complete list of cast and crew items, so this is an area of Star Wars collecting that is ripe for bootleg items. So collector beware.

Big Ticket: The Cream of the Collectible Crop:

Moving out of the realm of the amateur and casual Star Wars collector, big-ticket items allow many Star Wars fans to become collectors and keep what they feel is a certain amount of "respectability" in their hobby. These are the items that carry a high initial price tag, and would be more often found in a museum than a teenager's room.

Notable among these collectibles are items such as

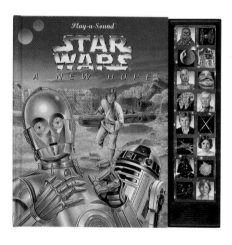

R2-D2 and C-3PO cookie jar,
The Star Wars Storybook (hardcover),
Play-a-Sound Star Wars book,
Imperial Star Destroyer toy (Power of the Force).

Legends in 3 Dimensions' bust series sculpted by Greg Aronowitz, sculptures by Randy Bowen, art prints by Ralph McQuarrie and collector's plates by The Hamilton Collection. While these items are collectible in their own right, they often fall under the two-markets rule. Statue, art and plate collectors are after them as well as Star Wars collectors, something which can drive prices up on certain items.

In addition to the sculptures and more fine-art Star Wars collectibles, prop replicas are an area of interest among some of the more serious collectors. Notable items among the replicas include Icons' lightsaber replicas, Don Post Studios' deluxe Darth Vader, Boba Fett and Scout Trooper helmets, as well as a life-sized Stormtrooper offered by The Sharper Image, among others.

However, for the investment-minded, big-ticket items are very slow to appreciate. Due to their high price tag, demand is kept fairly low, since not every Star Wars fan will be able to afford a Stormtrooper to stand in the living room.

Additionally, Lopez warns that since Lucasfilm only granted a few licenses to produce replica props, much of what you see out in the marketplace is bootleg. Sometimes the bootlegs have authentic origins, perhaps being originally cast from an actual prop, such as a Stormtrooper rife. More often however, a fan with a love of mechanical design and the right materials crafted the replica in the garage.

Beyond Big Ticket: the Holy Grails of Star Wars Collecting

You've reached nirvana. These are the ultimate collectibles, actual props and costumes from the movies, well-deserving of the label: ultra-rare and ultra-collectible.

Lopez, who recently vacationed in Tunisia (a.k.a. Tatooine in "Star Wars" and "The Phantom Menace") to scout out shooting locations and possibly nab a lost gaffi stick from a sand dune, explains that this is an arena of collecting usually left to people with the major bucks. "It's really not that mainstream of a collecting area, because almost nothing is in circulation, and anything that does come up usually commands a price in the thousands to hundreds of thousands of dollars," Lopez says.

And he would know. The prize piece of his collection is a square-foot section from the Death Star surface used for close-up special effects shots in "Return of the Jedi," a piece he dropped a sizable chunk of change to acquire.

However, before you lay down $500 for the net backpack in which Chewbacca carried the blasted-apart C-3PO during the final scenes of "The Empire Strikes Back," be warned that there are a lot of fakes out there, with probably more fakes being sold than the real things.

The Bizarre

A chapter about non-toy Star Wars items wouldn't be complete without a mention of these — the few, the weird, the items that make you scratch your head

Return of the Jedi music carrying case,
Star Wars gift wrap,
Darth Vader soap.

and wonder what Lucasfilm was thinking. For a collector with a bit of money and a sense of humor, collecting oddball Star Wars items could be a definite niche in the marketplace.

Weird items range from Wilton Star Wars cake pans (including a Boba Fett cake mold), to glue sticks packaged with Ewok figures made in Italy, to Australian Star Wars Dog Chow, and loads of others. Needless to say, there are a ton of weird products out there with the Star Wars logo emblazoned proudly across the top. Start hunting and keep smiling.

What We'll All Be Talking About

With a tidal wave of "The Phantom Menace" merchandise poised to strike virtually every retail market in the coming months, there's no doubt that it will have an effect on Star Wars collecting. What will it be?

Most likely, with the new movie's release, collectors and collections will be divided into three eras, Vintage Star Wars, The Interim Years and The Prequel Years. Prices and activity in each collectible period may fluctuate for a period until the third prequel hits theaters in 2005.

One thing that is sure to happen, Lopez says, is that the market will diversify as young kids are once again enthralled by "Star Wars."

"For the last ten years, older collectors have really been driving the market," Lopez says. "That's why we're only seeing what collectors want — toys, high-end merchandise and promotional items that Lucasfilm puts out to maintain brand interest. With the new film, little kids will be jazzed about "Star Wars," and will want anything with "The Phantom Menace" characters on it. You can bet that the Lucasfilm licensees are going to respond and crank out notebooks, preschool toys, erasers, bowls, clothes, bed sheets, soap and shampoo dispensers and nearly everything else we saw before. In addition, there will be a major tie-in with Pepsi and Taco Bell, which may include all the Pepsi brands, including Frito-Lay. There's going to be a lot of stuff out there."

However, with all the new "The Phantom Menace" products coming out, it's safe to say that it will be awhile before any of them gain value as collectibles. Why? When "Star Wars" was released in 1977, it took everyone by surprise, and as a result, organized Star Wars collecting took a few years to get geared up and moving. In 1999, Star Wars collectors are lean, savvy and ready to pounce. Stockpiling of Phantom merchandise is going to be the norm among many collectors for the next few years.

With all the attention being paid to the new movie, what's the hapless vintage or interim collector to do? Good question. On one hand, classic Star Warts collectors could find themselves up a creek as manufacturers opt to produce merchandise based on the new movie rather than the 22-year-old movie. On the other hand, vintage items could skyrocket in value as an even larger portion of the population, crazed by "The Phantom Menace," goes back and takes another look at the original films and their merchandise. Either way, it's going to be a very active time for Star Wars collectors.

Star Wars metal lunchbox, "All I Need To Know" commercial poster.

The Force will be with you . . .

Despite the picture painted in this chapter, as far as collecting goes, many collectors feel that Star Wars collecting is in its infancy, with a lot of room for expansion, both in the number of collectors and the prices they're willing to pay for anything related to "Star Wars." Parts of the market, such as toy collecting, matured very fast, but many segments are still virtually ignored by collectors, providing plenty of room for the new collector looking for some bargain collectibles.

If you're thinking of getting in, don't wait too long. As time goes by, many areas are showing signs of an impending boom in prices that could keep new collectors out. However, if the last 20 years have shown us anything, it's that as long as there is "Star Wars," there will always be plenty of merchandise to tempt the collector.

By Steve Fritz

A true story.

The Chelsea district of New York City is notorious for its open-air flea markets. From the corner of 26th Street and the Avenue of the Americas you can walk one block any way and bump right into an abandoned parking lot loaded with dealer tables piled high with all manner of paraphernalia, memorabilia and out-and-out strangeness. Bargains can be had, but you better know what you're doing before you ask said dealer what he or she wants for that pretty goo gaw that just grabbed your eye.

Case in point. I'm at such an establishment on 25th Street. On one of the tables is, of all darn things, a Darth Vader speaker phone. The item is in extremely good condition. I can't detect a bit of chipped paint or plastic anywhere on it. It also comes with the instruction book. The proprietor of the table wanted $100 for the speaker phone.

As is the case with any such type of financial transaction, some haggling was to be expected. I gave it my best. The proprietor would have nothing to do with it. Finally, I put the item down and went on my way.

My reason for this was, quite frankly, I

Luke Skywalker in Bespin Fatigues (1980 The Empire Strikes Back line), Greedo carded and loose (1978 Star Wars line).

was not sure if the item was 1) still being manufactured; and, more importantly, 2) if a Darth Vader Speaker Phone is truly worth $100 off of a dealer table, particularly as it came without the original box.

Now you see why there's such a need for a book such as *A Movie Fan's Extreme Guide to Collectibles from a Galaxy Far, Far Away.*

You see, Star Wars collecting is a very established hobby. It's been so for many a year. A woman named Linda Kyro published the first amateur magazine, the Star Wars Collectors Trading Post, for nearly a decade. Then she saw the writing on the wall.

Actually, Kyro saw it in the form of movie posters trumpeting a brand spanking new Star Wars film, "The Phantom Menace." She also saw the newsstands which have recently been flooded with all manner of Star Wars publications, the one I write for, *Beckett Sci-Fi Collector*, among them.

Actually, the first is responsible for the second.

Over the mists of time, a lot of people have forgotten how huge a phenomenon the first three Star Wars films actually were (and still are). Each one was the biggest grossing film of its respective year. Further, a lot of people bought tons of licensed merchandise due to the first three films. Now here it is over a decade later and it appears it's starting all over again.

In fact, I wouldn't be surprised if the mania surrounding the collecting aspect of "The Phantom Menace" is twice what it was the last time. The first three films concentrated on one generation of collectors. They were basically young fans who were in total thrall with the adventures of Luke Skywalker, Princess Leia and Han Solo. "The Phantom Menace" is undoubtedly going to strike a chord with two generations: the original Star Wars fans who still love the first three movies . . . and their kids.

Another thing about this new generation of kids: They are much more collecting savvy than their parents. The original Star Wars collectors were the type who were pleased just to have found a certain action figure at a toy store or read the further adventures of the original three heroes in a Marvel comic at a local drug store. Their kids know about such things as retailer exclusive. They haunt comic book shops for alternative covers of the Dark Horse lines of Star Wars titles.

X-Wing with Dagobah background play set, Marvel Comic No. 2, Marvel Comic inside spread, Marvel Comic No. 1.

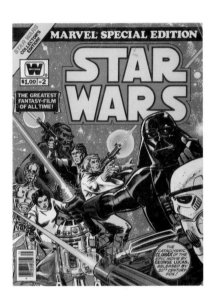

Further, these kids might easily buy two of each item. They'll buy two of the action figures so they can rip one out of the packaging and pose it in all manner of ways. The other they'll carefully store as an investment.

With their comics they'll read one and wrap the other one in a plastic bag with cardboard backing.

To top it off, these kids know there are a lot of magazines, Web sites and other forms of information out there that specialize in the latest information, pricing and otherwise, that they'll need for their collections. While it's my personal opinion that I write for one of the best publications, I don't take any guff from the fact I know these youngsters are comparing Beckett to two to three more. Heck, they're all racked up against each other. Don't tell me I don't know the score.

Which probably explains why Kyro (our erstwhile publisher) sadly stepped out of the field. She was of the first generation of collectors. She saw that an operation such as Beckett has resources at its disposal she could never match. Personally, I'd love to collect her magazine for its historical value, but that's just me. The last time I talked to her, Kyro told me she's concentrating on finishing off her collection of 1977-to-1982 merchandise. Here's hoping she gets everything she wants at the absolutely best price possible. She's earned her props.

Which leads to the next major question. Say you are just getting started and want to build a collection of your own. Where do you start?

There are some basic premises when it comes to collecting Star Wars memorabilia. The first, and the most important, is there's going to be a ton of it in a galaxy-wide array of types. I break the variety into several distinct categories:

1) Action Figures, Dolls, Model Kits and Statues;

2) Books and Comics;

3) Trading Cards and Similar Collectibles;

4) Games and Collectible Card Games;

5) Actual Movie Memorabilia;

6) Miscellaneous.

For more details on these items, check the rest of the contents of this book. There's a lot of valuable information in there.

On the other hand, let's take a look at one of my particularly favorite categories: books and comics. If you are collecting

**Star Wars Insider poster,
The Empire Strikes Back folder,
Question and Answer Book About Space (hardcover),
The Empire Strikes Back Official Poster Monthly No. 1.**

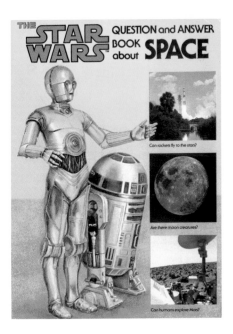

the comics, are you interested in the original titles published by Marvel Comics or the later ones published by Dark Horse? Story-wise, I think Dark Horse supersedes the Marvel stuff by leap years. On the other hand, the Marvel books are harder to find because they are 20 years older and hark back to the day when a lot of kids used to read those comics instead of storing them in plastic bags. Guess which commands the higher prices?

Let's take something that would appear slightly simpler, the Star Wars collectible card game (CCG). Only one company has ever done it: Decipher. Like most CCGs, cards were issued in three very distinctive scarcity levels: common, uncommon and rare. So, it should figure that one rare card should be worth about the same as another, right? Wrong.

The first edition of any of Decipher's Star Wars cards comes with a signature black border, while later editions have a white one. Also, the first print run is usually also the smallest of the lots. As such, if someone offered to buy a black-bordered Luke Skywalker card from you at a price of a white border, you'd better think about it. There's a 25 percent to 50 percent difference in value between the two, with the black bordered card being all the more valuable.

Then there's another key element to collecting a CCG, and that's called "playability." If someone offered you a one-up trade of his Luke Skywalker for your Darth Vader (assuming they're both first editions), again it's time to think twice about it. A Mint Luke is about $60. A Mint Vader is about $80. The reason for the difference is the playability. I can win a lot more games with that Vader card than with the Luke. Don't think any veteran Star Wars player doesn't know that.

These are the types of factors taken into account when devising the prices of these various items.

My next major bit of knowledge to share with you: As there are a galaxy of different Star Wars products out there, there's also a virtual ton of each item available. If walking down an aisle of any major toy store isn't enough to convince you, let me give you another example.

One of the best ways to find out about Star Wars merchandise is to go out on to the World Wide Web. Boot up your fave Web browser and go to the search section. Type in the words "Star Wars

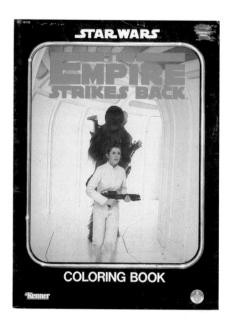

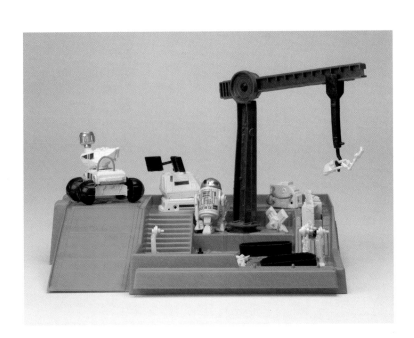

**Softcover book included with original Star Wars Official Soundtrack, Droid Factory play set,
The Empire Strikes Back coloring book.**

toys" and see what happens. If you get less than 100 different selections, it's time to check out another browser.

Quite frankly, Lucasfilm Ltd., the producers of the Star Wars series, made darn sure there are a lot of licenses passed out, both during the original films and with the new series. They have one of the largest toy manufacturers in the world, Hasbro, handling their toy lines. Hasbro has to fill the needs of a number of major toy chains. There's going to be a lot of product out there.

So my third piece of advice is equally simple: Just because one toy dealer is selling an action figure for $10 doesn't mean the guy at the table a few feet away isn't going to be selling it for $8. Be a smart shopper. Dare to compare and don't take any guff from anyone claiming an item is flying off the shelf. What's flying off one dealer's shelf is lingering at another's.

Which leads to my next major piece of advice. There's going to be so MUCH Star Wars merchandise released over the few years that it will be virtually impossible to collect it all. That said, stick to what you like. If you like to read, the books and comics are the way to go. If you're a more social type, there's not only the CCG's, but some fine role-playing, board and electronic games out there. If you want to impress your friends when you throw a party at your house, then get a nice display case and collect action figures, dolls, or if you really have some money to throw around, ceramic statuettes. But most important of all, make sure it's something you are going to like to do or show off 20 years from now. What's the real value of an item if it's stored in a trunk in your attic? Not much at all.

From there, actually collecting is a pretty simple science. Keep your items in their original packaging as much as possible. In the case of things like the statues, sure you'll want to display them . . . but keep the boxes in a nice dry place just in case you do want to get rid of it some day. Believe me, collectors will give you a lot more if the original packaging is readily available. The value of said item can double if it comes with its original box.

As for sources of information, take some time to scour the Web. It's an incredible resource that's getting bigger and bigger every day. Comic book shops and toy stores are incredible places to

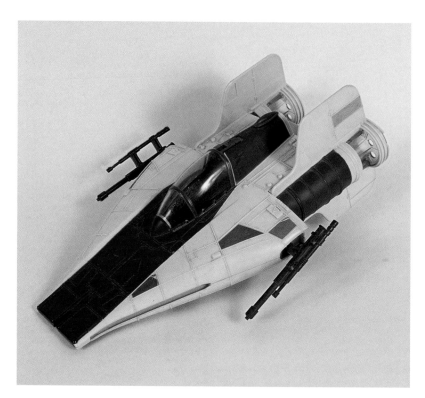

(Above) A-Wing Fighter toy (1978-85 Star Wars accessory), (Opposite) A-Wing Fighter toy (1995-98 Power of the Force accessory)

meet fellow collectors. Hit them for the latest conventions — the Internet's another incredible source for this info — those places offer many items you'll be hard pressed to find anywhere else.

But more important than anything else, shop. After you shop some, shop some more. Then shop again before you even think about purchasing anything. With the incredible amount of Star Wars merchandise out there, it's very easy to see such things as a Darth Vader Speaker Phone over and over again if you put your mind to it.

In fact, I did just that the next day after my excursion in Chelsea. I found one at a Radio Shack with its original packaging for a lot less than $100.

Star Wars: Episode I — The Phantom Menace

It was in May of 1980 that Time magazine stumbled upon a little-known bit of trivia that would later turn out to be oh so significant. Seems a film released that year called "The Empire Strikes Back," a sequel to the 1977 box office smash "Star Wars," was subtitled "Episode V." So, would that mean "Star Wars" was actually Episode IV? Begging of course, the question, "What happened to Episodes I-III?" At the time, nobody realized the original "Star Wars," the first of what will be six Star Wars films, was actually Episode IV of a much longer saga stored somewhere in the deep recesses of the mind of its creator, George Lucas.

"Star Wars," now referred to by knowing fans by its subtitle, "Episode IV — A New Hope," was the most feasible film for Lucas to make in terms of special effects technology available in 1977. Now, a full 22 years later, Lucas has come out of his hiding of sorts and deemed it an appropriate time to let us all know what happened an even longer time ago, in a galaxy far, far away.

"Star Wars: Episode I — The Phantom Menace" is unquestionably the most hyped film in history. (That's 22 years of hype, to be exact.) And along with a new Star Wars film comes new characters and new collectibles. The world got its first glimpse of a STAP and Battle Droid in the fall of 1998, just in time for Christmas, in the form of an Episode I Sneak Preview toy from Kenner. Then came Mace Windu, a 3 3/4-inch action figure available only by

Episode I teaser poster (fan club Version A),

Darth Vader with Removable Helmet (Power of the Force) revealing Anakin Skywalker,

Obi-Wan Kenobi action figure (1978 Star Wars) now known as an older version of Episode I's Ewan McGregor.

mailing in six proofs-of-purchase from any Star Wars figures, followed closely by the Gian Speeder & Theed Palace play set that fell under the Star Wars Action Fleet line.

It was brilliant marketing. Writing on the back of the boxes of each collectible gave fans the tiniest hint of the plot of the upcoming prequel, whetting our appetites just enough for a movie that wouldn't come out for five more months. ("The small planet of Naboo has been invaded. . . ." according to the back of the Gian Speeder box.)

And who can forget the Episode I teaser poster that depicts Anakin Skywalker casting a shadow eerily similar to the villain he would someday become? By February 1999, three months after the poster's release, the item was selling for $50 to $150 on the secondary market. Originally available from the fan club for a mere $15, the value shot up primarily due to rumors that a very limited number were printed.

At the time this book was printed, there were precious few Episode I collectibles available, but the deluge was expected to strike the U.S. by the start of summer of '99. Just as Episode I shows that Lucas hasn't lost his filmmaking touch, The Phantom Menace collectibles show that Lucasfilm Ltd. and its licensees still have their fingers on the pulse of the adults and children who can't wait for the first action figure from Episode II, tentatively scheduled for release in 2002.

Mace Windu

SPECS: Higher-up member of the Jedi Council.

Actor Samuel L. Jackson made no attempt to hide his boyish desire to play even a small role in the new Star Wars movie, and George Lucas was listening. Jackson, playing the role of Windu, endeared himself immediately to Star Wars fans everywhere with his memorable line in the first Episode I teaser movie trailer: "You refer to the prophecy of the one who will bring balance to the Force. And you believe it is this boy?" Although he didn't wield a lightsaber in that first trailer, that first Mace Windu action figure came with a blue lightsaber that looks like it could have been taken from one of the several Luke Skywalker '90s Power of the Force figures.

Mace Windu Episode I Sneak Preview action figure, with a lightsaber similar to those found in several Luke Skywalker Power of the Force figures.

Cool
Collectibles

✓ Mace Windu 3 3/4-inch action figure, Episode I (Kenner)
.... $15 loose, $30 in package

Battle Droid

SPECS: Members of the bad guys' army in Episode I.

They're not Stormtroopers, but they basically serve the same function. Images of the computer-generated Battle Droid characters had fans buzzing months before "The Phantom Menace" came out. Similarities can be seen in the Battle Droid and the droid 8D8 from "Return of the Jedi," and one could also make the argument that the Battle Droids are merely EV-9D9 look-alikes with a new paint job. Regardless, they are to Episode I what the Stormtroopers were to Episodes IV-VI: fierce fighting machines that shoot first, ask questions later. Fans got their first look at the STAP, the Battle Droid's vehicle of choice, when the Sneak Preview action figure came out months before the film. (The box says it's a "small, one-pilot repulsor-lift vehicle outfitted with two laser cannons.") Viewers got a chance to see the STAP in action for the first time near the end of the teaser trailer.

STAP and Battle Droid Episode I Sneak Preview toy, with a droid similar to those found in the 8D8 (1983 Return of the Jedi) and EV-9D9 action figures (Power of the Force).

Cool
Collectibles

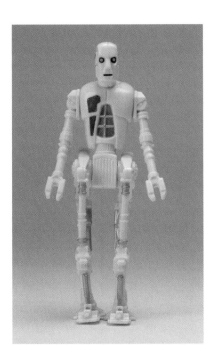

✓ STAP and Battle Droid, Episode I (Kenner)
....$10 loose, $20 in package

Others

SPECS: Comparisons between Episodes I and IV.

Let's see . . . . where have we seen that Gian Speeder before? Perhaps it reminds you of Luke Skywalker's Landspeeder in Episode IV. And the Battle Droid? Looks suspiciously similar in function to the Stormtroopers that debuted in "Star Wars." Indeed, the creators of "The Phantom Menace" haven't forgotten their roots. Much of Episode I takes place where Episode IV began: the desert planet of Tatooine, apparently the home of Luke Skywalker AND Luke's father before him, Anakin. After all, this is the same far, far away galaxy as in Episodes IV-VI. Perhaps it makes sense that the vehicles and robots and human characters would be similar in nature. Yoda, several hundred years old

Gian Speeder & Theed Palace play set (Episode I Sneak Preview), Vanity Fair magazine with "The Phantom Menace" cover, Yoda mouse pad.

Cool
Collectibles

✓ Gian Speeder & Theed Palace play set, Star Wars Action Fleet
(Galoob) .... $10 loose, $20 in package

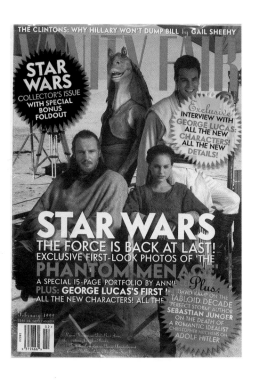

in "The Empire Strikes Back," is as strong as ever in "The Phantom Menace." The Emperor of "Return of the Jedi," we learn, was once a Senator named Palpatine. And C-3PO and R2-D2, who George Lucas has promised will appear in each and every Star Wars film, were there to observe it all (although C-3PO doesn't seem quite finished in Episode I). Princess Leia's birth mother is in Episode I in the form of a young queen, and a Wookie similar to Chewbacca even holds a seat on the Galactic Senate. Collectors are no doubt scrambling today to guess which alien pulled from a background scene that hardly anybody noticed will have an action figure that will be worth thousands of dollars 10 years from now.

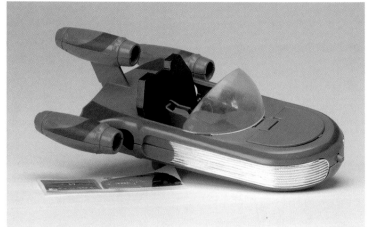

The Emperor (1983 Return of the Jedi action figure) shows up as a younger man in Episode I. Other featured collectibles include early versions of C-3PO (1979 Star Wars 12-inch action figure shown here) and R2-D2 (Power of the Force action figure), as well as vehicles similar to the Landspeeder (1978-85 Star Wars accessory).

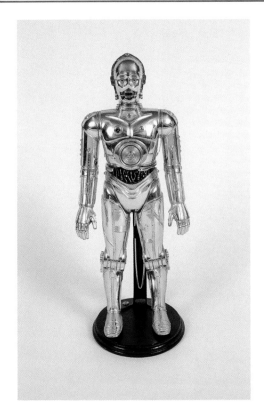

More collectibles related to Episode I: Obi-Wan Kenobi folder (look for the younger Obi-Wan Phantom Menace items), Chewbacca Power of the Force action figure (look for the Wookie Senator), Barada 1985 Power of the Force action figure (keep your eyes peeled for all kinds of bizarre aliens) and Prince Leia Power of the Force figure (look for many laser gun-toting Queen Amidala figures).

Star Wars: Episode IV — A New Hope

The movie that started it all, referred to simply as "Star Wars" by an audience that had no reason at the time to suspect that it was actually "Episode IV," certainly has aged well. Asked in 1998 to name the top 100 movies of all time, the American Film Institute placed "Star Wars" No. 15, behind just "Schindler's List" among films released since 1975. Although many critics will tell you "The Empire Strikes Back" was actually technically the best film of the original trilogy, there's no replacing the refreshing originality of Episode IV.

No one really knew what to think of "Star Wars" when it first came out in 1977. When the Special Edition version of the film was released in 1997, many publications reprinted their original review of "Star Wars" that had run 20 years earlier. Most reviewers at the time dismissed the film as a trend that would soon pass. More

A long
time ago
in a galaxy
far, far away...

STAR WARS

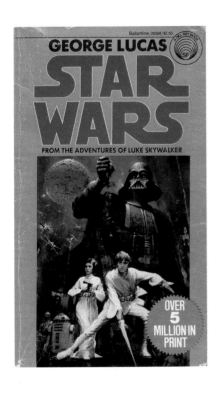

**Teser "B" theatrical poster,
Star Wars softcover novel,
Marvel Comic No. 24.**

than two decades later, fans are still introducing the films to their children, trying to explain how the special effects were so revolutionary for their time.

And then there's the collectibles. You could literally decorate your entire house with Star Wars-related items (some people no doubt have). From bedspreads to kitchenware, they made it all, and now rabid fans are trying to scoop it back up, creating the most active marketplace around for movie memorabilia.

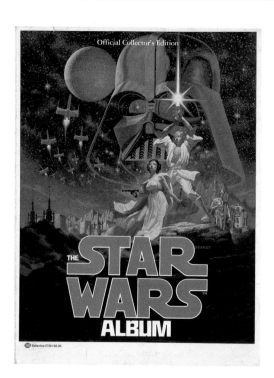

Star Wars Album poster,
The Star Wars Storybook
(softcover),
Time magazine (Feb. 1997),
The World of Star Wars
book.

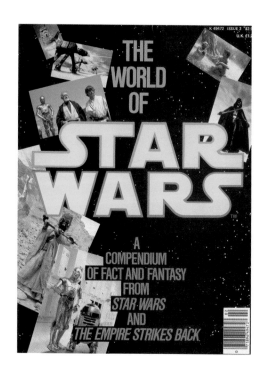

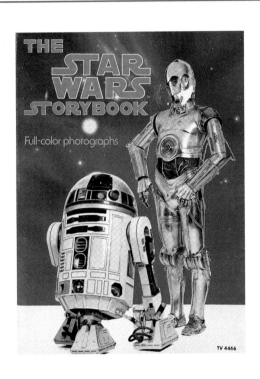

TV 4466

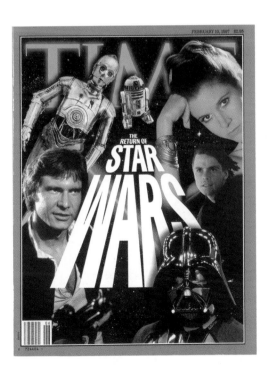

Luke Skywalker

SPECS: The "hero" in the "hero journey" of Episodes IV-VI.

If George Lucas' story was indeed inspired by Joseph Campbell's writings concerning the journey of the hero, then Luke is indeed the main man in question. From his humble beginnings as a farm boy on a sweltering desert planet, to the revelation that he is the son of Darth Vader (a.k.a. Anakin Skywalker) and the sister of Princess Leia, to his ascent into Jedi Knight-dom, young Skywalker plays a pivotal role in the original trilogy, which in turn resulted in a pivotal role in the vast universe of Star Wars collectibles. There are literally hundreds of Luke-related items, ranging in value from $2 to thousands of dollars. As Star Wars collecting grew in popularity, so did the size of Luke's muscles in his collectibles. The classic Star Wars

Cool
Collectibles

**Luke Skywalker action figure from original Star Wars line,
Luke Skywalker X-Wing pilot action figure,
Luke Skywalker Jedi Knight Special Edition action figure.**

✓ Luke Skywalker 3 3/4-inch action figure, classic Star Wars (Kenner) .... $30 loose, $350 in package

✓ Luke Skywalker 12-inch action figure, classic Star Wars (Kenner) .... $150 loose, $325 in package

✓ Luke Skywalker: X-Wing Pilot 3 3/4-inch action figure, classic Star Wars (Kenner) .... $12 loose, $150 in package

✓ Luke Skywalker: Jedi Knight Power of the Force Special Edition 3 3/4-inch action figure (Kenner) .... $40 loose, $100 in package

✓ X-Wing collector plate (Hamilton) $40

✓ Luke Skywalker cup (Sigma Ceramics) $30

✓ Han and Luke T-shirt (Star Tours) $25

✓ Luke Skywalker and Yoda placemat (Sigma) $20

✓ Luke Skywalker jigsaw puzzle (Kenner) $20

✓ X-Wing model kit (Structors) $20

✓ The Empire Strikes Back Luke collector's glass (Burger King) $10

✓ Darth Vader and Luke Skywalker pajamas (Wilker Brothers) $10

✓ Landspeeder, classic Star Wars (Kenner) .. $20 loose, $80 in package

action figures provide a more, shall we say, "realistic" version of Skywalker's physique, while the Power of the Force line from the '90s depicts what Luke might have looked like on steroids.

**Luke Skywalker
12-inch action figure,
X-Wing ship from
the Power of the Force line,
Landspeeder from the classic
Star Wars accesories line,
Luke Skywalker glass from
Burger King.**

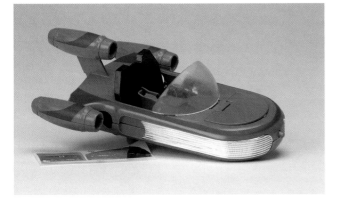

✓ X-Wing Fighter Power of the Force vehicle (Kenner)
.... $10 loose, $40 in package

✓ Luke Skywalker coloring book (Kenner) $5

✓ Luke Skywalker soap (Omni Cosmetics) $5

✓ Luke Skywalker with lightsaber magnet (Ata Boy) $5

✓ Return of the Jedi Storybook (Random House) $5

✓ X-Wing Hologarm key chain (A.H. Prismatic) $5

✓ Luke Skywalker game card from Star Wars Two-Player Customizable
Game (Decipher) $5

Luke Skywalker soap,
X-Wing collector's plate,
Star Wars novel (featuring old-
school Luke drawing on the
cover),
The Empire Strikes Back coloring
book with Bespin Luke on the
cover.

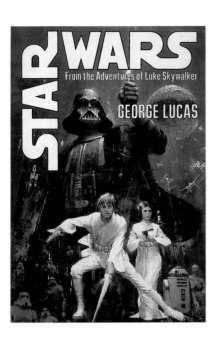

Han Solo

SPECS: The perfect Force-less foil for Luke Skywalker.

It was a hot topic of debate for anyone under 20 in the late '70s and early '80s: Who would you rather be, Luke Skywalker or Han Solo? If you thought it was cooler just to blast your enemies instead of using an old Jedi mind trick, Han Solo was your man. Unquestionably a good guy, Solo still was many of the things Luke wasn't: cocky, smooth-talking, cunning and never one to back away from a straight fight. If you're more of the Solo kind, you had to have the Han Solo Laser Rifle, a nice replica of the one used in the films. In fact, when it comes to collectibles, Solo can hold his own with any of the Star Wars characters, certainly in terms of quantity. There's a slew of books depicting the further adventures of our favorite smuggler. The man wore many different hats (and jackets, and pants, and shirts, etc.), all of which are depicted in the action figures.

Cool
Collectibles

Han Solo
12-inch action figure, two variations from the classic Star Wars line of action figures (note the size of the heads).

✓ Chewbacca and Han Solo toothbrush (Oral B) $10

✓ Han Solo bookmark (Random House) $10

✓ Han Solo's Rescue pop-up book (Random House) $5

✓ Poster with Millennium Falcon and second Death Star (Portal) $10

✓ Han Solo and the Lost Legacy novel (Ballantine) $2

✓ Millennium Falcon game card from Star Wars Two-Player ....
   Customizable Game (Decipher) $5

✓ Millennium Falcon Collector Plate (Hamilton) $40

✓ Han Solo and Princess Leia medallion (Craft House) $30

✓ Han Solo and Chewbacca glass (Coca-Cola) $5

✓ Han Solo and Chewbacca jigsaw puzzle (Kenner) $2

✓ Han Solo in Carbonite key chain (Placo, FAO Schwartz exclusive) .$10

✓ Millennium Falcon model kit (Structors) $30

✓ Hoth Tissue Box with Han Solo $20

✓ Millennium Falcon magnet (A.H. Prismatic) $3

✓ Han Solo pewter miniature $25

✓ Han Solo with larger head 3 3/4-inch action figure, classic Star Wars
   line (Kenner) ....$40 loose, $700 in package

✓ Han Solo with smaller head 3 3/4-inch action figure, classic Star Wars

Millenium Falcon ship from the Power of the Force line,
12-inch Han Solo in Hoth Gear,
Han Solo and the Lost Legacy softcover novel,
Han Solo action figure with carbonite
from the Power of the Force line,
Millenium Falcon collector's plate.

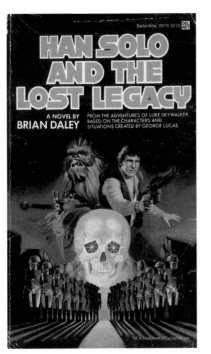

line (Kenner) ....$30 loose, $600 in package

✓ Han Solo 12-inch action figure, classic Star Wars line (Kenner)
......................................$250 loose, $500 in package

✓ Han Solo in Carbonite, 1985 Star Wars: Power of the Force line
(Kenner)$100 loose, $250 in package

✓ Millenium Falcon, Power of the Force (Kenner)
......................................$25 loose, $60 in package

Star Wars
commercial poster,
Millenium Falcon card from
Collectible Card Game,
Han Solo and Chewbacca
toothbrush.

Princess Leia

SPECS: The heroine of Episodes IV-VI.

Strong with the Force is she. That's because the only Force-wielding female in the original trilogy is Luke's sister, which means she's also the daughter of Darth Vader, and, as we learn in the films, the Force is strong in that family. We dare you to think of any of your female friends from the '70s who didn't want to be the determined and attractive Princess Leia. When young women played with Star Wars toys, they played with Princess Leia, whose fashion show is a featured element of the 1998 interactive CD-ROM "Star Wars: Behind the Magic." The interesting choice of outfits in Jabba's palace in "Return of the Jedi" not withstanding, Leia and her related collectibles may be best known for the cinnamon-bun hairdo in the original "Star Wars." At the height of Star Wars' popularity, her Halloween costume was a hit among girls ages 5-15.

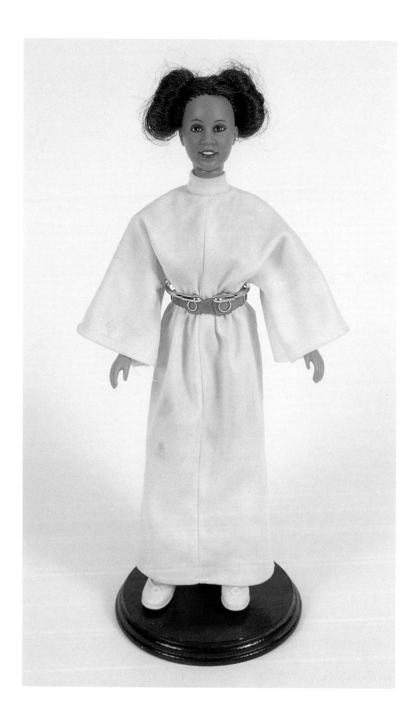

Cool
Collectibles

**Princess Leia 12-inch action figure,
Leia action figure from
classic Star Wars line,
Leia in Hoth Gear action figure.**

✓ Princess Leia 12-inch action figure, classic Star Wars (Kenner)
.... $125 loose, $250 in package

✓ Princess Leia 3 3/4-inch action figure, classic Star Wars (Kenner)
.... $40 loose, $300 in package

✓ Princess Leia Hoth Outfit 3 3/4-inch action figure, The Empire Strikes Back (Kenner) .... $20 loose, $125 in package

✓ Princess Leia as Jabba's Prisoner 3 3/4-inch action figure, Power of the Force (Kenner) .... $2 loose, $15 in package

✓ Princess Leia photo autographed by Carrie Fisher $60

✓ Princess Leia T-shirt (Changes) $15

✓ The Courtship of Princess Leia novel $10

✓ Princess Leia Halloween card (Drawing Board) $10

✓ The Empire Strikes Back notebook (Stuart Hall) $5

✓ Princess Leia soap (Omni Cosmetics) $5

Carrie Fisher
autographed photo,
Princess Leia as Jabba's
Slave Power of the Force
action figure,
Princess Leia soap,
Rebel Blockade Runner
(Princess Leia's ship)
Power of the Force
vehicle.

SPECS: One-half of the Star Wars saga's dynamic droid duo.

R2-D2, referred to as "Artoo-Detoo" on some collectibles, is your basic astromech droid from a galaxy far, far away. What CAN'T this 3-foot tall bundle of electricity do? We already know he can: project a 3-D movie, perform on-the-spot repairs on an X-wing, communicate with ANY other machine (Death Star, Millennium Falcon, etc.), cut through rope, open locked doors . . . the list goes on and on, and will expand further in Episodes I-III as Artoo and his pal C-3PO continue to witness the entire Star Wars saga. Despite the fact that he never utters a single English word, R2-D2 has more personality than most human characters in films today and remains one of the most highly collected Star Wars figure. Can you imagine not having an R2-D2 to play with while growing up? His distant relative,

Radio-controlled disc-firing R2-D2 toy from Japan, R2-D2 action figure from classic Star Wars line, Kenny Baker-signed action figure.

Cool Collectibles

✓ Remote control R2-D2 with firing discs (from Japan) $500

✓ R2-D2 3 3/4-inch action figure, classic Star Wars ....
.... $15 loose, $150 in package

✓ R2-D2 bank (Roman Ceramics) $50

✓ R2-D2 3 3/4-inch action figure, Power of the Force (Kenner), signed by
Kenny Baker $30

✓ R2-D2 van model (Structors) $35

✓ C3-PO and R2-D2 blue rain jacket with pockets (Adam Joseph) ... $30

✓ R2-D2 Underoos (Union Underwear) $15

✓ R2-D2 with sensorscope 3 3/4-inch action figure, The Empire Strikes .
Back .. .. $10 loose, $60 in package

✓ R2-D2 Pizza Hutt box (1997) $5

✓ R2-D2 cake candle (Wilton) $5

R5-D4, makes a cameo in the original "Star Wars," and various astromech droids with striking similarities to Artoo show up throughout all the films.

R2-D2 with sensorscope action figure, R2-D2 cake candle, Pizza Hut promo box, R5-D4 action figure.

C-3PO

SPECS: R2-D2's sometimes annoying but always faithful companion.

Fluent in more than six million forms of communication, C-3PO (or "See-Threepio"), a protocol droid, can calculate the probabilities of successfully navigating an asteroid field faster than he can blink. It was C-3PO who spoke some of the first words in the original "Star Wars." "This is madness . . . we're doomed" immediately established C-3PO as the worrywart, contrasting R2-D2's level-headed optimism. In fact, one of the most memorable exchanges in recent film history wasn't between two people, but instead two bickering droids. As R2-D2 asks C-3PO, in a series of whistles and beeps, if he thinks Luke likes him, Threepio responds, "No, I don't think he likes you at all." Artoo lets out another hopeful inquiring bleep, to which C-3PO states point blank, "No, I don't like you either."

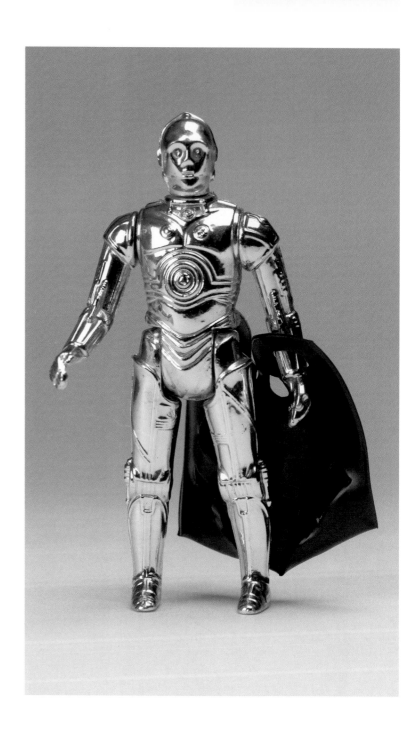

Cool
Collectibles

✓ See-Threepio (Removable Limbs) 3 3/4-inch action figure, The Empire Strikes Back (Kenner) . . . . $10 loose, $60 in package

✓ C-3PO and R2-D2 Talking Alarm Clock (Bradley Time) $40

✓ The Empire Strikes Back R2-D2 and C-3PO collector's glass (Burger King) $20

✓ C-3PO Action Figure case (Kenner) . . . . $15 loose, $40 in package

✓ C-3PO Pez dispenser $2

C-3PO action figure with removable limbs, C-3PO Pez dispenser, Burger King glass.

Chewbacca

SPECS: Faithful sidekick to Han Solo.

Yet another character who conveys a tremendous amount of emotion without ever uttering a word, Chewy is, understandably, especially popular among Han Solo fans. Who can forget the scene in "The Empire Strikes Back" when Chewbacca howls in anguish as the decision was made to close the bay doors at the Hoth Rebel Base, literally leaving Luke and Han out in the cold? The 12-inch Chewbacca action figure came with a rather neat laser bow caster that fit snugly into the Wookie's hand (or is it a paw?), and Kenner recently released a decent real-size bow caster replica.

Cool Collectibles

Chewbacca 12-inch action figure with bowcaster, Chewbacca Pez dispenser, Chewbacca bubble bath.

✓ Chewbacca 12-inch action figure, classic Star Wars (Kenner)
....$75 loose, $150 in package

✓ Chewbacca Bubble Bath (Omni Cosmetics) $10

✓ Chewbacca boxer shorts (Briefly Stated) $5

✓ Chewbacca cake candle (Wilton) $5

✓ Chewbacca Pez dispenser $2

Obi-Wan Kenobi

SPECS: Jedi Knight and mentor to both Luke Skywalker and Luke's father, Anakin.

Another of the few characters to appear (in some form or another) in each and every Star Wars film, Ben Kenobi didn't exactly die when struck by Darth Vader's lightsaber, he merely became one with the Force. Not a huge hit among collectors (although it's a sure bet the younger Kenobi in Episode I will be), some nice Obi-Wan items can be found for a reasonable price. In the original Star Wars action figure line, there were two Obi-Wan variations, one with gray hair and one with white, although both were produced in nearly equal numbers, so one doesn't hold a higher premium than the other.

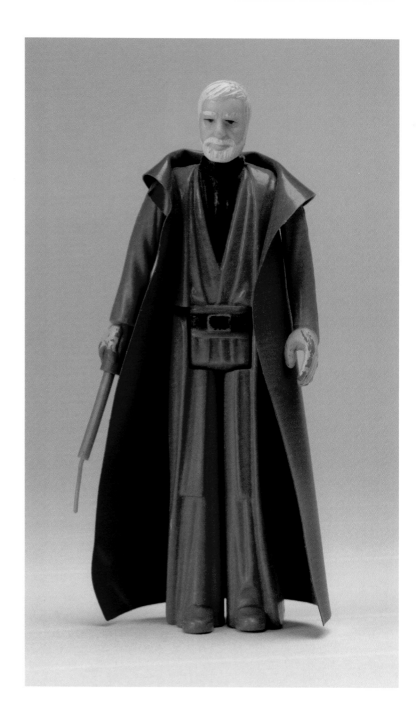

Cool
Collectibles

Obi-Wan Kenobi
action figure
from classic
Star Wars line,
Obi-Wan Kenobi card
from Collectible
Card Game,
12-inch action figure.

✓ Ben (Obi-Wan) Kenobi 3 3/4-inch action figure, classic Star Wars
(Kenner) .... $15 loose, $250 in package

✓ Obi-Wan Kenobi 12-inch with dark blue insert, Power of the Force
(Kenner) .... $30 loose, $60 in package

✓ Ben Kenobi bookmark (Random House) $10

✓ Obi-Wan Kenobi keychain (Rawcliffe) $10

✓ Ben Kenobi collector's cup (Coca-Cola) $5

✓ Obi-Wan Kenobi game card from Star Wars Two-Player Customizable
Game (Decipher) $5

Darth Vader

SPECS: Dark Lord of the Sith, and indeed, Luke's father.

One of the most famous movie villains of all time, it turns out that deep down inside, this Vader guy ain't so bad. With the introduction of the two ferocious villains in Episode I, Darth Maul and Darth Sidious, we learned that "Darth" was Vader's title, not his first name as many had assumed for 20-plus years. Regardless, the guy is bad, and that's "bad" in a good way. Vader's collectibles are far out: from ceramic heads to posters with his ominous silhouette in the background. We learn more about the character in Episode I, which explores a time when Vader was merely Anakin Skywalker with a world of potential ahead of him.

Cool Collectibles

Darth Vader action figure from classic Star Wars line, David Prowse signed photo, Darth Vader bank.

✓ Darth Vader 3 3/4-inch action figure, classic Star Wars (Kenner) .... $12 loose, $250 in package

✓ Darth Vader cookie jar with R2-D2 and C-3PO on other side (Sigma) $100

✓ Darth Vader photo autographed by David Prowse $40

✓ Darth Vader ceramic bank (from Australia) $30

✓ Darth Vader's Tie Fighter, Power of the Force (Kenner) .... $12 loose, $30 in package

Tusken Raiders and Jawas

SPECS: Natives of Tatooine.

Nameless (and in the case of the Jawas, faceless) creatures that generally cause trouble on the home planet of Luke and Anakin, these guys don't speak a word of English and, unlike the Ewoks, never really took off as collectibles. The saving grace collectibles-wise is the Jawa with the plastic cape, produced in far smaller quantity than the cloth-caped Jawa. Otherwise, the Jawas and Tusken Raiders (also known as Sand People) don't have individual characteristics. The Jawas drive Sandcrawlers and buy and sell droids, while the Raiders … well, they just… you know… raid things.

**Tusken Raider
from the classic Star Wars line,
Jawa with vinyl cape.**

Cool
Collectibles

✓ Jawa 3 3/4-inch action figure, classic Star Wars with plastic cape
   (Kenner) ....$300 loose, $3,200 in package

✓ Radio-controlled Sandcrawler $300

✓ Jawa 3 3/4-inch action figure, classic Star Wars (Kenner)
   ....$15 loose, $250 in package

✓ Sand People 3 3/4-inch action figure, classic Star Wars (Kenner)
   ....$15 loose, $250 in package

✓ Droid Factory, Star Wars accessory ......$75 loose, $200 in package

Grand Moff Tarkin / Stormtrooper / Death Squad Commander

SPECS: Occupants of the original Death Star.

Tarkin lasted just one movie, refusing to evacuate the Death Star when its destruction appeared imminent, but collectors seem strangely fascinated by Tarkin collectibles, probably because the first action figure didn't come out until the '90s. Although he ranked somewhere between Darth Vader and The Emperor in the bad guys' chain of command, he couldn't really hold a candle to Vader in terms of fan appeal. The Stormtroopers are another story. Although it has been rumored among die-hard fans that the men in white are all clones of each other, a conversation between two Stormtroopers about the recent flurry of activity on the Death Star ("Do you know what's going on? Maybe it's just a drill.") in Episode IV would suggest a little individuality.

Cool
Collectibles

**Stormtrooper action figure
from classic Star Wars line,
Death Squad gunner
from classic Star Wars line,
12-inch Grand Moff Tarkin.**

✓ Stormtrooper 3 3/4-inch action figure, classic Star Wars (Kenner)
.....................................$15 loose, $225 in package

✓ Death Squad Commander 3 3/4-inch action figure, classic Star Wars
(Kenner)..............................$12 loose, $225 in package

✓ Grand Moff Tarkin and Imperial Gunner with Interrrogator Droid 12
inch action figures, (Kenner / FAO Schwarz).......................
.....................................$20 loose, $60 in package

✓ Grand Moff Tarkin 12-inch action figure, Power of the Force (Kenner)
.....................................$15 loose, $30 in package

✓ Stormtrooper chess set (Danbury Mint).......................$25

Greedo / Hammerhead / Walrus Man / Snaggletooth

SPECS: Regulars at the cantina in Mos Eisley Spaceport.

One of the many things that makes the Star Wars saga so fascinating are the amazing characters and creatures who come and go in the backgrounds of scenes. An interesting variation in Snaggletooth action figures has kept collectors on their toes: The first Snaggletooth figure was too tall and the wrong color, blue; later versions were shortened and changed to red. Greedo nearly stole the show in his confrontation with Han Solo early in Episode IV when he threatened to highjack the Millennium Falcon, to which Solo proclaimed, "Over my dead body." Greedo's response: "That's the idea."

Cool
Collectibles

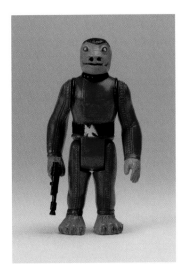

**Hammerhead action figure
from classic Star Wars line,
the two variations of
Snaggletooth.**

✓ Snaggletooth 3 3/4-inch blue action figure, classic Star Wars (Kenner)
....$175 loose

✓ Greedo 3 3/4-inch action figure, classic Star Wars (Kenner)
.....................................$10 loose, $150 in package

✓ Hammerhead 3 3/4-inch action figure, classic Star Wars (Kenner)
.....................................$8 loose, $150 in package

✓ Snaggletooth 3 3/4-inch red action figure, classic Star Wars (Kenner)
.....................................$8 loose, $150 in package

✓ Walrus Man 3 3/4-inch action figure, classic Star Wars (Kenner)
.....................................$10 loose, $125 in package

Death Star Droid / Power Droid

SPECS: Robotic occupants of the original Death Star.

The Death Star Droid and Power Droid have each appeared just three times in all the Star Wars sets over the years. Neither has appeared since 1983. Both made appearances in one set for each of the three original films. The most highly sought after of the two is the '78 Star Wars Death Star Droid, followed closely by the Power Droid from the same series. Neither played a significant role in the trilogy, although one droid did serve for some comic relief when it scrambled away whimpering from a growling Chewbacca in Episode IV.

Cool
Collectibles

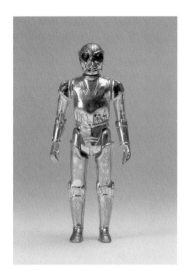

✓ Power Droid 3 3/4-inch action figure, classic Star Wars (Kenner)
.... $10 loose, $125 in package

✓ Death Star Droid 3 3/4-inch action figure, classic Star Wars (Kenner)
.... $10 loose, $150 in package

✓ Death Star World, The Empire Strikes Back Micro Set (Kenner)
.... $75 loose, $150 in package

✓ Destory the Death Star board game (Kenner) $20

✓ Escape from the Death Star jigsaw puzzle (Kenner) $10

**Power Droid action figure
from classic Star Wars line,
Death Star Droid action figure,
Death Star Micro World play set.**

Star Wars: Episode V — The Empire Strikes Back

Possibly a forebearer of what will come in Episodes II and III, Episode V is by far the darkest and scariest film of the original trilogy. It's also arguably the best.

"The Empire Strikes Back" introduced several unforgettable characters (Boba Fett, Yoda, Lando Calrissian, etc.) while maintaining the charm and thrill of the original. The true definition of a sequel (it wasn't merely a remake of the first one like so many other sequels), Episode V took the Star Wars saga to new depths, shocking us with the idea that Darth Vader was Luke Skywalker's father and kindling possible romantic sparks between Han Solo and Princess Leia.

And when it comes to collectibles, the aforementioned

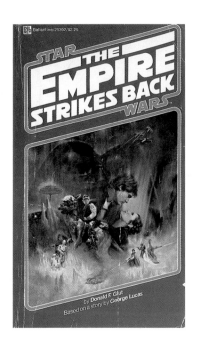

**The Empire Strikes Back
advance poster,
original softcover novel,
Empire baseball cap.**

Fett rules the roost. The guy who leads Darth Vader to Cloud City just ahead of Han Solo has become one of the trilogy's most popular figures.

And Yoda, the venerable Jedi Master, could do things like no other Muppet before him. And then there were the Snow-speeders, which rivaled the legendary X-Wings in coolness and collectibles stature, and the AT-ATs, which wreaked havoc on so many kids' action figure collections.

In the end of Episode V, you're left with the sense that the best thing that happened in the film is none of the major good guys were killed, although you were fearing for Han Solo's life when Fett got away with him, frozen carbonite chamber and all. Indeed, the "happy ending" of "The Empire Strikes Back" is simply the idea that the rebels lived to fight another day.

**The Empire Strikes Back folder,
Empire Storybook hardcover,
Time magazine (May 1980),
Washington Post Empire review.**

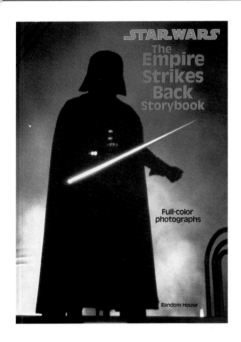

Boba Fett

SPECS: The galaxy's most feared bounty hunter.

When it comes to the ratio of screen time minutes to value of collectibles, Boba Fett rules the Star Wars universe. He's introduced halfway through Episode V, becomes a general annoyance to Han Solo and then gets offed (albeit it accidental) early in Episode VI (by, appropriately enough, Solo). His only memorable line is, "He's no good to me dead," but that hasn't slowed the growth in popularity of his collectibles. His name appears more than 50 times in our checklist, and that doesn't include countless collage posters and books prominately featuring his likeness and the likeness of his equally popular ship, the Slave 1. Heading the list is his 3 3/4-inch action figure from the classic Star Wars series (even though the character didn't appear in Star Wars), and the 12-inch action figure produced by Kenner in 1979, one of just two figures of that size from The Empire Strikes Back line (IG-88,

Cool Collectibles

Boba Fett
12-inch action figure,
action figure from
classic Star Wars line,
The Empire Strikes Back
bedspread.

✓ Boba Fett 3 3/4-inch action figure, classic Star Wars (Kenner) . . . .
. . . . $40 loose, $1,300 in package

✓ Boba Fett 12-inch action figure, classic Star Wars (Kenner) . . . .
. . . . $250 loose, $600 in package

✓ Slave 1 ship, classic Star Wars accessory (Kenner) . . . .
. . . . $50 loose, $200 in package

✓ Boba Fett stein $50

✓ Boba Fett and Chewbacca place mat (Sigma) $20

✓ Boba Fett: Bounty on Bar-Kooda comic book $20

✓ Boba Fett cosume (Ben Cooper) $30

✓ The Empire Strikes Back bedspread with Darth Vader and Boba Fett
. . . . $20

✓ Slave 1 ship, Power of the Force accessory (Kenner) . . . .
$8 loose, ... $20 in package

✓ Boba Fett mug (Applause) $15

✓ Boba Fett with backpack 3 3/4-inch action figure, Power of the Force
(Kenner) . . . . $6 loose, $15 in package

✓ Boba Fett 3 3/4-inch action figure, Power of the Force (Kenner) . . . . . .
. . . . $4 loose, $12 in package

✓ Boba Fett Learn to Read and Write note pad (Stuart Hall) $10

✓ Slave 1 ship model (Structors) $10

✓ Boba Fett watch (Hope Industries) $6

✓ Boba Fett spiral notebook (Stuart Hall) $5

another very valuable piece, is the other). Fett is rumored to have a prominent role in Episode II, but it's likely that his appeal to fans will remain a mystery. Boba Fett collectibles tend to be extremely valuable for one reason — an intensely high demand.

Slave 1 Power of the Force ship, Boba Fett Power of the Force action figure, Boba Fett statue, action figure with backpack.

Carded action figure from classic Star Wars line, Star File trading card, Boba Fett trading card, Darkhorse comic.

Boba Fett™

Lando Calrissian

SPECS: Scoundrel-turned-good guy who helps rescue Han Solo from Jabba the Hut.

Who would have thought, after he was first introduced in Episode V as a traitor to Han Solo, that Lando Calrissian would go on to play a major role in the destruction of the second Death Star and become one of the Rebel Alliance's all-time great heroes? The character who was seconds away from getting choked to death by Chewbacca now has more than 10 action figures of his likeness. One of the more interesting variations of all the Star Wars figures is the regular Lando and the Lando with much whiter eyes and a huge white-teeth grin on his face. However, since both pieces were produced in nearly equal quantities, both have identical values. Say what you want about Lando, but his home of Cloud City provides some of the most scenic and beautiful shots in the original Star Wars trilogy.

Cool Collectibles

Lando Calrissian
action figure,
Bespin Control Room
micro play set,
Lando in disguise.

✓ Lando Calrissian General Pilot 3 3/4-inch action figure, 1985 Power of the Force (Kenner) .... $10 loose, $125 in package

✓ Bespin Control Room, The Empire Strikes Back Micro Set (Kenner) .... $20 loose, $50 in package

✓ Lando Calrissian Skiff Disguise 3 3/4-inch action figure, Return of the Jedi (Kenner) .... $20 loose, $50 in package

✓ Tie Fighters in Cloud City Collector Plate (Hamilton) $40

✓ Lando Calrissian mug (Sigma Ceramics) $30

✓ Lando Calrissian and the Starcave of Thonboka novel .... (Random House) $15

✓ The Empire Strikes Back Lando Calrissian collector's glass .... (Burger King) $10

✓ Lando Calrissian bookmark (Random House) $10

✓ Lando Calrissian and Boush paint by number (Craftmaster) $5

✓ Lando Calrissian coloring book (Kenner) $5

Cloud City
collector's plate,
Lando Calrissian
action figure,
Lando Lili-Ledy figure,
Lando Burger King
glass.

SPECS: Jedi Master in Episodes I, V and VI.

Don't judge him by his size. The diminuitive Yoda is tracked down by Luke on a swamp planet on which Yoda appears to be the only thing that can talk, but we find out in Episode I that his roots run much deeper than that, back to a time when the Old Republic was still in power. Like Obi-Wan Kenobi and Anakin Skywalker, Yoda doesn't exactly die, he instead lives on through the Force. Yoda and his wisdom have been good fodder for collectibles, including an "All I Need to Know I learned from Star Wars" poster with Yoda sayings: "Size matters not." "Try not. Do. Or do not. There is no try." "Adventure . . . Excitement . . . A Jedi craves not these things." Be sure and check out the Yoda magic 8-ball, which provides answers such as, "The Force is not clear on this one." The character also provides one of the most gut-wrenching lines of the original trilogy. When, in "The Empire Strikes Back," Kenobi told Yoda that Luke Skywalker was the last hope for the good guys, Yoda left us hanging with, "No. There is another." We didn't find out until "Return of the Jedi" that the "other" is Princess Leia, Luke's sister.

Cool Collectibles

**Yoda action figure with brown snake,
Yoda magic 8-ball question answerer.**

✓ Yoda with brown snake 3 3/4-inch action figure, Return of the Jedi
(Kenner) .... $30 loose, $100 in package

✓ Yoda with orange snake 3 3/4-inch action figure, The Empire Strikes
Back (Kenner) .... $25 loose, $100 in package

✓ Yoda hand puppet $50

✓ Yoda: The Jedi Master magic 8-ball (Kenner) $50

✓ Yoda salt and pepper shaker $40

2-1B and FX-7

SPECS: Medical droids.

Once again, two background characters from the trilogy make it to the big-time via the collectibles route. 2-1B, referred two as "Too-Onebee" on one of his action figure cards, is the droid who assists Luke Skywalker after his encounter with the Wampa snow creature at the beginning of Episode V. FX-7, with his multiple arms, also aids the good guys on the Hoth Rebel Base. Their respective action figures have respectable values if you didn't take them out of the package. The thin, plastic arms of the FX-7 figure could have been easily torn off by a playful child. FX-7 didn't appear after the 1983 Return of the Jedi series.

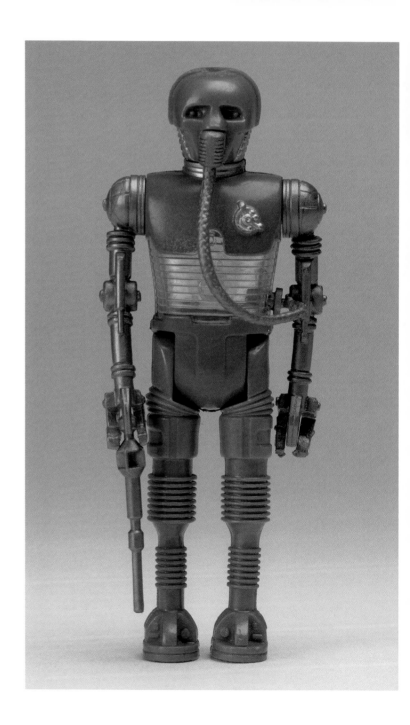

Cool Collectibles

**2-1B action figure,
FX-7 action figure,
2-1B Power of the Force
action figure.**

✓ 2-1B 3 3/4-inch action figure, The Empire Strikes Back (Kenner) . . . . . .
. . . . $12 loose, $75 in package

✓ FX-7 3 3/4-inch action figure, The Empire Strikes Back (Kenner) . . . . . .
. . . . $10 loose, $50 in package

✓ 2-1B socks (Factors) $10

✓ 2-1B 3 3/4-inch action figure, Power of the Force (Kenner) . . . .
. . . . $2 loose, $6 in package

✓ 2-1B candy $2

AT-AT Commander and AT-AT Driver

SPECS: Bad guys manning the Empire's All Terrain Armored Transports.

It's the general consensus of most Star Wars fans that the ice planet of Hoth is one of the neatest ideas in all the Star Wars movies. (Of course, that was before the underwater scenes of Episode I.) Once the Empire discovered the rebel base on the ice planet of Hoth, it sent the dreaded AT-ATs in to attack. Han and Leia fled to an asteroid field, Luke took off for Dagobah, and the rest is history. But the AT-ATs and their on-board personnel live on in the form of action figures, play set, cups, mugs, pins . . . you name it. The AT-AT, of course, isn't to be confused with the AT-STs in "Return of the Jedi."

AT-AT toy from classic Star Wars line, AT-AT Driver 12-inch action figure, AT-AT Driver action figure.

Cool
Collectibles

✓ AT-AT vehicle, The Empire Strikes Back (Kenner) ....
.... $125 loose, $400 in package

✓ AT-AT Driver 12-inch action figure, Collector Series (Kenner) $100

✓ AT-AT Driver 3 3/4-inch action figure, The Empire Strikes Back ....
(Kenner) .... $10 loose, $75 in package

✓ AT-AT Commander 3 3/4-inch action figure, The Empire Strikes Back
(Kenner) .... $10 loose, $50 in package

✓ AT-AT model kit (Structors) $30

✓ AT-AT mug (Rawcliffe) $15

✓ The Empire Strikes Back postcard with AT-AT $10

✓ AT-AT keychain (Rawcliffe) $10

✓ AT-AT game card from Star Wars Two-Player Customizable Game ....
(Decipher) $5

✓ AT-AT puzzle with candy (Tombola Eggs) $5

**AT-AT Commander action figure,
Blizzard 2 card (featuring an AT-AT)
from Collectible Card Game,
The Empire Strikes Back postcard.**

Bespin Security Guard and Cloud Car Pilot

SPECS: Employees of Lando Calrissian.

Although it seemed a rather peaceful place, Cloud City (also known as Bespin) turned into a trap for our heroes. One can possibly see a parallel between Bespin and the peaceful planet of Naboo in Episode I. Cloud Cars would certainly be no match for Imperial Tie Fighters, but they were enough to make Han Solo more than a little nervous. They were also apparently cool enough in the eyes of viewers to spawn a nice little line of collectibles, including several Cloud City play sets that are worth quite a bit even out of the original package. The Bespin Security Guard action figures were made with both white and black figures in both The Empire Strikes Back and Return of the Jedi series, but all hold nearly the same values.

Twin-pod Cloud Car ship from The Empire Strikes Back micro set, Cloud Car pilot action figure, Bespin Security Guard action figure.

Cool Collectibles

✓ Bespin World, The Empire Strikes Back micro set (Kenner) . . . .
. . . . $90 loose, $200 in package

✓ Cloud Car, Star Wars accessory (Kenner) . . . .
. . . . $30 loose, $125 in package

✓ Twin Pod Cloud Car, die-cast vehicle (Kenner) . . . .
. . . . $20 loose, $60 in package

✓ (Twin Pod) Cloud Car Pilot 3 3/4-inch action figure, The Empire Strikes
Back (Kenner) . . . . $20 loose, $60 in package

✓ Bespin Control Room, The Empire Strikes Back micro set (Kenner)
. . . . $20 loose, $50 in package

✓ Bespin Security Guard, black, 3 3/4-inch action figure, The Empire
Strikes Back (Kenner) . . . . $10 loose, $50 in package

✓ Bespin Security Guard, white, 3 3/4-inch action figure, The Empire
Strikes Back (Kenner) . . . . $10 loose, $50 in package

✓ Bespin tissue box $20

✓ Twin Pod Cloud Car paper cup (James River-Dixie) $20

✓ Bespin postcard (Star Tours) $5

Bossk / Zuckuss / 4-LOM / IG-88 / Dengar

SPECS: Bounty hunters hired in Episode V to track down Luke Skywalker.

And you thought Mos Eisley offered a wretched hive of scum and villany? Check out the lineup assembled by Darth Vader to track down his son and Han Solo in "The Empire Strikes Back." Vader, of course, really just had an interest in his son, Luke, but the bounty hunters were likely enticed by the opportunity to return Han Solo to Jabba the Hut. None of these guys ended up making the cut, as it was Boba Fett, the king of the bounty hunters, who tracked down Solo and paved the way for Vader's intervention at Cloud City. But that didn't stop Kenner from producing action figures for all of these thugs. Heading the way is the IG-88 12-inch action figure, one of just two 12-inchers produced from The Empire Strikes Back. Several bounty hunter-related books, games and comics were also produced.

Cool Collectibles

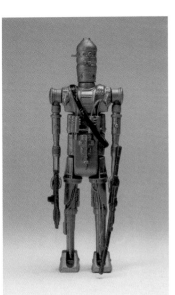

**IG-88 12-inch
action figure,
4-LOM action figure,
IG-88 action figure.**

✓ IG-88 12-inch action figure, classic Star Wars (Kenner) ....
.... $400 loose, $1,100 in package

✓ 4-LOM 3 3/4-inch action figure, The Empire Strikes Back (Kenner)
.... $15 loose, $175 in package

✓ IG-88 (Bounty Hunter) 3 3/4-inch action figure, The Empire Strikes
Back (Kenner) .... $15 loose, $120 in package

✓ Bossk (Bounty Hunter) 3 3/4-inch action figure, The Empire Strikes
Back (Kenner) .... $8 loose, $100 in package

✓ Zuckuss 3 3/4-inch action figure, The Empire Strikes Back (Kenner)
.... $8 loose, $100 in package

✓ Dengar 3 3/4-inch action figure, The Empire Strikes Back (Kenner)
.... $10 loose, $50 in package

✓ Battle of the Bounty Hunters pop-up book (Dark Horse) $20

✓ 4-LOM 3 3/4-inch action figure, Power of the Force (Kenner) ....
.... $2 loose, $6 in package

✓ Bossk 3 3/4-inch action figure, Power of the Force (Kenner) ....
.... $2 loose, $6 in package

✓ Bossk candy $2

Bossk action figure,
4-LOM Power of the Force
action figure,
Boba Fett Power of the Force
action figure,
Dengar action figure.

Imperial Stormtrooper (Hoth Battle Gear) / Imperial Tie Fighter Pilot / Imperial Commander

SPECS: Bad guys.

These Imperial menaces to society starting showing up with The Empire Strikes Back series of action figures in 1980. The Hoth Battle Gear Stormtrooper is a variation of the original Stormtrooper from the classic Star Wars line, with some slight uniform modifications to better adapt to the cold weather. The Imperial Tie Fighter characters first showed up in "Star Wars" and are featured in the final dogfight in Episode IV, but the respective action figure didn't find its way to the market until the 1980 series of toys. It seemed the primary role of the Imperial Commander characters in Episode V was the botch things up, then get strangled to death from a touch of the Force by a ticked off Darth Vader. The larger Tie Fighter ships were designed to accommodate the 3 3/4-inch pilot action figures in their cockpits. The larger Tie Fighter produced in

TIE Interceptor ship from classic Star Wars line, TIE Fighter Pilot action figure, Imperial Commander action figure.

Cool Collectibles

✓ Tie Interceptor, classic Star Wars (Kenner) ....
....$75 loose, $150 in package

✓ Imperial Tie Fighter Pilot 3 3/4-inch action figure, The Empire Strikes
Back (Kenner) ....$15 loose, $100 in packge

✓ Imperial Commander 3 3/4-inch action figure, The Empire Strikes Back
(Kenner) ....$10 loose, $60 in package

✓ Stormtrooper (Hoth Gear) 3 3/4-inch action figure, The Empire Strikes
Back (Kenner) ....$10 loose, $60 in package

✓ Snowtrooper 12-inch action figure, Star Wars Action Collection .....
(Kenner) ....$20 loose, $40 in package

✓ Tie Fighters plate (Hamilton) $40

✓ Tie Fighter Collector's PC game (LucasArts) $30

✓ Tie Fighter model (Structors) $20

✓ Tie Fighter necktie (Ralph Marlin) $15

✓ Tie Fighter, Power of the Force (Kenner) ....$10 loose, $25 in package

the '90s Power of the Force line is an off-green color, which in the films was reserved only for Darth Vader's Tie Fighter.

Imperial Stormtrooper (Hoth Battle Gear) action figure, TIE Fighters collector's plate, TIE Fighter Power of the Force ship, 12-inch Snowtrooper.

Lobot / Ugnaught

SPECS: Occupants of Cloud City.

Lobot, an assistant to Lando Calrissian on Bespin, appears to be part human, part droid. He's got a pretty cool set of headphones seemingly fused to his head that allow him to communicate with his boss. Although he appears very briefly, he plays a key role in allowing Lando, Princess Leia, Chewbacca and C-3PO to escape Cloud City when the place is run over with Stormtroopers. The Ugnaughts, workers in Bespin's inner chambers, get even less screen time than Lobot and are most remembered for playing catch with C-3PO's arms and legs as a frustrated Chewbacca tries to gather the parts of the disabled droid. The Ugnaught action figure came with a small plastic briefcase that was easily lost by kids who, at the time, didn't realize they were playing with what would become a $50 collectible.

Cool
Collectibles

**Ugnaught action figure,
Lobot action figure.**

✓ Bespin World, The Empire Strikes Back Micro Set (Kenner) ....
.... $90 loose, $200 in package

✓ Bespin Freeze Chamber, The Empire Strikes Back Micro Set (Kenner)
.... $40 loose, $100 in package

✓ Bespin Gantry, The Empire Strikes Back Micro Set (Kenner) ....
.... $20 loose, $50 in package

✓ Ugnaught 3 3/4-inch action figure, The Empire Strikes Back (Kenner)
.... $8 loose, $50 in package

✓ Lobot 3 3/4-inch action figure, The Empire Strikes Back (Kenner) .....
.... $10 loose, $40 in package

✓ Beneath Cloud City rub-down transfer (American Publishing Presto
Magix) $10

✓ Cloud City invitation (Drawing Board) $10

✓ Ugnaughts iron-on applique $10

✓ Cloud City gift tag (Drawing Board) $5

✓ Cloud City toy (Taco Bell) $5

Rebel Commander and Rebel Soldier (Hoth Battle Gear)

SPECS: The good guys running the show on Hoth.

Nearly every principal Star Wars character has appeared in a collectible in "Hoth Gear." Well, these two good guys appear in Hoth gear, and never again. The Rebel Commander, presumably based on the character who gives the order to begin evacuation of the base after Han Solo discovers the Imperial Probe Droid, came with a blaster rifle that could be hung around his shoulder or placed in his hand. The rather generic Rebel Soldier could serve in your Hoth play set as any of the rebels who 1) successfully evacuate the base, 2) stay to fight the Stormtroopers in Hoth Gear or 3) get crushed by an AT-AT. The Soldier figure, which can easily be confused with the Luke Skywalker in Hoth Gear figure, came with a tiny blaster pistol. The Hoth Ice Planet play set featured a rotating laser canon and a stand for an Imperial Probe Droid.

Hoth Ice Planet play set, Rebel Commander action figure, Rebel Soldier action figure.

Cool Collectibles

✓ Hoth Ice Planet, Star Wars accessory (Kenner) ....
.... $60 loose, $200 in package

✓ Assualt on Hoth board game (West End Games) $50

✓ Rebel Commander 3 3/4-inch action figure, The Empire Strikes Back ....
(Kenner) .... $8 loose, $50 in package

✓ Rebel Soldier (Hoth Gear) 3 3/4-inch action figure, The Empire Strikes
Back (Kenner) .... $8 loose, $50 in package

✓ Hoth Ice Planet Adventure board game (Kenner) $20

✓ Imperial Probe Droid (orange), 1997 Power of the Force (Kenner) ....
.... $8 loose, $20 in package

✓ Battle on Hoth paint by number set (Craftmaster) $10

✓ Hoth Ice Planet Adventure jigsaw puzzle (Kenner) $10

✓ Imperial Probe Droid (green), 1997 Power of the Force (Kenner) ....
.... $4 loose, $10 in packge

✓ Heroes on Hoth spiral notebook (Stuart Hall) $5

**Hoth Ice Planet
Adventure Set,
Deluxe Probe Droid Power
of the Force action figure,
Luke Skywalker with Wampa
12-inch figure pack,
Hoth Rebel Soldier Power
of the Force action figures.**

Star Wars: Episode VI — Return of the Jedi

And then there's Episode VI, the most hotly contested of all the Star Wars films. There's actually a chapter in a 1998 book dedicated to the films called, "Why Return of the Jedi Sucked." That's probably a bit harsh, as the film did serve up some excellent battle scenes and a nice resolution between father-and-son team Darth Vader and Luke Skywalker.

Indeed, Episode VI (the name was changed from "Revenge of the Jedi" just before the film was released) wasn't without its good side (and neither is Vader, we find out).

The Emperor was pretty darn impressive, with his Force-powered electroshock therapy inflicted upon Skywalker. And the climactic lightsaber duel between Vader and Luke Skywalker is the best sword fight of the trilogy. If you go back and compare the special effects of Episode IV and Episode VI, you'll see there's really no comparison. And if you go back and compare the detail and quality of the action figures and

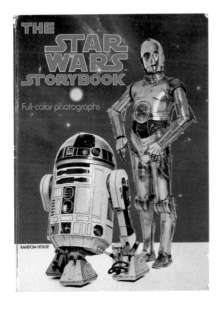

**Revenge of the Jedi advance
theatrical poster,
Return of the Jedi
bedspread,
The Star Wars Storybook
hardcover.**

other collectibles, you'll notice the same thing.

But there's always the Ewoks, and that isn't necessarily a good thing. Sure, they're cute, but the images of the furry guys twirling around on an Imperial Speeder Bike and swinging from vines in full Tarzan-mode was a bit too childlike for many of the trilogy's older fans.

The denouement — a sing-along with the Ewoks and our heroes on the forest moon of Endor — was dramatically improved in the Special Edition version released in theaters in 1997. That version features a crowd of celebrating citizens tearing down a statue of The Emperor in the galaxy's capital city of Coruscant (prominately featured in Episode I) in place of the Ewok music, and ends up being by far the Special Edition's best contribution to the trilogy.

AT-ST Driver action figure,
Return of the Jedi "A" Sheet
poster reprint,
Marvel Comic Jedi No. 1,
Official Collectors Edition
program.

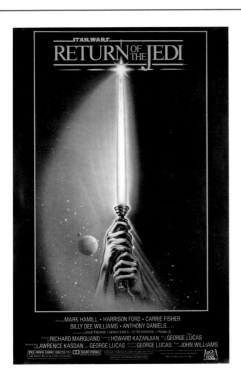

Anakin Skywalker and The Emperor

SPECS: The human in Darth Vader and his boss

The bomb Darth Vader dropped on Star Wars fans everywhere ("No, Luke . . . I am your father. . . ."), was one of the most crucial turning points in the saga. Turns out Obi-Wan Kenobi fibbed a little in Episode IV when he told Luke that Vader had betrayed and murdered Luke's father. (The venerable Kenobi contended that what he told Luke was true, "from a certain point of view," in the sense that Anakin Skywalker had been betrayed by the Dark Side and transformed into Darth Vader.) Kenner took advantage of the helmetless Vader in Episode VI with a "Darth Vader with Removable Helmet" figure as well as an Anakin Skywalker figure in the 1985 Power of the Force series. That figure has a very high value, as it had one of the lowest production runs of the already rare '85 POF series. Look for many more Anakin figures based on the slave boy Skywalker in Episode I. Anakin should eventually get his butt kicked by Kenobi in Episode III, only to return the favor in Episode IV. The Emperor, meanwhile, will appear in Episodes I-III as the benevolent Senator Palpatine.

Cool Collectibles

The Emperor action figure, Darth Vader with removable helmet action figure, The Emperor Power of the Force action figure.

✓ Anakin Skywalker 3 3/4-inch action figure, Power of the Force ......
(Kenner) ....$30 loose, $2,500 in package

✓ The Emperor 3 3/4-inch action figure, Power of the Force (Kenner) ....
....$8 loose, $75

✓ The Emperor 3 3/4-inch action figure, Return of the Jedi (Kenner) .....
......................................$8 loose, $40 in package

✓ Darth Vader 3 3/4-inch action figure with Removable Helmet, 1998
Power of the Force (Kenner) ....$5 loose, $12 in package

✓ Clone Emperor Palpatine, 1999 Star Wars Expanded Universe (Kenner)
......................................$5 loose, $12 in package

✓ The Emperor , 1997 Electronic Power FX (Kenner) ....
......................................$4 loose, $10 in package

✓ The Emperor, 1993 Star Wars Bend Ems (Kenner) ....
......................................$4 loose, $10 in package

✓ Emperor Palpatine 3 3/4-inch action figure, 1997 Power of the Force
(Kenner) ....$2 loose, $6 in package

✓ Emperor T-shirt (American Marketing Enterprise) $20

✓ The Emperor mug (Applause) $15

SPECS: Natives of the forest moon of Endor.

Ah, the Ewoks, a point of much contention among Star Wars fans. Cute or cop-out? George Lucas' original idea called for a planet full of mean ole Wookies, but somebody somewhere decided cuddly teddy bear-like creatures would be more kid-friendly (and presumably easier to market as dolls, action figures, etc.). Unlike the Tusken Raiders and Jawas from Episode IV, the Ewoks, which dominate the final half of Episode VI, were given individual names. Although you'd be hard-pressed to pick out names in the Ewok-speak in the film, much less tell one little furry guy from the other, the corresponding action figures in the Return of the Jedi series were called Chief Chirpa, Logray (Ewok Medicine Man), Teebo, Wicket W. Warrick (played by actor Warwick Davis, who has several small roles in Episode I), Paploo and Lumat. An Ewok named Warok appeared in the 1985 Power of the Force series along with his buddy Romba.

Cool Collectibles

**Paploo action figure,
Logray (Ewok Medicine Man),
Chief Chirpa action figure.**

✓ Wicket 3 3/4-inch action figure, Power of the Force (Kenner) .... $15 loose, $200 in package

✓ Paploo 3 3/4-inch action figure, Return of the Jedi (Kenner) .... $20 loose, $50 in package

✓ Chief Chirpa 3 3/4-inch action figure, Return of the Jedi (Kenner) .... $10 loose, $40 in package

✓ Logray (Ewok Medicine Man) 3 3/4-inch action figure, Return of the .. Jedi (Kenner) .... $10 loose, $40 in package

✓ Ewoks bedspread $30

✓ 1984 Ewoks calendar (Ballantine) $10

✓ Ewok Adventure coloring book (Little Golden) $5

✓ Ewoks centerpiece (Drawing Board) $5

✓ The Ewoks Join the Fight book (Random House) $5

✓ The Ewoks Join the Fight tape $5

✓ Paploo 3 3/4-inch action figure, ... Return of the Jedi (Kenner) .... $20 loose, $50 in package

✓ Chief Chirpa 3 3/4-inch action figure, Return of the Jedi (Kenner) .... $10 loose, $40 in package

✓ Logray (Ewok Medicine Man) 3 3/4-inch action figure, Return of the Jedi (Kenner) .... $10 loose, $40 in package

✓ Ewoks bedspread $30

✓ 1984 Ewoks calendar (Ballantine) $10

✓ Ewok Adventure coloring book (Little Golden) $5

✓ Ewoks centerpiece (Drawing Board) $5

✓ The Ewoks Join the Fight book (Random House) $5

✓ The Ewoks Join the Fight tape $5

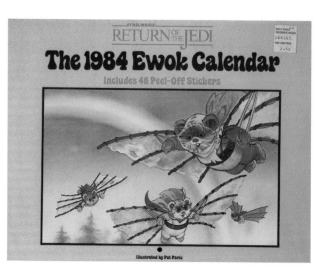

Trilogy bedspread,
Ewok centerpiece,
The Ewoks Join the Fight book,
Ewok calendar.

✓ Paploo 3 3/4-inch action figure, Return of the Jedi (Kenner) . . . .
. . . .$20 loose, $50 in package

✓ Chief Chirpa 3 3/4-inch action figure, Return of the Jedi (Kenner) . . . . .
. . . . $10 loose, $40 in package

✓ Logray (Ewok Medicine Man) 3 3/4-inch action figure, Return of the
Jedi (Kenner) . . . . $10 loose, $40 in package

✓ Ewoks bedspread $30

✓ 1984 Ewoks calendar (Ballantine) $10

✓ Ewok Adventure coloring book (Little Golden) $5

✓ Ewoks centerpiece (Drawing Board) $5

✓ The Ewoks Join the Fight book (Random House) $5

✓ The Ewoks Join the Fight tape $5

✓ Paploo 3 3/4-inch action figure, Return of the Jedi (Kenner) . . . .
. . . .$20 loose, $50 in package

✓ Chief Chirpa 3 3/4-inch action figure, Return of the Jedi (Kenner) . . . . .
. . . . $10 loose, $40 in package

✓ Logray (Ewok Medicine Man) 3 3/4-inch action figure, Return of the
Jedi (Kenner) . . . . $10 loose, $40 in package

✓ Ewoks bedspread $30

✓ 1984 Ewoks calendar (Ballantine) $10

✓ Ewok Adventure coloring book (Little Golden) $5

✓ Ewoks centerpiece (Drawing Board) $5

✓ The Ewoks Join the Fight book (Random House) $5

✓ The Ewoks Join the Fight tape $5

The Ewoks Join the Fight cassette,
Ewok Toothbrush,
Wicket night light.

Admiral Ackbar / Nien Nunb / General Madine

SPECS: Key players in the destruction of the second Death Star.

Episode VI features the widest assortment of weird-looking characters than any of the two previous Star Wars films. Admiral Ackbar, who briefed the rebels before the attack run on the second Death Star, and Nien Nunb, Lando Calrissian's co-pilot during that attack, are just two examples. Ackbar spoke English, but Nunb chattered in to Calrissian in some kind of alien dialect. General Madine is the human of the bunch, who assisted Ackbar in the briefing of the rebel pilots. The Madine action figure is the key collectible of this bunch, as it has made just one appearance thus far in all the Star Wars action figures, while Nunb and Ackbar both have multiple figures.

Cool
Collectibles

**Admiral Ackbar action figure,
Nien Nunb action figure,
General Madine action figure.**

✓ Admiral Ackbar 3 3/4-inch action figure, Return of the Jedi (Kenner)
....$8 loose, $40 in package

✓ General Madine 3 3/4-inch action figure, Return of the Jedi (Kenner)
....$8 loose, $40 in package

✓ Nien Nunb 3 3/4-inch action figure, Return of the Jedi (Kenner) ......
....$8 loose, $40 in package

✓ Admiral Ackbar 12-inch action figure, 1996 Power of the Force
(Kenner) ....$15 loose, $30 in package

✓ Admiral Ackbar costume (Ben Cooper) $20

✓ Admiral Ackbar, Star Wars Bend Ems (Kenner) ....
....$4 loose, $10 in package

✓ Admiral Ackbar bookmark (Random House) $10

✓ Admiral Ackbar mask (Don Post) $10

✓ Admiral Ackbar 3 3/4-inch actio figure, 1997 Power of the Force
(Kenner) ....$2 loose, $6 in package

✓ Nien Nunb 3 3/4-inch action figure, 1997 Power of the Force (Kenner
....$2 loose, $6 in package

AT-ST Driver and Biker Scout

SPECS: Troublemakers on the forest moon of Endor.

The AT-STs, two-legged Imperial walkers similar to AT-ATs, showed up in Episode VI, and a host of toys followed. The AT-ST drivers were seen only briefly and were defeated all too easily by the pesky Ewoks. The Speeder Bike was one of the coolest vehicles in all the trilogy and was piloted by the Biker Scouts, who were basically variations on the old Stormtrooper theme.

Cool
Collectibles

**AT-ST Driver action figure,
Biker Scout action figure,
Speeder Bike toy from classic Star
Wars line.**

B-Wing Pilot and A-Wing Pilot

SPECS: The Rebel flying aces of Episodes IV-VI.

Although they were never as popular among fans as the ultra-hip X-Wings, A-Wings and B-Wings, and their respective pilots, still make nice collectibles. Of special note is the A-Wing Fighter that came in the 1985 Droids cartoon series, worth around $600 if it's still sealed in the original packaging. The high value is the result of a low production run due to the lack of success of the TV series. The action figures for the A-Wing and B-Wing pilots are strikingly similar, with the exception of the uniform color. Neither made much of an appearance on the screen, but their ships could be seen in the attacks on both Death Stars.

A-Wing ship from classic Star Wars line,
A-Wing pilot action figure,
B-Wing pilot action figure.

Cool Collectibles

✓ A-Wing Fighter, 1985 Droids Cartoon (Kenner) ....
.... $200 loose, $600 in package

✓ A-Wing Fighter, classic Star Wars accessory (Kenner) ....
.... $150 loose, $500 in package

✓ A-Wing Pilot 3 3/4-inch action figure, 1985 Droids Cartoon (Kenner) ...
.... $80 loose, $250 in package

✓ A-Wing Pilot 3 3/4-inch action figure, Power of the Force (Kenner) ...
.... $40 loose, $125 in package

✓ B-Wing Pilot 3 3/4-inch action figure, Power of the Force (Kenner) ...
.... $8 loose, $40 in package

✓ B-Wing Pilot 3 3/4-inch action figure, Return of the Jedi (Kenner) ....
.... $8 loose, $40 in package

✓ B-Wing collector's plate (Hamilton) $40

✓ A-Wing model (Structors) $20

✓ B-Wings Attack jigsaw puzzle (Craftmaster) $10

✓ B-Wing, Millennium Falcon, Tie Fighter bookmark
(A.H. Prismatic) $5

Bib Fortuna and Gamorrean Guard

SPECS: Employees of Jabba the Hut.

Bib Fortuna and the Gamorrean Guards, both rather weak of mind and easily influenced by the old Jedi mind trick, greet Luke Skywalker at the beginning of Episode VI. All are presumably destroyed in the explosion of Jabba's sail barge, as the good guys fly off to safety. The first "act" of "Return of the Jedi" was really entirely independent from the rest of the film but made for some memorable action sequences, including Luke's head-over-heels-flip-while-catching-his-lightsaber-in-mid-air off a plank, and Han Solo's accidental knocking off of Boba Fett ("Boba Fett? Where?!?"). Keep your eyes open for a Gamorrean Guard figure in a 1985 Power of the Force package — it can command a nifty premium.

Cool Collectibles

Gamorrean Guard action figure, Bib Fortuna Power of the Force action figure, Big Fortuna The Empire Strkes Back action figure.

✓ Gamorrean Guard 3 3/4-inch action figure, Power of the Force (Kenner) .... $8 loose, $250 in package

✓ Luke with Bib Fortuna 12-inch action figure, 1997 Exclusive (Kenner) .... $60 loose, $150 in package

✓ Bib Fortuna 3 3/4-inch action figure, Return of the Jedi (Kenner) .... $8 loose, $40 in package

✓ Gamorrean Guard 3 3/4-inch action figure, Return of the Jedi (Kenner) .... $8 loose, $40 in package

✓ Bib Fortuna, Star Wars Bend Ems (Kenner) .... $10 loose, $25 in package

✓ Bib Fortuna mug (Applause) $15

✓ Gamorrean Guard cap (Sales Corporation of America) .... $ 15

✓ Gamorrean Guard, Star Wars Bend Ems (Kenner) .... $4 loose, $10 in package

✓ Bib Fortuna 3 3/4-inch action figure, 1997 Power of the Force (Kenner) .... $2 loose, $6 in package

✓ Gamorrean Guard 3 3/4-inch action figure, 1997 Power of the Force (Kenner) .... $2 loose, $6 in package

Sail Barge
characters and others

SPECS: The many aliens, creatures and bounty hunters who appear on Jabba's sail barge.

Perhaps we could have included Boussh in the Princess Leia section, but the diminutive bounty hunter has really taken on a life of its own. Not the least bit feminine when holding a thermal detonator, Boussh figures are available with removable helmets that reveal their true identity: Princess Leia, all dressed up in an attempt to rescue Han Solo from Jabba the Hut. Like Mos Eisley in Episode IV, the sail barge at the beginning of "Return of the Jedi" is alive with creatures of all sorts, some familiar-looking (Jawas), some not (Klaatu). Many have shown up in the form of action figures, and some were rumored to reappear in Episode I. As far as non-sail barge items go, the Emperor's Royal Guard figures are in relatively high demand, again due to low production numbers.

Cool Collectibles

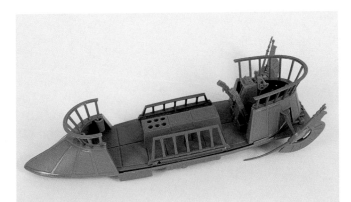

✓ Yak Face 3 3/4-inch action figure, Power of the Force (Kenner) . . . .
. . . . $175 loose, $2,000 in package

✓ Tatooine Skiff, classic Star Wars accessory (Kenner) . . . .
. . . . $400 loose, $700 in package

✓ Nikto 3 3/4-inch action figure, Power of the Force (Kenner) . . . .
. . . . $15 loose, $600 in package

✓ Amanaman 3 3/4-inch action figure, Power of the Force (Kenner) . . . . .
. . . . $125 loose, $250 in package

✓ Barada 3 3/4 inch action figure, Power of the Force (Kenner) . . . .
. . . . $50 loose, $125 in package

✓ Emperor's Royal Guard 3 3/4-inch action figure, Return of the Jedi
(Kenner) . . . . $10 loose, $60 in package

✓ 8D8 3 3/4-inch action figure, Return of the Jedi (Kenner) . . . .
. . . . $10 loose, $40 in package

✓ Rancor Keeper 3 3/4-inch action figure, Return of the Jedi (Kenner) . . .
. . . . $8 loose, $40 in package

✓ Emperor's Royal Guard 3 3/4-inch action figure, 1997 Power of the
Force (Kenner) . . . . $2 loose, $6 in package

✓ Princess Leia in Boussh Disguise 3 3/4-inch action figure, 1996 Power
of the Force (Kenner) . . . . $2 loose, $6 in package

**Yak Face action figure,
Tatooine Skiff toy from
classic Star Wars line,
Nikto action figure.**

Barada from the 1985
Power of the Force line,
Emperor's Royal Guard
Power of the Force action figure,
8D8 action figure,
Emperor's Royal Guard 1985
Power of the Force action figure.

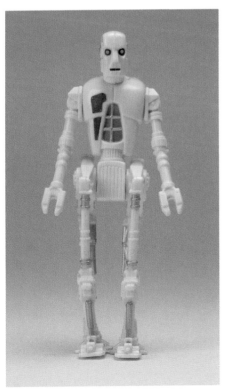

Rancor Keeper action figure,
Ishi Tib Power
of the Force action figure,
Return of the Jedi comic,
Leia in Boushh Disguise
Power of the Force action
figure.

Klaatu action figure,
Weequay action figure,
Jabba's Sail Barge
micro collection,
Ree-Yees action figure.

APPAREL

Hats, caps and visors

Thinking Cap Company

○ Rebel Forces Cap

○ Imperial Forces cap

○ Yoda cap

Sales Corporation of America

○ Return of the Jedi Logo printed hat

○ Luke and Darth Vader Dueling printed hat

○ Darth Vader and Royal Guards printed hat

○ Gamorrean Guard printed hat

○ Gamorrean Guard knitted hat

Fresh Caps

○ Yoda Video cap

○ Darth Vader Video cap

○ Stormtrooper Video cap

○ Darth Vader Injection mold mesh cap

○ X-wing Glitter cap

Ralph Marlin

○ Gamorrean Guard knitted hat

○ Star Wars Logo white outline cap

○ Star Wars Logo white outline with black embroidery cap

Jackets and ponchos

Adam Joseph Industries

○ C3-PO and R2-D2 blue rain jacket with pockets

○ C3-PO and R2-D2 blue rain poncho

○ Darth Vader and Royal Guards silver rain poncho

Jeans

Liberty Trouser Company

○ Star Wars brown pants overall pattern

Overalls

Liberty Trouser Company

○ Star Wars blue overalls pattern

Shorts

Liberty Trouser Company

○ Star Wars navy shorts overall pattern

T-Shirts

PATTI MARSH PRODUCTIONS

○ Wicket color-me

○ Princess Kneesaa color-me

○ Kneesaa and Wickett color-me

○ Latara and Teebo color-me

○ Ewok Group color-me

Portal

○ "All I need to know"

Lucas Arts

○ TIE Fighter Video Game

○ Space Scene

○ Death Star

Factors

○ Darth Vader

○ Han Solo

Center for the Arts

○ Art of Star Wars white

American Marketing Enterprise

○ Galaxy 1 art

○ Han Solo

○ Chewbacca

○ Emperor

○ Rancor Beast

The Empire Strikes Back pillowcase (Bibb Co.)

Princess Leia soap (Omni Cosmetics)

○ Poster Art

○ Villains

Ralph Marlin

○ Star Wars

Embroidery

○ Darth Vader

○ Yoda

○ Stormtrooper

San Diego Comic Con

○ Star Wars Day 1995

○ Star Wars Day 1994

OTHERS

○ Creatures

○ Good Guys

○ Bad Guys

○ C-3PO

○ Yoda

○ Darth Vader

○ R2-D2 and C-3PO busting through

○ Han Solo busting through

○ Han Solo in Carbonite

○ Darth Vader "I want you"

○ Shadows of the Empire

○ Emperor Palpatine

○ Boba Fett firing at you

○ Darth Vader busting out

○ Star Wars two-sided

○ Empire Strikes Back two-sided

○ Return of the Jedi two-sided

○ Rebel Wear/Star Wars

○ Imperial Wear/Darth Vader

○ Stormtrooper black and white

○ C-3PO black and white

○ Princess Leia black and white

○ Boba Fett black and white

○ Darth Vader black and white

○ Yoda black and white

○ Chewbacca black and white

○ Darth Vader Video

○ Yoda Video

○ Stormtrooper Video

Hildebrandt iron-on

○ R2-D2 and C-3PO

○ Darth Vader

○ Han and Chewbacca

○ Luke and C-3PO

○ Stormtrooper

○ Princess Leia

○ Jawa

○ Darth Vader with Fighter

○ Star Wars Logo

Iron-On Patches

○ Brotherhood of the Jedi Knights

○ May the Force be with You

○ Star Wars Logo

○ Darth Vader Lives

Center for the Arts in San Francisco

○ Art of Star Wars black

Production/Lucasfilm

○ THX from Overland Park Kansas

Sweatshirts

JVC

○ Darth Vader

Bathrobes

Wilker Brothers

○ Darth Vader

**Luke Skywalker soap
(Omni Cosmetics)**

**Darth Vader soap
(Omni Cosmetics)**

**Yoda soap
(Omni Cosmetics)**

○ TESB repeat pattern bathrobe

○ May The Force Be With You bathrobe

Pajamas

Wilker Brothers

○ Darth Vader and Luke Skywalker TESB

○ Darth, R2-D2, C-3PO, Luke, and Chewie

○ R2-D2 pajamas

○ R2-D2 and C-3PO, ROTJ pajamas

○ Wicket the Ewok blue pajamas

Socks / hosiery

FACTORS

○ 2-1B

Charleston Hosiery Mills

○ Ewoks: Wicket on a vine

Underwear

Union Underwear

○ R2-D2 Underoos

○ Boba Fett Underoos

○ C-3Po Underoos

○ Darth Vader Underoos

○ Princess Leia Underoos

○ Luke Skywalker Underoos

○ Yoda Underoos

○ Wicket Underoos

Ralph Marlin

○ Darth Vader black repeat silk boxer shorts

○ Star Wars boxer shorts

BRIEFLY STATED

○ Chewbacca boxer shorts

Star Tours

○ First Ten Years sweatshirt

○ Star Tours hat

Han Solo / Chewbacca toothbrush (Oral B)

○ TIE Interceptor T-shirt

○ X-wings T-shirt

○ Han and Luke T-shirt

○ Ewoks T-shirt

○ Star Tours T-shirt

APPAREL ACCESSORIES

Belts

Lee

○ Return of the Jedi fabric: red, black, and gray, with SW and ROTJ Logos

○ Return of the Jedi

○ Ewok tan

○ Darth Vader

○ Return of the Jedi brown

○ The Empire Strikes Back vinyl

Buckles

LEATHERSHOP

○ Star Wars

○ C-3PO and R2-D2

○ Darth Vader

○ TIE Fighter / X-wing

Unlicensed

○ Star Wars belt buckle

○ May the Force Be with You

Neckties

Ralph Marlin

○ Fighter Jets silk

○ Darth Vader silk (with tie-in collector's tin)

○ Darth Vader repeat sillk

○ Rebellion Starships blueprint repeat silk

○ Imperial Starships blueprint repeat silk

○ Darth Vader video polyester

○ Stormtrooper video polyester

Wicket toothbrush (Kenner)

- ○ Yoda video polyester
- ○ Star Wars poster art polyester
- ○ Production painting
- ○ Character tie
- ○ Character tie No. 2
- ○ TIE Fighter
- ○ Star Wars foreign video art
- ○ TESB foreign video art
- ○ ROTJ foreign video art
- ○ Concept art

Return of the Jedi towel set (Bibb Co.)

Umbrellas

Adam Joseph
R2-D2 and C-3PO

AUTOGRAPHS

8 X 10s

○ Anthony Daniels	25.00	40.00
○ Billy Dee Williams	30.00	50.00
○ Caroline Blakistan	18.00	30.00
○ Carrie Fisher	40.00	60.00
○ Clive Revill	12.00	20.00
○ David Prowse	25.00	40.00
○ Declan Mulholland	15.00	25.00
○ Femi Taylor	15.00	25.00
○ Frank Oz	15.00	25.00
○ George Lucas	60.00	100.00
○ Harrison Ford	75.00	125.00
○ Jack Purvis	12.00	20.00
○ James Earl Jones	40.00	60.00
○ Jeremy Bulloch	30.00	50.00
○ John Hollis	25.00	40.00
○ John Morton	15.00	25.00
○ Julian Glover	15.00	25.00
○ Kenneth Colley	15.00	25.00
○ Kenny Baker	15.00	25.00
○ Liam Neeson	25.00	40.00

○ Maria De'Aragon	15.00	25.00
○ Mark Hamill	30.00	50.00
○ Michael Sheard	15.00	25.00
○ Mike Carter	15.00	25.00
○ Natalie Portman	50.00	80.00
○ Peter Cushing	30.00	50.00
○ Peter Mayhew	30.00	50.00
○ Phil Brown	15.00	25.00
○ Samuel L. Jackson	40.00	60.00
○ Shelagh Fraser	12.00	20.00
○ Sir Alec Guiness	50.00	80.00
○ Terence Stamp	15.00	25.00
○ Warwick Davis	15.00	25.00

BED AND BATH

Bedspreads / Comforters / Quilts

BIBB CO.

- ○ Star Wars
- ○ The Empire Strikes back with Darth Vader and Boba Fett
- ○ Return of the Jedi with multiple characters
- ○ Return of the Jedi with Ewoks bedspread

Blankets

BIBB CO.

- ○ Star Wars
- ○ The Empire Strikes Back
- ○ Return of the Jedi

Return of the Jedi bedspread (Bibb Co.)

Curtains / Drapes

BIBB CO.

- ○ Star Wars
- ○ The Empire Strikes Back
- ○ ROTJ Montage 1
- ○ ROTJ Montage 2

Darth Vader bubble bath (Omni Cosmetics)

Pillowcases

BIBB CO.

◯ Star Wars

◯ The Empire Strikes Back

Sheets

BIBB CO.

◯ Star Wars

◯ The Empire Strikes Back

◯ Return of the Jedi

Sleeping Bags

BIBB CO.

◯ Star Wars

◯ The Empire Strikes Back

◯ Return of the Jedi

◯ Ewoks

Towels

BIBB CO.

◯ Star Wars

◯ The Empire Strikes Back

◯ ROTJ Ewoks, heroes, and Jabba's Palace

◯ ROTJ Bath Towel and Wash Mitt set

Nouveau from Bibb Designs (australia)

◯ ROTJ eight round scenes and spaceships on white

Washclothes

BIBB CO.

◯ Star Wars

◯ The Empire Strikes Back

◯ Return of the Jedi

Personal care kits

Omni Cosmetics

◯ Princess Leia beauty bag

Bubble bath

Omni Cosmetics

◯ R2-D2

◯ Princess Leia

◯ Chewbacca

◯ Jabba the Hutt

◯ Wicket

◯ Yoda

◯ Darth Vader

Combs / brushes

ADAM JOSEPH

◯ R2-D2 and C-3PO pop-up comb

◯ Princess Leia pop-up comb

◯ Max Rebo Band Comb-n-keeper

◯ Landspeeder Comb-n-keeper

◯ Kneesaa Comb-n-keeper

◯ Wicket and Kneesaa Comb-n-keeper

Shampoo

Omni Cosmetics

◯ Chewbacca

◯ Princess Leia

◯ Luke Skywalker

◯ Yoda

◯ R2-D2

◯ Darth Vader

◯ Wicket

◯ Jabba the Hutt

◯ Refill

Soap

OMNI COSMETICS

◯ Luke Skywalker

◯ Princess Leia

◯ Yoda

◯ Darth Vader

The Art of The Empire Strikes Back book (Random House)

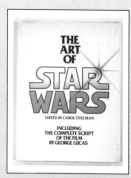

The Art of Star Wars book (Random House)

○ Gamorrean Guard

○ Wicket

○ C-3PO

○ Boxed set: Luke Skywalker, Princess Leia, Yoda and Chewbacca

○ Boxed set: R2-D2, Lando Calrissian, C-3PO and Darth Vader

ENGLAND

○ C-3PO

○ R2-D2

○ R2-D2 and C-3PO boxed set

○ Wicket and Woklings boxed set

The Star Wars Sketchbook (Random House)

Toiletry sets

ENGLAND

○ Return of the Jedi shower gel

○ Ewoks foam bath and soap

Toothbrushes

KENNER

○ Star Wars electronic toothbrush

○ Wicket electronic toothbrush

Oral B

○ Luke Skywalker

○ Princess Leia

○ Chewbacca & Han Solo

○ R2-D2 and C-3PO

○ Darth Vader

○ Ewoks

○ Jabba the Hutt dental check-up postcard

○ Ewok dental check-up postcard

○ Luke Skywalker and Darth Vader dental check-up postcard

Travel kits

OMNI COSMETICS

○ Luke Skywalker belt kit, blue bag

○ Ewoks personal care kit, red bag

○ Princess Leia beauty bag

BOOKS

Activity

Random House

○ Artoo Detoo's Activity Book $1.25 printed price

○ Artoo Detoo's Activity Book $1.50 printed price

○ Artoo Detoo's Activity Book $1.95 printed price

○ Luke Skywalker's Activity Book $1.25 printed price

○ Luke Skywalker's Activity Book $1.95 printed price

Return of the Jedi Sketchbook (Random House)

○ Chewbacca's Activity Book no printed price

○ Chewbacca's Activity Book $1.25 printed price

○ Chewbacca's Activity Book $1.50 printed price

○ Chewbacca's Activity Book $1.95 printed price

○ Darth Vader's Activity Book $1.25 printed price

○ Darth Vader's Activity Book $1.95 printed price

○ Iron-on Transfer Book

○ Star Wars Punch Out and Make It Book

○ TESB Mix and Match Book $2.95 printed price

○ TESB Mix and Match Book $3.50 printed price

○ TESB Mix and Match Book $3.95 printed price

○ The Empire Strikes Back Punch Out and Make It Book

○ Yoda's Activity Book

○ Star Wars Word Puzzles

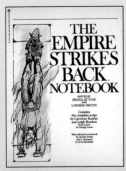

The Empire Strikes Back Notebook (Random House)

- ○ Return of the Jedi Punch Out and Make It Book
- ○ ROTJ Picture Puzzle Book
- ○ ROTJ Dot to Dot Fun
- ○ ROTJ Things to do and Make Book
- ○ ROTJ Word Puzzle Book with barcode
- ○ ROTJ Word Puzzle Book without barcode
- ○ ROTJ Monster Activity Book
- ○ ROTJ Mazes
- ○ ROTJ Book of Mazes

FUN WORKS

- ○ Millenium Falcon Punch Out and Make It book

LITTLE GOLDEN

- ○ Scratch and Sniff book

Random House (CANADA)

- ○ ROTJ Word Puzzle Book

The Star Wars Intergalactic Passport (Random House)

Art / sketch

Freidlander

- ○ The Art of Dave Dorman
- ○ Art of Dave Dorman hardcover

Random House

- ○ Art of Star Wars softcover
- ○ Art of Star Wars hardcover
- ○ Art of Star Wars (1994)
- ○ Star Wars Sketchbook
- ○ Art of The Empire Strikes Back softcover
- ○ The Empire Strikes Back Sketchbook
- ○ The Empire Strikes Back Notebook
- ○ Art of The Empire Strikes Back (1994)
- ○ Art of Return of the Jedi softcover
- ○ Art of Return of the Jedi (1994)
- ○ Return of the Jedi Sketch Book
- ○ The Art of Star Wars (1994 Edition) $18 half price

- ○ The Art of TESB (1994 Edition) $18 half price
- ○ The Art of ROTJ (1994 Edition) $18 half price

Topps Publishing

- ○ Art of Star Wars Galaxy Volume 1
- ○ Art of Star Wars Galaxy Volume 1 hardcover
- ○ Art of Star Wars Galaxy Volume 2 foil cover
- ○ Art of Star Wars Galaxy Volume 2
- ○ Art of Star Wars Galaxy Volume 3
- ○ The Art of Galaxy II Foil Cover $35 half price

Art portfolios

- ○ Random House
- ○ Star Wars Portfolio
- ○ The Empire Strikes Back Portfolio
- ○ Return of the Jedi Portfolio

Classico

- ○ Post Art Portfolio

Chronicle

- ○ The Art of Ralph McQuarrie

An Ewok Adventure coloring book (Little Golden)

Blank books

Antioch

- ○ Truce at Bakura wth matching bookmark
- ○ Crystal Star with matching bookmark
- ○ Courtship of Princess Leia with matching bookmark
- ○ Space Battle with bookmark
- ○ Book of Days

Chronicle Books

- ○ Star Wars Log Book

The Empire Strikes Back coloring book (Kenner)

Random House

○ My Jedi Journal

○ Intergalactic Passport

○ Technical Journal hardcover

Starlog Publications

○ Technical Journal #1

○ Technical Journal #1 Foil Cover

○ Technical Journal #2

○ Technical Journal #3

○ Second Edition with updated information
   on Special Edition

○ Technical Journal #1 Tatooine

○ Technical Journal #2 Rebel Forces

○ Technical Journal #3 Imperial Forces

Zanart

○ Star Wars Blueprint Portfolio

Unlicensed

○ Sci-Fi Blueprints

Bookmarks

Random House

○ Luke Skywalker

○ Darth Vader

○ Princess Leia

○ R2-D2

○ Lando Calrissian

○ Chewbacca

○ Ben Kenobi

○ Han Solo

○ Wicket

○ Admiral Ackbar

○ Imperial Guard

○ Stormtrooper

Return of the Jedi coloring book (Kenner)

○ Jabba the Hutt

○ Admiral Ackbar

A.H. Prismatic

○ B-Wing, Falcon, TIE Fighter

○ Falcon, Vader, Star Destroyer

○ X-wing, TIE Interceptor, AT-AT

Antioch, TASSLED

○ Courtship of Princess Leia

○ Crystal Star

○ Lost City of the Jedi

○ Zorba the Hutt

○ Glove of Darth Vader

○ Truce at Bakura

○ Han Solo

○ Darth Vader

○ Princess Leia

○ Luke Skywalker

○ Lando Calrissian

○ Ben Kenobi

○ Chewbacca

ANTIOCH, Shapemarks

○ Stormtrooper

○ Boba Fett

○ R2-D2

○ Yoda

○ Tusken Raider

○ C-3PO

○ Dancing Girl

Fantasma

○ Darth Vader 3-D

BANTAM

○ Darth Vader die-cut

Question and Answer Book About Space softcover (Random House)

TITAN BOOKS (GERMANY)

○ ROTJ bookmark

Bookplates

RANDOM HOUSE

○ R2-D2 and C-3PO

○ Darth Vader

ANTIOCH

○ Dark Empire

Coloring books

Kenner

○ Leia, Chewbacca and C-3PO

○ Luke Skywalker

○ R2-D2

○ Yoda

○ Darth Vader and Stormtroopers

○ Max Rebo Band

○ Luke Skywalker-Bespin

○ Lando in battle

○ Wicket's World

○ Wicket the Ewok

Dragon Books (England)

○ Droids

○ Ewoks

FERNANDEZ EDITORES (LITTLE GOLDEN — MEXICO)

○ Heroes and Villains

○ Galactic Adventures

○ Activity Book

Little Golden

○ A Galaxy of Creatures, Characters, and Droids

○ An Ewok Adventure

Question and Answer Book About Computers (Random House)

Comic paperbacks

Random House

○ Star Wars

Marvel

○ The Empire Strikes Back

○ Return of the Jedi

○ World of Fire

Educational

Random House

○ Attack on Reading Comprehension

○ Attack on Reading Word Study

○ C-3PO's Book About Robots

○ Star Wars Book About Flight

○ Question and Answer Book about Space hardcover

○ Library Edition of Question and Answer Book about Space

○ Question and Answer Book about Space softcover

○ Question and Answer Book About Computers

○ ROTJ Multiplication

○ ROTJ Addition and Subtraction

○ ROTJ Reading and Writing

○ ROTJ Spelling with barcode

○ ROTJ Spelling without barcode

○ ROTJ Early Numbers

○ ROTJ ABC Readiness

LITTLE GOLDEN

○ Spelling

Games

Random House

○ Jedi Master's Quiz Book (blue cover)

Question and Answer Book About Space hardcover (Random House)

Checklist

○ Jedi Master's Quiz Book (black cover)

○ From The Blob to Star Wars Quiz Book

Prima publishing

○ Rebel Assault Guide

○ Super Empire Strikes Back Hintbook

○ Super Star Wars Hintbook

○ X-wing Strategy Guide

○ uper Return of the Jedi Hintbook

○ Official Strategy Guide: Jedi Knights

SUPER NINTENDO

Super Return of the Jedi Hintbook

The Empire Strikes Back Mix-Match Storybook (Random House)

Guides

Random House

○ A Guide to the Star Wars Universe

○ A Guide to the Star Wars Universe second edition

○ Essential Guide to Characters

○ Essential Guide to Vehicles and Vessels

○ The Essential Guide to Weapons and Technology

Scholastic

○ Rebel Alliance Scrapbook

○ Galactic Empire Scrapbook

Paradise Press

○ The World of Star Wars

"Making of" books

Citadel Press

○ Empire Building

Random House

○ The Star Wars Compendium

○ The Star Wars Album

○ Star Wars the Making of the Movie

The Empire Strikes Back softcover novel

○ Once Upon a Galaxy

○ The Making of Return of the Jedi

○ The Secrets of Shadows of the Empire

Australia

○ The Star Wars Album

Germany

○ The Star Wars Album

Netherlands

○ The Star Wars Album

Paradise Press

○ The Star Wars Compendium

Mechanical

Random House

○ Star Wars Pop-Up Book

○ The Empire Strikes Back Pop-Up Book

○ The Empire Strikes Back Panorama Book

○ Return of the Jedi Pop-Up Book

○ Han Solo's Rescue Pop-Up Book hardcover

○ Ewok's Save the Day Pop-Up Book hardcover

○ Mos Eisley Cantina Pop-Up Book

○ Star Wars Lift the Flap Book

Dark Horse

○ Battle of the Bounty Hunters Pop-Up Book

Little Brown

○ Rebel Alliance Pop-Up Book

○ The Galactic Empire Pop-Up Book

Little Golden

○ A Droid's Tale

Play-a-Sound Star Wars book (Publications International)

PUBLICATIONS INTERNATIONAL

○ Star Wars: A New Hope Play-a-Sound

Non-fiction

Chronicle

○ Vintage Toys postcard book

○ From Star Wars to Indiana Jones softcover

○ Star Wars to Indiana Jones hardcover

○ Behind the Scenes postcard book

○ Aliens and Creatures postcard book

Abrams

○ Geoge Lucas the Creative Impulse

Bible Voice

○ The Force of Star Wars

Random House

○ Industrial Light and Magic: Into the Digital Realm

○ Skywalk Trade paperback

○ The Quotable Star Wars

Starlog

○ Science Fiction Heroes and Heroines

○ Toys

○ Villians

○ Heroes

Ballantine

○ Star Wars The Magic of Myth

Bantam

○ The Magic of Myth hardcover

JAPAN

○ George Lucas the Creative Impulse

○ From Concept to Screen to Collectible

○ Harrison Ford

Unknown

○ The Films of Harrison Ford

Novels

○ Star Wars paperback

○ First edition

○ Second edition June 1977 Berkey Cover

○ "Now a Spectacular"

○ Third-Sixth

○ Seventh June 1977 "Best Movie of the Year"

○ Eigth

○ Ninth July 1977 "Best Movie" no photos

○ 10th-12th

○ 13th August 1977

○ 14th

○ 15th August 1977

○ 16th-19th

○ 20th May 1978 "Over 5 Million in Print"

○ 21st-26th

○ 27th May 1983 "Over 5 Million" Star Wars in green

○ 28th-48th

○ 49th Title changed to A New Hope new cover

○ 1st Special Printing August 1977

○ 2nd Special Printing October 1977

○ 3rd Special Printing November 1977

○ 1st Special Printing July 1978

○ 2nd Special Printing January 1983

○ Star Wars hardcover Book Club

○ Star Wars hardcover (1995)

○ Splinter of the Mind's Eye hardcover

○ Splinter of the Mind's Eye paperback

Return of the Jedi softcover novel

Star Wars hardcover novel

Star Wars softcover novel

○ Han Solo at Stars End hardcover

○ Han Solo at Stars End paperback

○ Han Solo's Revenge hardcover

○ Han Solo's Revenge paperback

○ Han Solo and the Lost Legacy paperback

○ an Solo Adventures paperback

○ Han Solo Adventures Trade Paperaback

○ The Empire Strikes Back paperback

○ The Empire Strikes Back paperback 22nd printing

○ The Empire Strikes Back hardcover (1995)

○ The Empire Strikes Back Illustrated Edition

○ Return of the Jedi paperback

○ Return of the Jedi paperback 24th printing

○ Return of the Jedi hardcover (1995)

○ Return of the Jedi Illustrated Edition

○ Star Wars Trilogy paperback Boxed set

○ Star Wars Trilogy paperback

○ Star Wars Trilogy Trade paperback

○ Lando Calrissian and the Mindharp of Sharu paperback

○ Lando Calrissian and the Flamewing of Oseon paperback

○ Lando Calrissian and the Starcave of Thonboka paperback

○ Lando Calrissian Adventures paperback

○ Lando Calrissian Adventures Trade paperback

○ Han Solo and the Lost Legacy

○ The Phantom Menace novel by Terry Brooks

Bantam

○ Heir to the Empire hardcover

○ Heir to the Empire Book Club

○ Heir to the Empire paperback

○ Dark Force Rising hardcover

○ Dark Force Rising Book Club

○ Dark Force Rising paperback

○ Dark Force Rising Limited Edition

○ The Last Command hardcover

○ The Last Command Book Club

○ The Last Command paperback

○ Truce at Bakura hardcover

○ Truce at Bakura hardcover Book Club

○ Truce at Bakura paperback

○ Courtship of Princess Leia hardcover

○ Courtship of Princess Leia Book Club

○ Courtship of Princess Leia paperback

○ Jedi Search paperback

○ Dark Apprentice paperback

○ Champions of the Force

○ Jedi Academy Trilogy Boxed set

○ The Crystal Star hardcover

○ The Crystal Star hardcover Book Club

○ The Crystal Star paperback

○ Ambush at Corelli paperback

○ Assault on Selonia paperback

○ Showdown at Centerpoint paperback

○ Corellian Trilogy hardcover Book Club

○ Children of the Jedi hardcover

○ Children of the Jedi Book Club

○ Children of the Jedi paperback

○ Dark Saber hardcover

○ Dark Saber Book Club

○ Dark Saber paperback

○ Tales From Jabba's Palace paperback

○ Tales From the Mos Eisley Cantina paperback

○ X-wing Book 1: Rogue Squadron paperback

○ X-wing Book 2: Wedge's Gamble

○ X-wing: The Wraith

○ Kryto's Trap paperback

○ Black Fleet Crisis Book 1: Before the Storm

○ Black Fleet Crisis Book 2

○ Black Fleet Crisis Book

○ Shadows of the Empire hardcover

○ New Rebellion hardcover

Star Wars Radio Dramatization (Random House)

The Star Wars Storybook softcover (Random House)

○ Boxed sets

○ Corellian Trilogy

○ Jedi Academy Trilogy

○ Tales of the Empire

○ Specter of the Past, hardcover

○ Tales from the Empire

Berkely

○ Young Jedi Knights

○ Heirs to the Force

○ Shadow Academy

○ The Lost Ones

○ Light Sabers

○ Darkest Knight

○ Jedi Under Seige

○ Young Jedi Boxed set 1-3

○ Young Jedi hardcover 1-6

The Star Wars Storybook hardcover (Random House)

Costa Rica

○ The Empire Strikes Back softcover

England

○ Star Wars paperback "Greatest film of the Century"

○ Star Wars paperback "A Spectacular Motion Picture"

France

○ The Empire Strikes Back softcover

Germany

○ The Empire Strikes Back second cover paperback

○ Return of the Jedi softcover

○ Return of the Jedi photocover

○ Star Wars Trilogy paperback

○ Heir to the Empire

○ Dark Force Rising

○ The Last Command

○ The Truce at Bakura hardcover

Japan

○ Heir to the Empire

○ Dark Force Rising

Korea

○ Heir to the Empire softcover

Netherlands

○ Star Wars Trade paperback

○ Star Wars larger trade paperback

○ Star wars softcover photo cover

○ Return of the Jedi softcover

Spain

○ Heir to the Empire

○ Dark Force Rising

○ Last Command

Postcard books

chronicle

○ Alien Creatures

Scripts / screenplays

RANDOM HOUSE ILLUSTRATED SCREENPLAYS

○ A New Hope

○ The Empire Strikes Back

○ Return of the Jedi

Random House

○ Star Wars Radio Dramatization

○ The Empire Strikes Back Radio Dramatization

OSP

○ Star Wars

○ The Empire Strikes Back

○ Return of the Jedi

○ Boxed set of Scripts

Random House (Del Rey)

○ The Annotated Screenplays

The Empire Strikes Back Storybook hardcover (Random House)

Technical

Random House

○ Star Wars Blue Prints

Unlicensed

○ Star Destroyer Blueprints

Kids books

Random House

○ Star Wars Storybook

○ hardcover with Anthony's
   hand no bar code 1-5 printing

○ hardcover without Anthony's hand no barcode 7-9 printing

○ hardcover with barcode
   14-17 printing

○ hardcover with barcode no printing

○ Star Wars Storybook softcover

○ Star Wars Storybook softcover "TV4466"

○ The Empire Strikes Back Storybook hardcover

○ The Empire Strikes Back Storybook HC Book Club

○ The Empire Strikes Back Storybook softcover

○ Return of the Jedi Storybook hardcover

○ Return of the Jedi Storybook hardcover Weekly Readers

○ Return of the Jedi Storybook hardcover Book Club Edition

○ Return of the Jedi Storybook softcover

○ Star Wars Treasury

○ Star Wars Storybook Trilogy

○ Star Wars Step Up Book

○ Star Wars Step Up Book (1995)

○ The Empire Strikes Back Step Up Book

○ The Empire Strikes Back Step Up Book (1995)

○ Return of the Jedi Step Up Book

○ Return of the Jedi Step Up Book Weekly Readers

○ Return of the Jedi Step Up Book (1995)

○ Mystery of the Rebellious Robot $1.25 printed price

○ Mystery of the Rebellious Robot $1.95 printed price

The Mystery of the Rebellious Robot (Random House)

○ Mystery of the Rebellious Robot no printed price

○ Wookie Storybook without barcode

○ Wookie Storybook with barcode

○ Baby Ewoks Picnic Surprise

○ Three Cheers for Kneesaa

○ The Ewoks Hang-Gliding Adventure

○ Wicket Finds a Way

○ Ewoks Join the Fight with barcode

○ Ewoks Join the Fight no barcode

○ Ewoks Join the Fight no barcode no price

○ How the Ewoks Saved the Trees hardcover

○ How the Ewoks Saved the Trees softcover

○ Ewoks and the Lost Children

○ The Lost Prince hardcover

○ Escape from the Monster Ship

○ Shiny as a Droid

○ Fuzzy as an Ewok

○ The Red Ghost

Bantam

○ The Glove of Darth Vader

○ The Lost City of the Jedi

○ Zorba the Hutt's Revenge

○ Mission From Mount Yoda

○ Queen of the Empire

○ Prophets of the Dark Side

○ Illustrated Star Wars Universe

○ Galaxy of Fear Series

○ The Brain Spiders

○ The Swarm

Abrams

○ Monsters and Aliens from George Lucas

Berkeley

○ The Golden Globe

○ Lyric's World

○ Promises

The Star Wars Storybook softcover (Random House)

The Empire Strikes Back Panorama Book (Random House)

England

○ Return of the Jedi Storybook hardcover

JAPAN

○ Ewoks and the Lost Children

○ The Glove of Darth Vader

○ The Lost City of the Jedi

○ Queen of the Empire

○ Mission From Mount Yoda

○ Prophets of the Dark Side

○ Zorba the Hutt's Revenge

○ Monsters and Aliens from George Lucas

Netherlands

○ Star Wars storybook softcover

BUTTONS AND BADGES

Adam Joseph

○ Revenge of the Jedi with TM and ©LFL 1982

○ Return of the Jedi logo

○ Max Rebo

○ Gamorrean Guard

○ Teaser art

○ Darth Vader

○ Jabba the Hutt

○ Heroes in Forest

○ Chewbacca

○ Royal Guard

○ Yoda

CBS Fox Video

○ Fox Video button

○ Special Edition Video button

Star Wars Fan Club

○ Fan Club Logo button

Factors

○ May the Force Be With You

○ R2-D2

○ C-3PO

○ Luke Skywalker

○ Chewbacca

○ Ben Kenobi

○ Darth Vader

○ Darth Vadar Lives (sic)

○ Yoda

○ Chewbacca

○ Luke Skywalker

1978 Star Wars Calendar (Ballantine)

Adam Joseph

○ ROTJ with TM and ©LFL 1982

○ Return of the Jedi Logo

○ Max Rebo

○ Gamorrean Guard

○ Revenge of the Jedi poster art

○ R2-D2 and C-3PO

○ Darth Vader

○ Jabba the Hutt

○ Heroes in Forest

○ Chewbacca

○ Baby Ewok

○ Royal Guard

○ Yoda

○ Wicket the Ewok Logo

○ Ewoks Shoveling Snow

○ Basket on Head

○ Lessons in Forest

○ Sitting and Thinking

○ Flying

○ Wicket and R2-D2

○ Kneesaa and Baga

○ Feeding Baga

○ Baby Grouping

1984 Ewoks Calendar (Ballantine)

○ Wicket Tells a Story
○ Swinging on a Vine

Star Wars Trilogy

○ March 28, 1985 Button

10th Anniversary Convention

○ The First Ten Years
○ R2-D2 and C-3PO button
○ Darth Vader button

20th Century Fox Video

○ Promotional button

Star Badges

○ R2-D2
○ Chewbacca

Dark Horse Comics

○ Star Wars
○ Promotional button

Unlicensed

○ May The Force Be With You button
○ Revenge of the Jedi button

Star Trek Galore

○ Sisterhood of the Jedi Knights badge

GERMANY

○ Ewok
○ Teaser Art
○ Darth Vader
○ Max Rebo band
○ Style A Art
○ C-3PO
○ Vader with guards
○ R2-D2, C-3PO and Wicket
○ Jabba
○ Baby Ewok

○ Yoda
○ Gamorrean Guard
○ Luke Skywalker
○ Han Solo
○ Luke, Han and Leia
○ Sy Snootles
○ TIE Fighters
○ TIE Fighter and X-wing
○ TIE Fighters and X-wing

Star Tours

○ Round MGM sticker
○ Glow in the Dark MGM sticker
○ Sticker
○ Bumper sticker
○ Glow in the Dark sticker
○ Star Tours pin
○ Key chain
○ Black badge
○ Blue badge
○ C-3PO 35 Years pin
○ Button
○ Sticker sheet
○ Rex key chain
○ Badge
○ Sticker sheet

CALENDARS

Abrams

○ 1991 Lucasfilm

Andrews and McMeel

○ 1995 Magic Eye

Antioch

○ 1995
○ Book of Days

Return of the Jedi trading card package (Topps)

Return of the Jedi trading card package (Topps)

Ballantine

○ 1978 Star Wars (Luke Skywalker, Princess Leia, Han Solo)

○ 1979 Star Wars

○ 1980 Star Wars (poster art)

○ 1981 The Empire Strikes Back

○ 1984 Return of the Jedi

○ 1984 Ewok

○ 1990 Star wars trilogy

○ 1991 Star Wars trilogy

○ 1995 Star Wars trilogy

○ 1996 Star Wars

○ 1997 The Empire Strikes Back

○ 1997 Art of Star Wars

Capitol Distribution

○ 1995 Advanced Comics

Cedco

○ 1990

○ 1991

○ 1996

○ 1996 Date Book

○ 1997

○ 1997 Vehicles

○ 1997 Datebook

CHRONICLE BOOKS

○ 1997 Vehicles

Golden Turtle

○ 1997

Hallmark

○ 1995

Ink Group

○ 1998 Desk Calendar

Landmark General

○ 1995

Random House

○ 1978

○ 1979

○ 1980

○ 1981

○ 1984

Shooting Star Press

○ 1997

CERAMICS

○ Yoda stein

○ Boba Fett stein

○ Yoda salt and pepper shaker

Collector plates

○ Hamilton

○ Plate #1 Imperial Shuttle Plate

○ Plate #2 Snowspeeder

○ Plate #3 Millennium Falcon Plate

○ Plate #4 Star Destroyer

○ Plate #5 B-Wing

○ Plate #6 TIE Fighter

○ Plate #7 X-wing

○ Plate #8 Slave-1

Other

○ Han Solo

○ Crew in Cockpit

○ 1993 Movie Series

○ Star Wars

○ The Empire Strikes Back

○ Return of the Jedi

- ○ 1995 Ship Series
- ○ Millennium Falcon
- ○ Slave 1
- ○ Shuttle Tyderium
- ○ Characters
- ○ Luke Skywalker

Cookie jars

SIGMA

- ○ Hexagonal with droids on one side and Darth Vader on other

Cups and mugs

Sigma Ceramics

- ○ Luke Skywalker
- ○ Princess Leia
- ○ Han Solo
- ○ Chewbacca
- ○ C-3PO
- ○ Darth Vader
- ○ Lando Calrissian
- ○ Gamorrean Guard
- ○ Klaatu
- ○ Wicket
- ○ Biker scout

Applause

- ○ Darth Vader
- ○ Boba Fett
- ○ Stormtrooper
- ○ Tusken Raider
- ○ Han Solo
- ○ Emperor
- ○ Bib Fortuna
- ○ Gamorrean Guard
- ○ C-3PO
- ○ Princess Leia
- ○ Luke Skywalker

Rawcliffe

- ○ Shuttle Tyderium

Princess Leia trading card

- ○ TIE Fighter
- ○ AT-AT
- ○ AT-ST
- ○ Rebel Logo
- ○ Return of the Jedi
- ○ The Empire Strikes Back
- ○ Star Wars
- ○ Darth Vader
- ○ Yoda
- ○ Obi Wan Kenobi
- ○ Shadows of the Empire

Metalic Impresions

- ○ Star Wars Dimensional stein

Unlicensed

- ○ Darth Vader ceramic mug

Figurines

SIGMA

- ○ Han Solo
- ○ Princess Leia
- ○ R2-D2 and C-3PO
- ○ Darth Vader
- ○ Klaatu
- ○ Bib Fortuna
- ○ Wicket
- ○ Lando Calrissian

Sigma Ceramics

- ○ Lando Calrissian ceramic figurine

HOUSEHOLD ITEMS

- ○ C-3PO pencil tray
- ○ C-3PO picture frame

Music Boxes

- ○ Turret music box

Unlicensed

- ○ Yoda musical figurine

Luke Skywalker trading card

Tankards

UNLICENSED

○ Chewbacca copy

COMICS

MARVEL
1977-88 Star Wars

○ #1	40.00	80.00
○ #1A, 35 cent, cover/UPC	200.00	400.00
○ #1B, reprint	3.00	6.00
○ #2-4	12.50	25.00
○ #5-6	15.00	30.00
○ #7-44	7.50	15.00
○ #45-106	6.00	12.00
○ #107, last issue	25.00	50.00

1983 Star Wars Return of the Jedi Mini-Series

○ #1	3.00	6.00
○ #2-4	1.50	3.00

DARK HORSE
1991-92 Star Wars Dark Empire

○ #1	10.00	20.00
○ #1A, Platinum	20.00	40.00
○ #1B, Gold	20.00	40.00
○ #1C, Second print	2.00	4.00
○ #1D, Wizard edition	7.50	15.00
○ #2	10.00	20.00
○ #2A, Platinum	20.00	40.00
○ #2B, Gold	20.00	40.00
○ #2C, Second print	2.00	4.00
○ #3	5.00	10.00
○ #3A, Platinum	10.00	20.00
○ #3B, Gold	10.00	20.00
○ #3C, Second print	1.50	3.00
○ #4-	55.00	10.00
○ #4A-5A, Platinum	7.50	15.00
○ #4B-5B, Gold	7.50	15.00
○ #6	3.00	6.00

○ #6A, Platinum	7.50	15.00
○ #6B, Gold	7.50	15.00

1993-94 Star Wars Tales of the Jedi

○ #1	2.50	5.00
○ #2-5	2.00	4.00

1994 Star Wars Dark Empire II

○ #1	4.00	8.00
○ #1A, Platinum	5.00	10.00
○ #2-6	2.00	4.00
○ #2A-6A, Platinum	4.00	8.00

1994 Star Wars Droids

○ #1-6	1.50	3.00
○ 1994 Star Wars		

Tales of the Jedi: The Freedon Nadd Uprising

○ #1-2	1.50	3.00

1994-95 Star Wars Tales of the Jedi: Dark lords of the Sith

○ #1, bagged	2.00	4.00
○ #2-6	1.50	3.00

1995 Star Wars Droids

○ #1	1.50	3.00
○ #2-8	1.00	2.50

1995 Star Wars Empires End

○ #1-2	1.50	3.00

1995 Star Wars: Heir to the Empire

○ #1-6	1.50	3.00

1995 Star Wars: River of Chaos

○ #1-4	1.50	3.00

1995 Star Wars: Splinters of the Mind's Eye

○ #1-4	1.50	3.00

1995 Star Wars: Tales of the Jedi — The Sith War

○ #1-6	1.25	2.50

1995-99 Star Wars: X-wing Rogue Squadron

○ #1/2, Wizard MI	5.00	10.00
○ #1/2A, Wizard MI		
PLAT.	6.00	12.00

Han Solo trading card

Chewbacca trading card

○ #1-2	2.00	4.00
○ #3-35	1.50	3.00

1996 Star Wars: Battle of the Bounty Hunters

○ #1	10.00	20.00

1996 Star Wars: Shadows of the Empire

○ #1-6	2.00	4.00

1996 Star Wars: Tales of the Jedi — The Golden Age of Sith

○ #0	.75	1.50
○ #1-5	1.50	3.00

1997 Star Wars

○ #0-Amer.Ent.Exc.	10.00	20.00

1997 Star Wars: Crimson Empire

○ #1	3.00	6.00
○ #2-6	2.50	5.00

1997 Star Wars: Dark Force Rising

○ #1-6	1.50	3.00

1997 Star Wars: Tales of the Jedi — Redemption

○ #1-5	1.50	3.00

1997 Star Wars: Tales of the Jedi — The Fall of the Sith Empire

○ #1	2.00	4.00
○ #1A, signed	12.50	25.00
○ #2-5	1.50	3.00

1997-98 Star Wars: The Last Command

○ #1-6	1.50	3.00

1998 Star Wars: Crimson Empire II

○ #1-6	1.50	3.00

1998 Star Wars: Shadows of the Empire — Evolution

○ #1-5	2.50	5.00

Star Wars: Boba Fett

○ #1/2 Wizard MI	5.00	10.00
○ #1/2 Wizard MI Gold	7.50	15.00

○ Bounty On Bar-Kooda	2.50	5.00
○ Murder Most Foul	2.50	5.00
○ Twin Engines Of Destruction.	2.00	4.00
○ When The Fat Lady Sings	2.00	4.00
○ Death, Lies & Treachery	6.00	12.00

Star Wars: Jabba the Hut

○ Betrayal	1.25	2.50
○ The Dynasty Trap	1.25	2.50
○ The Gaar Suppoon Hit	1.25	2.50
○ The Hunger Of Pr.Nampi	1.25	2.50

England (Marvel U.K.)
○ Star Wars Weekly
○ TESB Weekly
○ TESB Monthly
○ ROJ Weekly

Annuals (hardcover)

○ Star Wars Annual
○ TESB Annual
○ Return of the Jedi Annual 1984
○ Return of the Jedi Annual 1985

England (Dark Horse U.K.)
○ Star Wars #1-#10

Grupo Editorial (Mexico)
○ Star Wars Special Edition Trade paperback
○ TESB Special Edition Trade paperback
○ ROTJ Special Edition Trade paperback
○ Trade paperback Volume 1
○ Trade paperback Volume 2
○ Trade paperback Volume 3

COSTUMES / MASKS

Promotora Textil Mexicana
○ C-3PO costume with mask
○ Darth Vader costume with mask

Darth Vader trading card

Costumes

Ben Cooper

○ Darth Vader costume blue box

○ Stormtrooper costume blue box

○ Darth Vader costume

○ Luke Skywalker costume

○ C-3PO costume

○ R2-D2 costume

○ Princess Leia costume

○ Chewbacca costume

○ Boba Fett costume

○ Darth Vader costume

○ C-3PO costume

○ Luke in Pilot costume

○ Princess Leia costume

○ Chewbacca costume

○ Stormtrooper costume

○ Boba Fett costume

○ Yoda costume, green version

○ Yoda costume, blue version

○ Wicket costume, TESB box, Revenge logo

○ Wicket costume, TESB box, Return logo

○ Wicket costume, ROTJ box, Revenge logo

○ Wicket costume, ROTJ box, Return logo

○ Admiral Ackbar costume, TESB box, Revenge logo

○ Admiral Ackbar costume, TESB box, Return logo

○ Admiral Ackbar costume, ROTJ box, Revenge logo

○ Admiral Ackbar costume, ROTJ box, Return logo

○ Gamorrean Guard costume, TESB box, Revenge logo

○ Gamorrean Guard costume, ROTJ box, Return logo

○ Klaatu costume, TESB box, Revenge logo

○ Klaatu costume, ROTJ box, Return logo

ENGLAND

○ C-3PO costume

○ Chewbacca costume

○ Darth Vader costume

○ Stormtrooper costume

**C-3PO
trading card**

Masks

Cesar (France)

○ Darth Vader two-piece

Don Post Studios

○ Chewbacca

○ Cantina Band member

○ Yoda with hair

○ Admiral Ackbar

○ Darth Vader mask

○ Darth Vader life size

○ Stormtrooper mask

○ C-3PO mask

○ Chewbacca mask

○ Cantina Band Member mask

○ Yoda mask

○ Gamorrean Guard mask

○ Admiral Ackbar mask

○ Wicket mask with fur

○ Wicket mask

○ Darth Vader mask, TESB label

○ Darth Vader mask

○ Chewbacca mask, large version

○ Chewbacca mask, small version

○ C-3PO mask, chrome version

○ C-3PO mask, small version

○ C-3PO mask, mid size version

○ C-3PO mask, large version

○ Stormtrooper mask

○ Tusken Raider mask

○ Gamorrean Guard rubber mask

○ Yoda rubber mask

○ Klaatu rubber mask

○ Wicket rubber mask

○ Chewbaccaa rubber mask

○ Admiral Ackbar rubber mask

○ Imperial Guard

○ Boba Fett

**Greedo
trading card**

**Luke Skywalker
trading card**

Rubies Costume Company

- ○ C-3PO
- ○ Chewbacca
- ○ Stormtrooper
- ○ Yoda
- ○ Darth Vader
- ○ Chewbacca
- ○ Princess Leia — wig
- ○ Princess Leia — no wig

FRANCE

- ○ C-3PO mask
- ○ Tusken Raider mask
- ○ C-3PO mask
- ○ Chewbacca mask
- ○ Stormtrooper mask

Play suits

ENGLAND

- ○ C-3PO outfit

Ponchos

- ○ C-3PO poncho
- ○ Darth Vader poncho

CRAFTS

MEXICO

- ○ Star Wars wall poster with stickers

Coloring sets

Rose Art

- ○ 3-D Crayon by Number

Figurine paint sets

- ○ Princess Leia
- ○ Yoda
- ○ Han Solo
- ○ Admiral Ackbar

- ○ Wicket
- ○ R2-D2 and C-3PO

Paint by number

- ○ Craftmaster
- ○ Battle on Hoth paint set
- ○ Darth Vader
- ○ Luke Skywalker
- ○ Princess Leia
- ○ Lando and Boussh
- ○ Jabba the Hutt
- ○ Max Rebo Band
- ○ R2-D2 and C-3PO
- ○ Wicket
- ○ Ewok Flyers
- ○ Ewok Village

Craft House

- ○ Star Wars Style C artwork

Paint sets

Craft House

- ○ Darth Vader and R2-D2 / C-3PO medallions
- ○ Han Solo and Princess Leia medallions
- ○ Luke and Yoda medallions

Poster sets

- ○ Star Wars play set

Rose Art Industries

- ○ A New Hope poster art

Iron-on appliques

- ○ Chewie iron-on
- ○ X-wing iron-on "Foto Dazzlers"
- ○ Princess Leia iron-on ROTJ
- ○ Hildebrandt iron-on with mini poster
- ○ Mask iron-on with mini poster

Sugar-Free Bubble Gum cards — Han Solo (Topps)

Sugar-Free Bubble Gum cards — Luke Skywalker (Topps)

- Droids iron-on with mini poster
- Luke Skywalker and C-3PO iron-on
- Han and Chewbacca iron-on with mini poster
- May The Force Be With You iron-on
- May The Force Be With You iron-on with mini poster
- Darth Vader Lives iron-on with mini poster
- Chewie iron-on
- C-3PO iron-on
- R2-D2 iron-on
- Ugnaughts iron-on

Rub-down transfers

American Publishing Presto Magix

- Star Wars activity set
- Battle on Endor
- Jabba the Hutt
- Ewoks at Home
- Poly-Bagged Sets
- Asteroid Storm
- Beneath Cloud City
- Cloud City Battle
- Dagobah Bog Planet
- Deck of the Star Destroyer

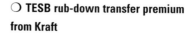

Sugar-Free Bubble Gum cards — Princess Leia (Topps)

- Ice Planet Hoth
- Rebel Base
- Ewok Village
- Jabba the Hutt
- Sarlac Pit
- Death Star
- Ewoks at Play

Rose Art Industries
- Super Stickers and Tatoo Station

England
- Sarlac Pit poly-bagged large set
- Ewok Village poly-bagged large set
- Jabba the Hutt poly-bagged small set
- The Ewoks poly-bagged small set

- TESB rub-down transfer premium from Kraft

Rubber stamps

Adam Joseph

- Chewbacca
- TIE Fighter
- Darth Vader
- Admiral Ackbar
- Gamorrean Guard
- C-3PO
- Wicket Three-in-One stamp set

Sewing kits

- Ewok Show and Sew cards

Stained glass

- C-3PO suncatcher
- Darth Vader suncatcher
- Princess Leia suncatcher
- R2-D2 and Yoda suncatcher
- Snowspeeders suncatcher
- R2-D2 Make It and Bake It
- Darth Vader Make It and Bake It
- Gamorrean Guard Make It and Bake It
- Jabba the Hutt and Salacious Crumb Make It and Bake It

Rose Art Industres

- Comic Maker
- Fun With Tatoos
- Activity Case
- Designer Desk

Return of the Jedi trading card package (Topps)

Star Wars trading card package (Topps)

CUPS / GLASSES

Collector's Cups

Burger King

- ○ Star Wars
- ○ Luke Skywalker
- ○ Return of the Jedi
- ○ Jabba the Hutt
- ○ Ewoks

PepsiCo

- ○ Darth Vader
- ○ Stormtrooper

Coke Star Wars numbered set of eight

- ○ Han and Chewbacca
- ○ Final Chase
- ○ Tusken Raiders, Jawas
- ○ Darth Vader
- ○ R2-D2 and C-3PO
- ○ Ben Kenobi
- ○ Luke and Leia
- ○ Vader and Kenobi duel

Coke Star Wars numbered set of 20

- ○ Stormtroopers
- ○ Chewbacca and Han Solo
- ○ Trapped in Trash Compactor
- ○ Duel of the Light Sabers
- ○ Vader, X-wing and TIE Fighter
- ○ Dogfight
- ○ Mos Eisley
- ○ Luke Skywalker
- ○ Skywalker with lightsaber
- ○ Vader and Grand Moff Tarkin
- ○ Chewbacca with Luke and Han
- ○ R2-D2 and C-3PO
- ○ Princess Leia
- ○ Tusken Raiders
- ○ Tusken Raiders II

Star Wars trading card package (Topps)

- ○ Jawas
- ○ Vader choking commander
- ○ Luke and Leia
- ○ Luke, Leia and Han
- ○ Ben Kenobi

Coke Star Wars unnumbered set of nine

- ○ Boba Fett
- ○ The Final Chase
- ○ Ben Kenobi
- ○ Darth Vader and Grand Moff Tarkin
- ○ Luke Skywalker and Princess Leia
- ○ R2-D2 and C-3PO
- ○ Han Solo
- ○ Chewbacca
- ○ Return of the Jedi Theatre Cup

Coke ROTJ 1983 set of 12 unnumbered

- ○ Han, Leia, and Chewie at Bunker
- ○ Bikers
- ○ Ackbar
- ○ Throne Room
- ○ Barge and Skiff
- ○ Bib Fortuna
- ○ Han Luke and Chewie
- ○ Luke and Darth
- ○ Moff Jerrjerrod
- ○ Klaatu, Jawas, Ishi
- ○ Wicket
- ○ Admiral Ackbar

Star Wars Movie Photo Cards pack (Topps)

Coke/Kenner ROTJ 1985 theatre promtion: "Win SW toys"

- ○ Kenner Theatre promotional cup with game piece

Peppridge Farms Tumblers

- ○ In-store ROTJ Cup
- ○ Rebels
- ○ Villians
- ○ Vehicles
- ○ Creatures

Glasses

BURGER KING Star Wars Glasses

- ○ Luke Skywalker
- ○ R2-D2 and C-3PO
- ○ Chewbacca
- ○ Darth Vader

BURGER KING The Empire Strikes Back Glasses

- ○ Luke Skywalker
- ○ R2-D2 and C-3PO
- ○ Lando Calrissian
- ○ Darth Vader

BURGER KING Return of the Jedi

- ○ Jabba the Hutt
- ○ Desert Tatooine
- ○ Ewoks
- ○ Throne Room

BURGER KING Massachusetts Plastic ROTJ Tumblers

- ○ Jabba the Hutt
- ○ Tatooine Desert
- ○ Emperor's Throne Room

Cristal Glasses (PepsiCo)

- ○ Stormtrooper

Holland

- ○ C-3PO glass

Sports Bottles

- ○ C-3PO
- ○ Stormtrooper

Wax / Paper

Pepsi

- ○ Special Edition game cup

Star Tours

- ○ Shorter silver ceramic mug

- ○ Tall mug
- ○ Plastic tumbler
- ○ C-3PO mug

FAN CLUBS

- ○ Lucasfilm/Star Wars Fan Club
- ○ Star Wars Insider #35 subscription edition

Membership kits

- ○ Official Star Wars Fan Club 1977-1987
- ○ Star Wars Fan Club membership card
- ○ Luke Skywalker wallet photo
- ○ A New Hope sticker
- ○ Color still
- ○ Star Wars Fan Club bookcover
- ○ 1985 Fan Club kit
- ○ Language sticker
- ○ 1993 membership kit
- ○ 1984 membership kit
- ○ TESB Fan Club card
- ○ Vader in Flames sticker
- ○ Yoda sticker
- ○ Lucasfilm membership card
- ○ ROTJ membership card
- ○ ROTJ Flicker postcard
- ○ Official Fan Club Special Items flyer
- ○ Letter with ROTJ kit
- ○ Letter with Yoda sticker
- ○ Merchandise flyer
- ○ Special product flyer — blue
- ○ Special product flyer — orange
- ○ ROTJ Storyboard
- ○ Letter with TESB poster
- ○ Questionnaire
- ○ Renewal letter 1986
- ○ Renewal letter 1985
- ○ ROTJ color flyer
- ○ TEST color flyer

Star Wars trading card package (Topps)

Star Wars trading card package (Topps)

Apparel

- ○ Official Star Wars Fan Club 1977-1987
- ○ Bantha Tracks T-shirt
- ○ Lucasfilm Logo T-shirt

Printed material

- ○ Official Star Wars Fan Club 1977-1987
- ○ TESB application form
- ○ ROTJ application sheet
- ○ Bantha Tracks #1-#34

Exclusive items

- ○ Official Star Wars Fan Club 1977-1987
- ○ The Empire Strikes Back boxed portfolio
- ○ The Empire Strikes Back poster album
- ○ Return of the Jedi poster album
- ○ Lucasfilm Fanclub 1987-1994
- ○ Lucasfilm Magazine #1-#17
- ○ Star Wars Fan Club 1994-Present
- ○ Star Wars Insider
- ○ 1997 Renewal Flyer Kit

FILM

Film clips

Ken Films (SUPER 8)

- ○ Star Wars
- ○ The Empire Strikes Back

Filmstrip / projector

KENNER

- ○ Star Wars Movie Viewer
- ○ Destroy the Death Star cartridge
- ○ Danger at Cantina cartridge

Star Wars Movie Photo Cards package (Topps)

The Empire Strikes Back trading card package (Topps)

- ○ Battle in Hyperspace cartridge
- ○ Assault on the Death Star cartridge
- ○ Star Wars Give-a-show Projector
- ○ The Empire Strikes Back Give-a-show Projector
- ○ Ewok Give-A-Show Projector

Slides

Willits Designs

- ○ The Empire Strikes Back
- ○ Luke Skywalker Edition Back A
- ○ Luke Skywalker Edition Back B
- ○ Rebel Alliance Edition Back A
- ○ Rebel Alliance Edition Back B
- ○ Imperial Attack Edition Back A
- ○ Imperial Attack Edition Back B
- ○ Millennium Falcon Edition Back A
- ○ Millennium Falcon Edition Back B
- ○ Yoda Edition

Video Cassettes

CBS / Fox Video

- ○ Star Wars video rental copy (1982)
- ○ Star Wars (1982)
- ○ Star Wars (1990)
- ○ Star Wars (1983)
- ○ Star Wars (1984)
- ○ tar Wars (1995)
- ○ The Empire Strikes Back (1984)
- ○ The Empire Strikes Back beta
- ○ The Empire Strikes Back (1990)
- ○ The Empire Strikes Back (1995)
- ○ Return of the Jedi (1990)
- ○ Return of the Jedi (1995)
- ○ From Star Wars to Jedi the Making of a Saga (1995)
- ○ Star Wars Trilogy Widescreen Edition (1995)
- ○ Making of Star Wars mail-in from Corn Pops
- ○ Trilogy Special Collector's Edition
- ✗ THX Trilogy boxed set

Return of the Jedi card No. 1 (Topps)

MGM

- ○ The Ewok Adventure
- ○ Ewoks: The Battle for Endor

OTHER

- ○ Star Wars Holiday Special (1978)

Video discs

- ○ Star Wars
- ○ The Empire Strikes Back
- ○ Return of the Jedi

Laser discs

- ○ Star Wars Extended Play
- ○ Star Wars Widescreen Extended Play
- ○ The Empire Strikes Back Extended Play
- ○ The Empire Strikes Back Widescreen Exteneded Play
- ○ Return of the Jedi Wide Screen Extended Play

Jim Henson Video

- ○ Muppet Babies "Time to Play"

FOOD CONTAINERS / PREMIUMS

Grocery items

Quality Bakers (New Zealand)

- ○ Card Set of 10
- ○ White toast bread wrapper
- ○ White sandwich bread wrapper

Beverage

Confection Concepts International (New Zealand)

- ○ Star Wars wrapper
- ○ Star Wars card set of 500
- ○ Plastic Card sleeve wall hangings
- ○ Star Wars display box (flat)

PepsiCo (Holland)

- ○ Wax Cup

England

- ○ Tesco Pepsi Flyer

Mexico

- ○ C-3PO poster
- ○ Darth Vader poster
- ○ Yoda poster
- ○ Darth Vader Pepsi Can
- ○ Darth Vader 1 liter bottle

England

- ○ 12 pack
- ○ 2 liter bottle
- ○ Can
- ○ 2 liter bottle 2 pack
- ○ Box

Diet Pepsi

- ○ 12 pack
- ○ 2 liter bottle
- ○ Can
- ○ 2 liter bottle 2 pack
- ○ Box

Pepsi Max

- ○ 12 pack
- ○ 2 liter bottle
- ○ Can
- ○ 2 liter bottle 2 pack
- ○ Box

Mountain Dew

- ○ 6 pack
- ○ 2 liter bottle
- ○ Can

7-UP

- ○ 6 pack
- ○ 2 liter bottle
- ○ Can

Return of the Jedi card No. 138 (Topps)

Return of the Jedi card No. 136 (Topps)

Return of the Jedi card No. 137 (Topps)

Other Pepsi items

- ○ Burger King set of 36 cards
- ○ The Empire Strikes Back Frisbee
- ○ The Empire Strikes Back Super Scene Collection with album and four sets of stickers
- ○ Return of the Jedi Burger King tray liner
- ○ Cherry Flavor Hi-C label
- ○ Return of the Jedi Cap HI-C premium
- ○ Return of the Jedi Sticker Sheet in mailer Hi-C premium

SINGAPORE

PepsiCo/British Petroleum Gas Stations

- ○ C-3PO mouse pad
- ○ Darth Vader mouse pad

Australia

- ○ Fun Meal box with Micro Machine

CANDY

Kinnerton Confections (England)

- ○ Box of shaped chocolates

Kent Gida (Turkey)

- ○ Wrapper
- ○ Stickers

Pez

- ○ Stormtrooper carded
- ○ Stormtrooper bagged
- ○ Darth Vader carded
- ○ Darth Vader bagged
- ○ C-3PO carded
- ○ C-3PO bagged
- ○ Yoda carded
- ○ Yoda bagged
- ○ Chewbacca carded
- ○ Chewbacca bagged
- ○ Display box

Europe

- ○ Stormtrooper
- ○ Chewbacca
- ○ Yoda

England

- ○ Premiums
- ○ Watch

Kinnerton Confections (England)

- ○ Die-cut Easter Egg container

Chupa Chups/Tombola Eggs

- ○ Twelve count display box
- ○ Display header card

OTHER

- ○ C-3PO candy head
- ○ Chewbacca candy head
- ○ Darth Vader candy head
- ○ Stormtrooper candy head
- ○ The Empire Strikes Back Series 1 candy head box
- ○ 2-1B candy head
- ○ Bossk candy head
- ○ Taun Taun candy head
- ○ Yoda candy head
- ○ The Empire Strikes Back Series 2 candy head box
- ○ Baby Ewok candy head
- ○ Darth Vader candy head
- ○ Jabba the Hutt candy head
- ○ Wicket candy head
- ○ Return of the Jedi candy head box
- ○ Full Set of candy heads
- ○ The Empire Strikes Back lemon flavored Chewbar wrapper

Bela Vista (Brazil)

- ○ Brin-Q

Return of the Jedi card No. 139 (Topps)

Return of the Jedi card No. 140 (Topps)

- ○ Packets, four different fronts 60 different numbered backs
- ○ Display box

Trebor Shaprs Limited

- ○ TESB Lemon Flavor Chewbar wrapper

Chupa Chups
Lazer Pop — Europe

- ○ Set of 9 wrappers
- ○ Set of 24 Stickers from wrappers

Tombola Eggs

- ○ Foil Wrapper
- ○ Three-Pack box
- ○ 36 count display box
- ○ Store Display of 15 ships and characters
- ○ Full Set of 20 toy prizes
- ○ Individual Tombola surprises
- ○ R2-D2
- ○ C-3PO
- ○ Princess Leia
- ○ Luke Skywalker
- ○ Stormtrooper
- ○ Darth Vader
- ○ Yoda
- ○ AT-AT puzzle
- ○ Han Solo
- ○ Chewbacca
- ○ Millennium Falcon
- ○ TIE Fighter
- ○ X-wing
- ○ Darth Vader TIE Fighter
- ○ Shuttle Tyderium
- ○ AT-AT
- ○ Space Battle puzzle
- ○ Yoda puzzle
- ○ Darth Vader puzzle

Return of the Jedi card No. 2 (Topps)

Cereal

- ○ Frosted Flakes
- ○ Corn Pops
- ○ Corn Flakes
- ○ Star Wars kite from Cheerios
- ○ Hildebrandt Mini poster from Cheerios
- ○ R2-D2 and C-3PO Mini poster from Cheerios
- ○ Star Destroyer Mini poster from Cheerios
- ○ X-wing and Characters Mini poster from Cheerios
- ○ Star Wars Tumbler (Mail away from Cheerios)
- ○ X-wing mobile
- ○ TIE Fighter mobile
- ○ Millennium Falcon mobile
- ○ Landspeeder mobile
- ○ Cocoa Puffs cereal box reproduction
- ○ Ben Kenobi cereal sticker
- ○ Stormtroopers cereal sticker
- ○ Frankenberry cereal box reproduction
- ○ R2-D2 and Luke Skywalker Eebel Eocket
- ○ C-3PO and Darth Vader Rebel Eocket
- ○ Chewbacca and Stormtrooper Rebel Rocket
- ○ Raisin Bran 20 oz
- ○ Corn Pops 10.9 oz
- ○ Corn Pops 15 oz
- ○ Apple Jacks 11 oz with comic strip

Kelloggs

- ○ Honey Nut Corn Flakes Making of SW video rebate 525g

Cookies / cakes

France

- ○ BNWRAPPER

DARTH VADER™

Return of the Jedi card No. 3 (Topps)

HAN SOLO™

Return of the Jedi card No. 4 (Topps)

Mexico

- ○ A1-A6 puzzle pieces
- ○ B1-B6
- ○ C1-C6
- ○ D1-D6
- ○ E1-E6
- ○ Natural Bran
- ○ Saltines Small
- ○ Mixed Flavors
- ○ Ritz large
- ○ Ricanelas

COOKIE WRAPPERS

- ○ Coco Choco
- ○ Combinado
- ○ Flippy
- ○ Merengu
- ○ Doro
- ○ Mamut
- ○ Arcoiris
- ○ Chokis
- ○ Polovomes
- ○ Roscas

EMPERADOR

- ○ Vanilla
- ○ Nuez
- ○ Chocolate

CREMIGOS

- ○ Chocolate
- ○ Vanilla
- ○ Strawberry

FRUTANA

- ○ Strawberry
- ○ Pineapple

PIRUFTAS

- ○ Limon
- ○ Fresta

Return of the Jedi card No. 5 (Topps)

PREMIUMS

- ○ Card set of 30
- ○ Card singles

PVC PREMIUMS

- ○ Boba Fett
- ○ Han Solo
- ○ C-3PO
- ○ Ben Kenobi
- ○ Princess Leia
- ○ Chewbacca

OTHER

- ○ Star Wars Cookie box vanilla
- ○ Star Wars Cookie box peanut butter
- ○ Star Wars Cookie box chocolate

FAST FOOD-RELATED

PIZZA HUT BOXES, SPECIAL EDITION, 1997

- ○ Darth Vader
- ○ Stormtrooper
- ○ R2-D2
- ○ C-3PO

Holland

- ○ Pizza Hut Cup

New Zealand

- ○ Pizza Hut Meal Bucket

Taco Bell

- ○ Cloud City Toy

Kentucky Fried Chicken

- ○ AT-AT

Australia

- ○ Pizza Hut
- ○ X-wing/TIE Fighter Spinner
- ○ Sandcrawler with R2-D2
- ○ Kentucky Fried Chicken
- ○ Kids Meal box

Return of the Jedi card No. 6 (Topps)

England

- ○ Pizza Hutt
- ○ England Pizza Hut menu

Mexico

- ○ Pizza Hut
- ○ Mexican Pizza Hut menu

Ice cream

Frigo (Spain)

- ○ Yoda ice creamstick
- ○ Boba Fett ice cream stick
- ○ Darth Vader ice cream stick

Snacks

BN (France)

- ○ Gaming Cards from snack chip bags
- ○ Moto Rangers
- ○ Ben Kenobi
- ○ Boba Fett
- ○ Death Star
- ○ Hoth

Smiths (Holland)

- ○ Film Cell Set with Binder and Projector
- ○ Paprika Grills
- ○ Gerookt Fume Grills
- ○ Cheetos Krips
- ○ Nacho Cheese Wavy Chips
- ○ Roasted Paprika Wavy Chips
- ○ Paprika Bugles

Japan

- ○ Tazo binder

Walker Crisps

- ○ Tazo Strip

Return of the Jedi card No. 7 (Topps)

Return of the Jedi card No. 8 (Topps)

Frito Lay

- ○ Set of 6 cards
- ○ Set of 20 discs

England

- ○ Uncut sheet of unproduced Tazos with four unpublished photos

Walker Chips

- ○ Set of wallet cards from Tazo binders

Smiths Chips (Holland)

- ○ Set of film cels with binder and mail-in projector

Bridge Farm Daries Ltd.

- ○ Strawberry yogurt container Princess Leia
- ○ Strawberry yogurt lid
- ○ Fudge yogurt lid

OTHER

- ○ Country Style Wonder Bread wrapper
- ○ Star Wars vitamins
- ○ Star Wars vitamins box flat
- ○ Vitamins press kit

ENGLAND

- ○ Dariylea cheese package

Theater promotions

- ○ Popcorn bucket

GAMES

Miniatures

- ○ Jabba the Hutt Miniatures boxed Set
- ○ Mos Eisley Cantina Miniatures boxed Set
- ○ Rebel Characters
- ○ Mos Eisley Cantina

○ Jabba's Palace

○ Zero G Assault Troopers

○ Miniature Pack #40501

○ Miniature Pack #40503

○ Miniature Pack #40502

○ Miniature Pack #40504

○ Miniature Pack #40505

○ Miniature Pack #40508

○ Miniature Pack #40525

○ Miniature Pack #40526

○ Miniature Pack #40527

○ Miniature Pack #40531

○ Miniature Pack #40532

○ Miniature Pack #40533

○ Miniature Pack #40534

Board games

Kenner

○ Destroy the Death Star

○ Escape from the Death Star

○ Yoda the Jedi Master

○ Hoth Ice Planet Adventure

Parker Brothers

○ Monopoly, Classic Trilogy Edition

○ Star Wars

○ Battle at the Sarlacc Pit

○ Battle at the Sarlacc Pit "Based on Lucasfilm Movie"

○ Wicket the Ewok Food-Gathering Game

○ The Ewoks Save the Trees

○ Death Star Assault

○ VCR game

West End Games

○ Assault on Hoth

Return of the Jedi card No. 9 (Topps)

○ Battle for Endor

○ Escape from the Death Star

CANADA

○ Escape from the Death Star

JAPAN

○ Endor

Card games

DECIPHER
Star Wars: A New Hope

○ Complete set (162)	150.00	250.00
○ Common cards (1-162)	.08	.20
○ Advance Prep.U1	.40	1.00
○ Advosze C2	.08	.20
○ Alt.To Fighting U1	.40	1.00
○ Arcona C2	.08	.20
○ Astromech Short. U2	.40	1.00
○ Attack Run R2	2.00	4.00
○ Beseiged R2	2.00	4.00
○ Besp.Mtrs.Void Spid. C2	.08	.20
○ Black 4 U2	.40	1.00
○ Blast the Door, Kid! C2	.08	.20
○ Blue Milk C2	.08	.20
○ Bowcaster R2	2.00	4.00
○ Brainiac R1	2.00	4.00
○ Captain Khurgee U1	.40	1.00
○ Cell 2187 R1	2.00	4.00
○ Chewbacca R2	2.00	4.00
○ Clak'dor VII R2	2.00	4.00
○ Come with Me C2	.08	.20
○ Comm. Evran Lajaie C1	.08	.20
○ Comm. V.Willard U2	.40	1.00
○ Comm.Prim.Ignition R2	2.00	4.00
○ Comm.Recharging R2	2.00	4.00
○ Conquest R1	2.00	4.00

Return of the Jedi card No. 90 (Topps)

○ Corella R1	2.00	4.00
○ Corellian C2	.08	.20
○ Corellian Slip C2	.08	.20
○ Dannik Jerrike R1	2.00	4.00
○ Danz Borin U2	.40	1.00
○ Dark Waters R2	2.00	4.00
○ Death Star R2	2.00	4.00
○ Death Star Gunner C1	.08	.20
○ Death Star Tract.Beam R2	2.00	4.00
○ Death Star Conf.Room U1	.40	1.00
○ Death Star Trench R2	2.00	4.00
○ Defel C2	.08	.20
○ Dejarik Holog. R1	2.00	4.00
○ Dianoga R2	2.00	4.00
○ Doikk Na'ts U2	.40	1.00
○ Double Agent R2	2.00	4.00
○ DS-61-4 R2	2.00	4.00
○ Eject! Eject! C2	.08	.20
○ Enh.TIE Lsr.Cannon C2	.08	.20
○ Evader U1	.40	1.00
○ Fire Extinguisher U2	.40	1.00
○ Garouf Lafoe U2	.40	1.00
○ Ghhhk C2	.08	.20
○ Gold 2 U1	.40	1.00
○ Grappling Hook C2	.08	.20
○ Greedo R1	2.00	4.00
○ Grimtaash C2	.08	.20
○ Hem Dazon R1	2.00	4.00
○ Het Nkik U2	.40	1.00
○ Houjix C2	.08	.20
○ Hunchback R1	2.00	4.00
○ Hyperwave Scan U1	.40	1.00
○ Hype R1	2.00	4.00
○ I Have A Bad Flng.About C2	.08	.20
○ I'm Here To Rescue You U1	.40	1.00
○ I'm On The Leader R1	2.00	4.00
○ Ackabel G'ont U2	.08	.20
○ Imperial Comm. C2	.08	.20

○ Imperial Holotable R1	2.00	4.00
○ Imperial Justice C2	.08	.20
○ Imperial Sq.Leader C3	.08	.20
○ Incom T-16 Skyhop. C2	.08	.20
○ Informant U1	.40	1.00
○ IT-0 R1	2.00	4.00
○ Jawa Blaster C2	.08	.20
○ Jawa Ion Gun C2	.08	.20
○ Kashyyyk C1	.08	.20
○ Kashyyyk C1	.08	.20
○ Kiffex R1	2.00	4.00
○ Krayt Dragon Bones U1	.40	1.00
○ Laser Gate U2	.40	1.00
○ Leia Seeker R2	2.00	4.00
○ Let The Wookie Win R1	2.00	4.00
○ Lirin Car'n U2	.40	1.00
○ Logistical Delay U2	.40	1.00
○ Lt. Pol Treidum C1	.08	.20
○ Lt. Shann Childsen U1	.40	1.00
○ Luke's Cape R1	2.00	4.00
○ Luke's Hunting Rifle U1	.40	1.00
○ M-HYD 'Binary' Droid U1	.40	1.00
○ Magn.Suction Tube R2	2.00	4.00
○ Magn.Suction Tube R2	2.00	4.00
○ Maneuver Check R2	2.00	4.00
○ Merc Sunlet C2	.08	.20
○ Mobq. A-1 Dlx. Floater C2	.08	.20
○ Monnok C2	.08	.20
○ Mosep U2	.40	1.00
○ Motti Seeker R2	2.00	4.00
○ Nalan Cheel U2	.40	1.00
○ Ng'ok C2	.08	.20
○ Officer Evax C1	.08	.20
○ Oo-na Goo-ta, Solo? C2	.08	.20

Star File Trading
Card — Boba Fet

Star Wars
card No. 10
(Topps)

Star Wars
card No. 11
(Topps)

Item		
○ Out Of Comm. U2	.40	1.00
○ Program Trap U1	.40	1.00
○ Quite A Merc. C2	.08	.20
○ R2-D2 R2	2.00	4.00
○ R2-Q2 C2	.08	.20
○ R3-T6 R1	2.00	4.00
○ R5-A2 C2	.08	.20
○ R5-D4 C2	.08	.20
○ RA-7 C2	.08	.20
○ Ralltiir C1	.08	.20
○ Ralltiir C1	.08	.20
○ Rebel Commander C2	.08	.20
○ Rebel Squad Ldr. C3	.08	.20
○ Rebel Tech C1	.08	.20
○ Rectenna C2	.08	.20
○ Red 2 R1	2.00	4.00
○ Red 5 R1	2.00	4.00
○ Red 6 U1	.40	1.00
○ Reegesk U2	.40	1.00
○ Remote C2	.08	.20
○ Reserve Pilot U1	.40	1.00
○ Ret. the Bridge R1	2.00	4.00
○ Rodian C2	.08	.20
○ Rogue Bantha U1	.40	1.00
○ Sabotage U1	.40	1.00
○ Sand.Droid Junkheap R1	2.00	4.00
○ Sand.Loading Bay R1	2.00	4.00
○ Saurin C2	.08	.20
○ Scanner Techs U1	.40	1.00
○ Sensor Panel U1	.40	1.00
○ Sniper U1	.40	1.00
○ Solomahal C2	.08	.20
○ Sorry About The Mess U1	.40	1.00
○ Spice Mines Of Kessel R1	2.00	4.00

Item		
○ Stunning Leader C2	.08	.20
○ Superlaser R2	2.00	4.00
○ SW-4 Ion Cannon R2	2.00	4.00
○ Swilla Corey C2	.08	.20
○ Tantive IV R1	2.00	4.00
○ Tatooine: Bluffs R1	2.00	4.00
○ Tech Mo'r U2	.40	1.00
○ Tentacle C2	.08	.20
○ There'll Be Hell To Pay U2	.40	1.00
○ They're On Dantooine R1	2.00	4.00
○ This Is Some Rescue! U1	.40	1.00
○ TIE Assault Squad. U1	.40	1.00
○ TIE Vanguard C2	.08	.20
○ Tiree U2	.40	1.00
○ Tractor Beam U1	.40	1.00
○ Trooper Davin Felth R2	2.00	4.00
○ Tzizvvt R2	2.00	4.00
○ U-3PO R1	2.00	4.00
○ Undercover U2	.40	1.00
○ Undercover U2	.40	1.00
○ URoRRuR'R'R U2	.40	1.00
○ URroRRuR'R'R Hunt. Rifle U1	.40	1.00
○ Victory-Class St.Dest. U1	.40	1.00
○ We Have A Prisoner C2	.08	.20
○ WED15-17 Septoid Droid U2	.40	1.00
○ Wedge Antilles R1	2.00	4.00
○ What're U Tryin' To Push U2	.40	1.00
○ Wookiee Roar R1	2.00	4.00
○ Y-wing Ass.Squad. U1	.40	1.00
○ Yavin 4-Brief.Room U1	.40	1.00
○ Yavin 4-Mass.Ruins U1	.40	1.00
○ You're All Clear Kid! R1	2.00	4.00
○ Zutton C1	.08	.20

Star Wars card No. 12 (Topps)

Star Wars card No. 58 (Topps)

Star Wars Cloud City

○ Complete set (180)	200.00	350.00
○ Common cards (1-180)	.04	.10
○ Ability, Ability C	.04	.10
○ Abyss U	.10	.25
○ Access Denied C	.04	.10
○ Advantage R	1.50	3.00
○ Aiiii! Aaa! Agggggggggg! R	1.50	3.00
○ All My Urchins R	1.50	3.00
○ All Too Easy R	1.50	3.00
○ Ambush R	1.50	3.00
○ Armed and Dangerous U	.10	.25
○ Artoo, come back at once! R	1.50	3.00
○ As Good As Gone C	.04	.10
○ Atmospheric Ass. R	1.50	3.00
○ Beldon's Eye R	1.50	3.00
○ Bespin U	.10	.25
○ Bespin U	.10	.25
○ Bespin: Cloud City U	.10	.25
○ Bespin: Cloud City U	.10	.25
○ Binders C	.04	.10
○ Bionic Hand R	1.50	3.00
○ Blasted Droid C	.04	.10
○ Blaster Proficiency C	.04	.10
○ Boba Fett R	20.00	40.00
○ Boba Fett's Blast.Rifle R	1.50	3.00
○ Bounty C	.04	.10
○ Brief Loss Of Control R	1.50	3.00
○ Bright Hope R	5.00	10.00
○ Captain Bewil R	1.50	3.00
○ Captain Han Solo R	15.00	30.00
○ Captive Fury U	.10	.25
○ Captive Pursuit C	.04	.10
○ Carbon-Freezing U	.10	.25

○ Carb.Chamber Console U	.10	.25
○ Chasm U	.10	.25
○ Chief Retwin R	1.50	3.00
○ Civil Disorder C	.04	.10
○ Clash Of Sabers U	.10	.25
○ Cloud Car C	.04	.10
○ Cloud Car C	.04	.10
○ Cloud City Blaster C	.04	.10
○ Cloud City Blaster C	.04	.10
○ Cloud City Engineer C	.04	.10
○ Cloud City Sabacc U	.10	.25
○ Cloud City Sabacc U	.10	.25
○ Cloud City Technician C	.04	.10
○ Cloud City Trooper C	.04	.10
○ Cloud City Trooper C	.04	.10
○ Cloud City-Carbonite U	.10	.25
○ Cloud City-Carb.Chamber U	.10	.25
○ Cloud City-Chasm Walk.C	.04	.10
○ Cloud City-Chasm Walk.C	.04	.10
○ Cloud City-Dining Room R	1.50	3.00
○ Cloud City-East Platform C	.04	.10
○ Cloud City-Guest Qtrs. R	1.50	3.00
○ Cloud City-Incinerator C	.04	.10
○ Cloud City-Incinerator C	.04	.10
○ Cloud City-Lower Corridor U	.10	.25
○ Cloud City-Lower Corridor U	.10	.25
○ Cloud City-Platform 327 C	.04	.10
○ Cloud City-Security Tower C	.04	.10
○ Cloud City-Upp.Pl.Corr.C	.04	.10
○ Cloud City-Upp.Pl.Corr.U	.04	.10
○ Clouds C	.04	.10
○ Clouds C	.04	.10
○ Comm. Desanne U	.10	.25
○ Computer Interface C	.04	.10

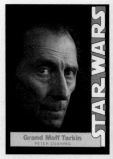

Star Wars card No. 6 (Topps)

Star Wars card No. 7 (Topps)

○ Courage of a Skywalker R	1.50	3.00
○ Crack Shot U	.10	.25
○ Cyborg Construct U	.10	.25
○ Dark Approach R	1.50	3.00
○ Dark Deal R	1.50	3.00
○ Dark Strike C	.04	.10
○ Dash C	.04	.10
○ Despair R	1.50	3.00
○ Desperate Reach U	.10	.25
○ Dismantle On Sight R	1.50	3.00
○ Dodge C	.04	.10
○ Double Back U	.10	.25
○ Dbl. Cross-No Good Swind. C	.04	.10
○ E Chu Ta C	.04	.10
○ E-3PO R	1.50	3.00
○ End This Dest.Conflict R	1.50	3.00
○ Epic Duel R	1.50	3.00
○ Fall Of The Empire U	.10	.25
○ Fall Of The Legend U	.10	.25
○ Flight Escort R	1.50	3.00
○ Focused Attack R	1.50	3.00
○ Force Field R	1.50	3.00
○ Forced Landing R	1.50	3.00
○ Frozen Assets R	1.50	3.00
○ Gambler's Luck R	1.50	3.00
○ Glancing Blow R	1.50	3.00
○ Haven R	1.50	3.00
○ He's All Yours, Bnty Hntr R	1.50	3.00
○ Heart Of The Chasm U	.10	.25
○ Hero Of A Thous. Devices U	.10	.25
○ Higher Ground R	1.50	3.00
○ Hindsight R	1.50	3.00
○ Hopping Mad R	1.50	3.00
○ Human Shield C	.04	.10

**Star Wars card
No. 8 (Topps)**

**Star Wars
sticker No. 2
(Topps)**

○ I Am Your Father R	1.50	3.00
○ I Don't Need Their Scum R	1.50	3.00
○ I Had No Choice R	1.50	3.00
○ Imperial Decree U	.10	.25
○ Imp.Trper.Dainsom U	.10	.25
○ Imp.Most Impressive R	1.50	3.00
○ Innocent Scoundrel U	.10	.25
○ Interrogation Array R	1.50	3.00
○ Into The Vent.Shaft, Lefty R	1.50	3.00
○ It's A Trap! U	.10	.25
○ Kebyc U	.10	.25
○ Keep Your Eyes Open C	.04	.10
○ Lando Calrissian R	10.00	20.00
○ Lando Calrissian R	10.00	20.00
○ Lando's Wrist Comlink U	.10	.25
○ Leia Of Alderaan R	1.50	3.00
○ Levitation Attack U	.10	.25
○ Lt. Cecius U	.10	.25
○ Lt. Sheckil R	1.50	3.00
○ Lift Tube Escape C	.04	.10
○ Lobot R	3.00	6.00
○ Luke's Blaster Pistol R	1.50	3.00
○ Mandalorian Armor R	1.50	3.00
○ Mostly Armless R	1.50	3.00
○ NOOOOOOOOO! R	1.50	3.00
○ Obsidian 7 R	1.50	3.00
○ Obsidian 8 R	1.50	3.00
○ Off The Edge R	1.50	3.00
○ Old Pirates R	1.50	3.00
○ Out Of Somewhere U	.10	.25
○ Path Of Least Res. C	.04	.10
○ Point Man R	1.50	3.00
○ Prepare The Chamber U	.10	.25
○ Princess Leia R	10.00	20.00
○ Projective Telepathy U	.10	.25

**Star Wars sticker
No. 40 (Topps)**

○ Protector R	1.50	3.00	
○ Punch It! R	1.50	3.00	
○ Put That Down C	.04	.10	
○ Redemption R	5.00	10.00	
○ Release Your Anger R	1.50	3.00	
○ Rend.Pt. On Tatooine R	1.50	3.00	
○ Rescue In The Clouds C	.04	.10	
○ Restricted Access C	.04	.10	
○ Rite Of Passage C	.04	.10	
○ Shattered Hope U	.10	.25	
○ Shocking Info.C	.04	.10	
○ Shocking Rev. C	.04	.10	
○ Slave I R	7.50	15.00	
○ Slip Sliding Away R	1.50	3.00	
○ Smoke Screen R	1.50	3.00	
○ Somersault C	.04	.10	
○ Sonic Bombardment U	.10	.25	
○ Special Delivery C	.04	.10	
○ Surprise R	1.50	3.00	
○ Surreptitious Glance R	1.50	3.00	
○ Swing-And-A-Miss U	.10	.25	
○ The Emperor's Prize R	1.50	3.00	
○ This Is Even Better R	1.50	3.00	
○ This Is Still Wrong R	1.50	3.00	
○ Tibanna Gas Miner C	.04	.10	
○ Tibanna Gas Miner C	.04	.10	
○ TIE Sentry Ships C	.04	.10	
○ Treva Horme U	.10	.25	
○ Trooper Assaut C	.04	.10	
○ Trooper Jerrol Blendin U	.10	.25	
○ Trooper Utris M'toc U	.10	.25	
○ Ugloste R	1.50	3.00	
○ Ugnaught C	.04	.10	
○ Uncontrollable Fury R	1.50	3.00	
○ Vlader's Bounty R	1.50	3.00	
○ Vader's Cape R	1.50	3.00	

Star Wars sticker No. 62 (Topps)

Star Wars sticker No. 63 (Topps)

○ We'll Find Han R	1.50	3.00	
○ We're The Bait R	1.50	3.00	
○ Weapon Levitation U	.10	.25	
○ Weapon Of An Ungrat.Son U	.10	.25	
○ Weather Vane U	.10	.25	
○ Weather Vane U	.10	.25	
○ Why Didn't You Tell Me? R	1.50	3.00	
○ Wiorkette U	.10	.25	
○ Wookiee Strangle R	1.50	3.00	
○ You Are Beaten U	.10	.25	

Star Wars Dagobah

○ Complete set (180)	200.00	350.00	
○ Common cards (1-180)	.04	.10	
○ 3,720 To 1 C	.04	.10	
○ 4-LOM R	5.00	10.00	
○ 4-LOM's Conc.Rifle R	1.50	3.00	
○ A Dangerous Time C	.04	.10	
○ A Jedi's Strength U	.50	1.25	
○ Anger, Fear Aggr. C	.04	.10	
○ Anoat U	.50	1.25	
○ Anoat U	.50	1.25	
○ Apology Accepted C	.04	.10	
○ Asteroid Field C	.04	.10	
○ Asteroid Field C	.04	.10	
○ Asteroid Sanctuary C	.04	.10	
○ Aster. don't concern Me R	1.50	3.00	
○ Astromech Translator C	.04	.10	
○ At Peace R	1.50	3.00	
○ Avenger R	5.00	10.00	
○ Away Put Your Weapon U	.50	1.25	
○ Aw, Can't get your ship Out C	.04	.10	
○ Bad Feeling Have I R	1.50	3.00	
○ Big One U	.50	1.25	
○ Big one U	.50	1.25	
○ Big one-ast.cave or sl.belly U	.50	1.25	

The Empire Strikes Back card No. 1 (Topps)

○ Big one-ast.cave or sl.belly U	.50	1.25	○ Egregious Pilot Error R	1.50	3.00	
○ Blasted Varmints C	.04	.10	○ Encampment C	.04	.10	
○ Bog-wing C	.04	.10	○ Executor R	12.50	25.00	
○ Bog-wing C	.04	.10	○ Executor-Comm. Stat. U	.50	1.25	
○ Bombing Run R	1.50	3.00	○ Executor-Control Stat. U	.50	1.25	
○ Bossk R	1.50	3.00	○ Executor-Holotheatre R	1.50	3.00	
○ Bossk's Mortar Gun R	1.50	3.00	○ Executor-Main Corridor C	.04	.10	
○ Broken Concentration R	1.50	3.00	○ Executor-Med.Chamber R	1.50	3.00	
○ Captain Needa R	2.50	5.00	○ Failure At The Cave R	1.50	3.00	
○ Close Call C	.04	.10	○ Fear C	.04	.10	
○ Closer? U	.50	1.25	○ Field Promotion R	1.50	3.00	
○ Comm. Chief C	.04	.10	○ Flagship R	1.50	3.00	
○ Commander Brandei U	.50	1.25	○ Flash Of Insight U	.50	1.25	
○ Commander Gherant U	.50	1.25	○ Found SomeoneYou Have U	.50	1.25	
○ Commande Nemet U	.50	1.25	○ Frustration R	1.50	3.00	
○ Control U	.50	1.25	○ Great Warrior C	.04	.10	
○ Control U	.50	1.25	○ Grounded Starfight.U	.50	1.25	
○ Corporal Derdram U	.50	1.25	○ Han's Toolkit R	1.50	3.00	
○ Corporal Vandolay U	.50	1.25	○ He Is Not Ready C	.04	.10	
○ Corrosive Damage R	1.50	3.00	○ Hiding In The Garbage R	1.50	3.00	
○ Dagobah U	.50	1.25	○ HoloNet Transmission U	.50	1.25	
○ Dagobah-Bog Clearing R	1.50	3.00	○ Hound's Tooth R	5.00	10.00	
○ Dagobah-Cave R	2.50	5.00	○ I Have A Bad Feeling R	1.50	3.00	
○ Dagobah-Jungle U	.50	1.25	○ I Want That Ship R	1.50	3.00	
○ Dagobah-Swamp U	.50	1.25	○ IG-2000 R	2.50	5.00	
○ Dagobah-Train.Area C	.04	.10	○ IG-88 R	10.00	20.00	
○ Dagobah-Yoda's Hut R	1.50	3.00	○ IG-88's Neural Inh.R	2.50	5.00	
○ Defensive Fire C	.04	.10	○ IG-88's Pulse Cannon R	2.50	5.00	
○ Dengar R	5.00	10.00	○ Imbalance U	.50	1.25	
○ Dengar's Blaster Carbine R	1.50	3.00	○ Imperial Helmsman C	.04	.10	
○ Descent Into The Dark R	1.50	3.00	○ Ineffective Maneuver U	.50	1.25	
○ Do, Or Do Not C	.04	.10	○ It Is The Future You See R	1.50	3.00	
○ Domain Of Evil U	.50	1.25	○ Jedi Levitation R	1.50	3.00	
○ Dragonsnake R	1.50	3.00	○ Knowledge And Defense C	.04	.10	
○ Droid Sensorscope C	.04	.10	○ Landing Claw R	1.50	3.00	
○ Effective Repairs R	1.50	3.00	○ Lando System? R	1.50	3.00	

The Empire Strikes Back card No. 138 (Topps)

The Empire Strikes Back card No. 158 (Topps)

Card		
○ Levitation U	.50	1.25
○ Lt. Commander Ardan U	.50	1.25
○ Lt. Suba R	2.50	5.00
○ Lt. Venka U	.50	1.25
○ Light Maneuvers R	1.50	3.00
○ Location, Location, Loc. R	1.50	3.00
○ Lost In Space R	1.50	3.00
○ Lost Relay C	.04	.10
○ Luke's Backpack R	1.50	3.00
○ Mist Hunter R	2.50	5.00
○ Moving To Att.Position C	.04	.10
○ Much Anger In Him R	1.50	3.00
○ Mynock C	.04	.10
○ Mynock C	.04	.10
○ Never Tell Me The Odds C	.04	.10
○ No Disintegrations! R	1.50	3.00
○ Nudj C	.04	.10
○ Obi-Wan's App. R	1.50	3.00
○ Order To Engage R	1.50	3.00
○ Pol.Neg.Power Coup.R	.04	.10
○ Portable Fusion Gen. C	.04	.10
○ Precision Targeting U	.50	1.25
○ Proton Bombs U	.50	1.25
○ Punishing One R	2.50	5.00
○ Quick Draw C	.04	.10
○ Raithal R	1.50	3.00
○ Raithal U	.50	1.25
○ Rebel Flight Suit C	.04	.10
○ Recoil In Fear C	.04	.10
○ Reflection R	1.50	3.00
○ Report To Lord Vader R	1.50	3.00
○ Res Luk Ra'auf R	1.50	3.00
○ Retractable Arm C	.04	.10
○ Rogue Asteroid C	.04	.10
○ Rogue Asteroid C	.04	.10
○ Rycar's Run R	1.50	3.00

Card		
○ Scramble U	.50	1.25
○ Shoo! Shoo! U	.50	1.25
○ Shot In The Dark U	.50	1.25
○ Shut him up or down U	.50	1.25
○ Size Matters Not R	1.50	3.00
○ Sleen C	.04	.10
○ Smuggler's Blues R	1.50	3.00
○ Something Hit Us! U	.50	1.25
○ Son Of Skywalker R	15.00	30.00
○ Space Slug R	1.50	3.00
○ Space Slug U	.50	1.25
○ Star Dest-Launch Bay C	.04	.10
○ Starship Levitation U	.50	1.25
○ Stone Pile R	1.50	3.00
○ Sudden Impact U	.50	1.25
○ Take Evasive Action C	.04	.10
○ The Dark Path R	1.50	3.00
○ The Professor R	1.50	3.00
○ There Is No Try C	.04	.10
○ They'd Be Crazy... C	.50	1.25
○ This Is More Like It R	1.50	3.00
○ This Is No Cave R	1.50	3.00
○ Those Reb. Won't Esc. Us C	.04	.10
○ Thru the force you will see R	1.50	3.00
○ TIE Avenger C	.04	.10
○ TIE Bomber U	.50	1.25
○ Tight Squeeze R	1.50	3.00
○ Trans. Terminated U	.50	1.25
○ Tunnel Vision U	.50	1.25
○ Unc. Is The Future C	.04	.10
○ Unexpected Interr. R	1.50	3.00
○ Vine Snake C	.04	.10
○ Vine Snake C	.04	.10
○ Visage Of The Emp. R	1.50	3.00
○ Visored Vision C	.04	.10
○ Voyeur C	.04	.10

The Empire Strikes Back card No. 224 (Topps)

The Empire Strikes Back card No. 59 (Topps)

The Empire Strikes Back card No. 98 (Topps)

○ Warrant Officer M'Kae	U.50	1.25		○ Collapsing Corridor R2	2.50	5.00	
○ Wars Not Make One Great U	.50	1.25		○ Comm. L.Skywalker R1	12.50	25.00	
○ We Can Still Out. Them R	1.50	3.00		○ ComScan Detection C2	.10	.25	
○ We Don't Need Their Scum R	1.50	3.00		○ Concussion Grenade R1	2.50	5.00	
○ WHAOOOOW! R	1.50	3.00		○ Crash Landing U1	.40	1.00	
○ What Is Thy Bidding, R	1.50	3.00		○ Dack Ralter R2	2.50	5.00	
○ Yoda R	15.00	30.00		○ Dark Dissension R1	2.50	5.00	
○ Yoda Stew U	.50	1.25		○ Death Mark R1	2.50	5.00	
○ Yoda's Gimer Stick R	1.50	3.00		○ Death Squadron U1	.40	1.00	
○ Yoda's Hope U	.50	1.25		○ Debris Zone R2	2.50	5.00	

Defenders of Freedom card (Topps)

○ Yoda, You Seek Yoda R	1.50	3.00		○ Deflector Shield Gen. U2	.40	1.00	
○ You Do Have Your Mom. U	.50	1.25		○ Derek 'Hobbie' Klivian U1	.40	1.00	
○ Zuckuss R	5.00	10.00		○ Direct Hit U1	.40	1.00	
○ Zuckuss' Snare Rifle R	3.00	6.00		○ Disarming Creature R1	2.50	5.00	
Star Wars Hoth				○ Dual Laser Cannon U1	.40	1.00	
○ Complete set (163)	200.00	350.00		○ E-web Blaster C1	.10	.25	
○ Common card (1-163)	.10	.25		○ Echo Base Operations R2	2.50	5.00	
○ 2-1B R1	2.50	5.00		○ Echo Base Trooper C3	.10	.25	
○ A Dk.Time For The Reb.C1	.10	.25		○ Echo Base Trooper Off.C1	.10	.25	
○ Admiral Ozzel R1	5.00	10.00		○ Echo Trooper Backpack C2	.10	.25	
○ Anakin's Lightsaber R1	10.00	20.00		○ EG-4 C1	.10	.25	
○ Artillery Remote R2	2.50	5.00		○ Electro-Rangefinder U1	.40	1.00	
○ AT-AT Cannon U1	.40	1.00		○ Evacuation Control U1	.40	1.00	
○ AT-AT Driver C2	.10	.25		○ Exhaustion U2	.40	1.00	
○ Atgar Laser Cannon U2	.40	1.00		○ Exposure U1	.40	1.00	
○ Attack Pattern Delta U1	.40	1.00		○ Fall Back! C2	.10	.25	
○ Bacta Tank R2	5.00	10.00		○ Frostbite C2	.10	.25	
○ Blizzard 1 R1	5.00	10.00		○ Frostbite C2	.10	.25	

Droids card No. 1 (Topps)

○ Blizzard 2 R2	4.00	8.00		○ Frozen Dinner R1	2.50	5.00	
○ Blizzard Scout 1 R1	5.00	10.00		○ Furry Fury R2	2.50	5.00	
○ Blizzard Walker U2	.40	1.00		○ FX-10 C2	.10	.25	
○ Breached Defenses U2	.40	1.00		○ FX-7 C2	.10	.25	
○ Cal Alder U2	.40	1.00		○ Gen.Carlist Rieekan R2	2.50	5.00	
○ Captain Lennox U1	.40	1.00		○ Gen.Veers R1	5.00	10.00	
○ Captain Piett R2	2.50	5.00		○ Golan Laser Battery U1	.40	1.00	
○ Cold Feet C2	.10	.25		○ He Hasn't Come Back Yet C2	.10	.25	

○ High Anxiety R1	2.50	5.00
○ Hoth U2	.40	1.00
○ Hoth U2	.40	1.00
○ Hoth Survival Gear C2	.10	.25
○ Hoth-Def.Perimeter C2	.10	.25
○ Hoth-Def.Perimeter C2	.10	.25
○ Hoth-Echo Comm.Ctr.U2	.40	1.00
○ Hoth-Echo Comm.Ctr.U2	.40	1.00
○ Hoth-Echo Corridor C2	.10	.25
○ Hoth-Echo Corridor U2	.40	1.00
○ Hoth-Echo Corridor U2	.40	1.00
○ Hoth-Echo Docking Bay C2	.10	.25
○ Hoth-Echo Docking Bay C2	.10	.25
○ Hoth-Echo Med Lab C2	.10	.25
○ Hoth-Ice Plains C2	.10	.25
○ Hoth-Main Pwr.Gen. U2	.40	1.00
○ Hoth-North Ridge C2	.10	.25
○ Hoth-North Ridge C2	.10	.25
○ Hoth-Snow Trench C2	.10	.25
○ Hoth-Wampa Cave R2	2.50	5.00
○ I thght smell bad outside R 1	2.50	5.00
○ I'd Just Soon Kiss Wookiee C2	.10	.25
○ Ice Storm U1	.40	1.00
○ Ice Storm U1	.40	1.00
○ Image Of The Dark Lord R2	2.50	5.00
○ Imperial Domination U1	.40	1.00
○ Imperial Gunner C2	.10	.25
○ Imperial Supply C1	.10	.25
○ Infantry Mine C2	.10	.25
○ Infantry Mine C2	.10	.25
○ It Can Wait C2	.10	.25
○ Jeroen Webb U1	.40	1.00
○ K-3PO R1	2.50	5.00
○ Lt. Cabbel U2	.40	1.00
○ Lightsaber Deficiency U1	.40	1.00
○ Lucky Shot U1	.40	1.00

○ Major Bren Derlin R2	2.50	5.00
○ Md. Rep.Blstr.Cann. C1	.10	.25
○ Medium Transport U2	.40	1.00
○ Meteor Impact? R1	2.50	5.00
○ Mournful Roar R1	2.50	5.00
○ Nice of U guys to drop by C2	.10	.25
○ Oh, Switch Off C2	.10	.25
○ One More Pass U1	.40	1.00
○ Ord Mantell C2	.10	.25
○ Ord Mantell U2	.40	1.00
○ Our 1st catch of the day C2	.10	.25
○ Perimeter Scan C2	.10	.25
○ Planet Def.Ion Cannon R2	2.50	5.00
○ Port.Fusion Gen. C2	.10	.25
○ Power Harpoon U1	.40	1.00
○ Probe Antennae U2	.40	1.00
○ Probe Droid C2	.10	.25
○ Probe Droid Laser U2	.40	1.00
○ Probe Telemetry C2	.10	.25
○ R-3PO R2	2.50	5.00
○ R2 Sensor Array C2	.10	.25
○ R5-M2 C2	.10	.25
○ Rebel Scout C1	.10	.25
○ Resp.Of Command R1	2.50	5.00
○ Rogue 1 R1	5.00	10.00
○ Rogue 2 R2	2.50	5.00
○ Rogue 3 R1	5.00	10.00
○ Rogue Gunner C2	.10	.25
○ Romas Navander U2	.40	1.00
○ Rug Hug R1	2.50	5.00
○ Scruffy lkng.Nerf Herder R2	2.50	5.00
○ Self-Destruct Mech.U1	.40	1.00
○ Shawn Valdez U1	.40	1.00
○ Silence Is Golden U2	.40	1.00
○ Snowspeeder U2	.40	1.00
○ Snowtrooper C3	.10	.25

Droids card No. 8.
(Topps)

Indigenous Force
Users No. 1
(Topps)

○ Snowtrooper Officer C1	.10	.25	
○ Stalker R1	10.00	20.00	
○ Stop Motion C2	.10	.25	
○ Surface Def.Cannon R2	2.50	5.00	
○ Tactical Support R2	2.50	5.00	
○ Tamizander Rey U2	.40	1.00	
○ Target The Main Gen. R2	2.50	5.00	
○ Tauntaun C2	.10	.25	
○ Tauntaun Bones U1	.40	1.00	
○ Tauntaun Handler C2	.10	.25	
○ That's It,Rebels R There U2	.40	1.00	
○ The First Trans.Is Away R1	2.50	5.00	
○ The shld.drs.must closed U1	.40	1.00	
○ This Is Just Wrong R1	2.50	5.00	
○ Tigran Jamiro U1	.40	1.00	
○ Too Cold For Speeders U1	.40	1.00	
○ Toryn Farr U1	.40	1.00	
○ Trample R1	2.50	5.00	
○ Turn It Off! Turn It Off! C1	.10	.25	
○ Tyrant R1	7.50	15.00	
○ Under Attack U1	.40	1.00	
○ Vehicle Mine C2	.10	.25	
○ Vehicle Mine C2	.10	.25	
○ Walker Barrage U1	.40	1.00	
○ Walker Sighting U2	.40	1.00	
○ Wall Of Fire U1	.40	1.00	
○ Wampa R2	2.50	5.00	
○ Weapon Malfunction R1	2.50	5.00	
○ WED-1016 Droid C1	.10	.25	
○ Wes Janson R2	2.50	5.00	
○ Who's Scruffy-Looking? R1	2.50	5.00	
○ Wyron Serper U2	.40	1.00	
○ Yaggle Gakkle R2	2.50	5.00	
○ You've failed for last time R1	2.50	5.00	
○ You'll Go To the Dag.Sys. R1	2.50	5.00	
○ Zev Senesca R2	2.50	5.00	

Star Wars: Jabba's Palace

○ Complete set (180)	175.00	350.00	
○ Common card (1-180)	.10	.25	
○ 8D8 R	2.00	4.00	
○ A Gift U	.40	1.00	
○ Abyssin C	.10	.25	
○ Abyssin Ornament U	.40	1.00	
○ All Wrapped Up U	.40	1.00	
○ Amanaman R	2.00	4.00	
○ Amanin C	.10	.25	
○ Anti.Laser Cannon U	.40	1.00	
○ Aqualish C	.10	.25	
○ Arc Welder U	.40	1.00	
○ Ardon 'Vapor' Crell R	2.00	4.00	
○ Artoo R	10.00	20.00	
○ Artoo, I Have A Bad Feeling. U	.40	1.00	
○ Attark R	2.00	4.00	
○ Aved Luun R	2.00	4.00	
○ B'omarr Monk C	.10	.25	
○ Bane Malar R	2.00	4.00	
○ Bantha Fodder C	.10	.25	
○ Barada R	2.00	4.00	
○ Baragwin C	.10	.25	
○ Bargaining Table U	.40	1.00	
○ Beedo R	2.00	4.00	
○ BG-J38 R	2.00	4.00	
○ Bib Fortuna R	4.00	8.00	
○ Blaster Deflection R	2.00	4.00	
○ Bubo U	.40	1.00	
○ Cane Adiss U	.40	1.00	
○ Chadra-Fan C	.10	.25	
○ Chevin C	.10	.25	
○ Choke C	.10	.25	
○ Corellian Retort U	.40	1.00	
○ CZ-4 C	.10	.25	
○ Den Of Thieves U	.40	1.00	

Galaxy card No. 38 (Topps)

Galaxy card No. 4 (Topps)

Galaxy card No. 6 (Topps)

○ Dengar's Mod.Riot Gun R	2.50	5.00
○ Devaronian C	.10	.25
○ Don't Forget The Droids C	.10	.25
○ Double Laser Cannon R	2.00	4.00
○ Droopy McCool R	2.00	4.00
○ Dune Sea Sabacc U	.40	1.00
○ Dune Sea Sabacc U	.40	1.00
○ Elom C	.10	.25
○ Ephant Mon R	2.00	4.00
○ EV-9D9 R	2.00	4.00
○ Fallen Portal U	.40	1.00
○ Florn Lamproid C	.10	.25
○ Fozec R	2.00	4.00
○ Galid R	2.00	4.00
○ Gamorrean Ax C	.10	.25
○ Gamorrean Guard C	.10	.25
○ Garon Nas Tal R	2.00	4.00
○ Geezum R	2.50	5.00
○ Ghoel R	2.50	5.00
○ Giran R	2.50	5.00
○ Gran C	.10	.25
○ H'nemthe C	.10	.25
○ Heart R	2.00	4.00
○ Hermi Odle R	2.00	4.00
○ Hidden Compartment U	.40	1.00
○ Hidden Weapons U	.40	1.00
○ Holoprojector U	.40	1.00
○ Hutt Bounty R	2.00	4.00
○ Hutt Smooch U	.40	1.00
○ I Must Be All.To Speak R	2.00	4.00
○ Information Exchange U	.40	1.00
○ Ishi Tib C	.10	.25
○ Ithorian C	.10	.25
○ J'Quille R	2.00	4.00
○ Jabba The Hutt R	10.00	20.00
○ Jabba's Pal.Sabacc U	.40	1.00

○ Jabba's Pal.Sabacc U	.40	1.00
○ Jabba's Pal.Aud.Chamber U	.10	.25
○ Jabba's Pal.Aud.Chamber U	.10	.25
○ Jabba's Pal.Droid Wkshop U	.40	1.00
○ Jabba's Pal.Dungeon U	.40	1.00
○ Jabba's Pal.Ent.Cavern U	.10	.25
○ Jabba's Pal.Ent.Cavern U	.10	.25
○ Jabba's Pal.Rancor Pit U	.40	1.00
○ Jabba's Sail Barge R	3.00	6.00
○ Jabba's Sail Brg.Pass.Dck.R	2.00	4.00
○ Jedi Mind Trick R	2.00	4.00
○ Jess R	2.00	4.00
○ Jet Pack U	.40	1.00
○ Kalit R	2.00	4.00
○ Ke Chu Ke Kukuta? C	.10	.25
○ Kiffex R	2.00	4.00
○ Kirdo III R	2.00	4.00
○ Kithaba R	2.00	4.00
○ Kitonak C	.10	.25
○ Klatooinian Rev. C	.10	.25
○ Klatuu R	2.00	4.00
○ Laudica R	2.00	4.00
○ Leslomy Tacema R	2.00	4.00
○ Life Debt R	2.00	4.00
○ Loje Nella R	2.00	4.00
○ Malakili R	2.00	4.00
○ Mandalorian Mishap U	.40	1.00
○ Max Rebo R	2.00	4.00
○ Mos Eisley Blaster C	.10	.25
○ Mos Eisley Blaster C	.10	.25
○ Murttoc Yine R	2.50	5.00
○ Nal Hutta R	2.50	5.00
○ Nar Shaddaa Wind Chimes U	.40	1.00
○ Nikto C	.10	.25
○ Nizuc Bek R	2.00	4.00
○ None Shall Pass C	.10	.25

Galaxy card No 64 (Topps)

Galaxy card No 73 (Topps)

Galaxy card No. 81 (Topps)

○ Nysad R	2.00	4.00		○ Tatooine Desert C	.10	.25
○ Oola R	2.00	4.00		○ Tatooine Great Pit Of Car. U	.40	1.00
○ Ortolan C	.10	.25		○ Tatooine Hutt Canyon U	.40	1.00
○ Ortugg R	2.00	4.00		○ Tatooine Jabba's Pal. U	.40	1.00
○ Palejo Reshad R	2.00	4.00		○ Taym Dren-garen R	2.50	5.00
○ Pote Snitkin R	2.00	4.00		○ Tessek R	2.50	5.00
○ Princess Leia Organa R	10.00	20.00		○ The Signal C	.10	.25
○ Projection Of A Skywalker U	.40	1.00		○ Thermal Detonator R	4.00	8.00
○ Pucumir Thryss R	2.00	4.00		○ Thul Fain R	2.50	5.00
○ Quarren C	.10	.25		○ Tibrin R	2.00	4.00
○ Quick Reflexes C	.10	.25		○ Torture C	.10	.25
○ R'kik D'nec R	2.00	4.00		○ Trandoshan C	.10	.25
○ Rancor R	3.00	6.00		○ Trap Door U	.40	1.00
○ Rayc Ryjerd R	2.00	4.00		○ Twi'lek Advisor C	.10	.25
○ Ree-Yees R	2.00	4.00		○ Ultimatum U	.40	1.00
○ Rennek R	2.00	4.00		○ Unfriendly Fire R	2.50	5.00
○ Resistance U	.40	1.00		○ Vedain R	2.00	4.00
○ Revealed U	.40	1.00		○ Velken Tezeri R	2.50	5.00
○ Saelt-Marae R	2.50	5.00		○ Vibro-Ax C	.10	.25
○ Salacious Crumb R	2.00	4.00		○ Vibro-Ax C	.10	.25
○ Sandwhirl U	.40	1.00		○ Vizam R	2.00	4.00
○ Sandwhirl U	.40	1.00		○ Vul Tazaene R	2.00	4.00
○ Scum And Villainy R	2.50	5.00		○ Weapon Levitation U	.40	1.00
○ Sergeant Doallyn R	2.50	5.00		○ Weequay Guard C	.10	.25
○ Shasa Tiel R	2.50	5.00		○ Weequay Hunter C	.10	.25
○ Sic-Six C	.10	.25		○ Weequay Marksman U	.40	1.00
○ Skiff C	.10	.25		○ Weequay Skiff Master C	.10	.25
○ Skiff C	.10	.25		○ Well Guarded U	.40	1.00
○ Skrilling C	.10	.25		○ Whiphid C	.10	.25
○ Skull U	.40	1.00		○ Wittin R	2.00	4.00
○ Snivvian C	.10	.25		○ Wooof R	2.00	4.00
○ Someone Who Loves You U	.40	1.00		○ Wortt U	.40	1.00
○ Strangle R	2.00	4.00		○ Wounded Wookiee U	.40	1.00
○ Tamtel Skreej R	2.00	4.00		○ Yarkora C	.10	.25
○ Tanus Spijek R	2.00	4.00		○ Yarna d'al'Gargan U	.40	1.00
○ Tatooine Desert C	.10	.25		○ You Will Take Me To Jabba C	2.00	4.00

Galaxy card No. 89 (Topps)

Jabba's Palace card No. 73 (Topps)

○ Yoxgit R	2.00	4.00		○ Caller U2	.40	1.00
○ Yuzzum C	.10	.25		○ Cantina Brawl R1	2.50	5.00
Star Wars Limited				○ Charming to the Last R2	2.50	5.00
○ Complete set (324)	600.00	900.00		○ Chief Bast U1	.40	1.00
○ Common card (1-324)	.10	.25		○ Collateral Damage C2	.10	.25
○ 2X-3KPR U1	.40	1.00		○ Collision C2	.10	.25
○ 5D6-RA-7 R1	2.50	5.00		○ Colonel Wullf Yularen U1	.40	1.00
○ A Disturbnce in the Force U1	.40	1.00		○ Combined Attack C2	.10	.25
○ A Few Maneuvers C2	.10	.25		○ Comlink C1	.10	.25
○ A Tremor in the Force U1	.40	1.00		○ Commander Praji U2	.40	1.00
○ Admiral Motti R2	2.50	5.00		○ Corelian Corvette U2	.40	1.00
○ Affect Mind R1	2.50	5.00		○ Counter Assault C1	.10	.25
○ Alderaan R1	2.50	5.00		○ Crash Site Memorial U1	.40	1.00
○ Alderaan U2	.40	1.00		○ CZ-3 C1	.10	.25
○ Alter U1	.40	1.00		○ Dantooine U1	.40	1.00
○ Alter U1	.40	1.00		○ Dantooine U1	.40	1.00
○ Assault Rifle R2	2.50	5.00		○ Dark Collaboration R1	2.50	5.00
○ Baniss Keeg C2	.10	.25		○ Dark Hours U2	.40	1.00
○ Bantha U2	.40	1.00		○ Dark Jedi Lightsaber U1	.40	1.00
○ Beggar R1	2.50	5.00		○ Dark Jedi Presence R1	2.50	5.00
○ Beru Lars U2	.40	1.00		○ Dark Maneuvers C2	.10	.25
○ Beru Stew U2	.40	1.00		○ Darth Vader R1	30.00	60.00
○ Biggs Darklighter R2	2.50	5.00		○ Dathcha U1	.40	1.00
○ Black 2 R1	4.00	8.00		○ Dead Jawa C2	.10	.25
○ Black 3 U1	.40	1.00		○ Death Star Plans R1	2.50	5.00
○ Blast Door Controls U2	.40	1.00		○ Death Star Sentry U1	.40	1.00
○ Blaster C2	.10	.25		○ Death Star Trooper C2	.10	.25
○ Blaster Rack U1	.40	1.00		○ Death Star-Central Core U2	.40	1.00
○ Blaster Rifle C1	.10	.25		○ Death Star-Detntion Block C1	.10	.25
○ Blaster Rifle C2	.10	.25		○ Death Star-Detntion Block U2	.40	1.00
○ Blaster Scope U1	.40	1.00		○ Death Star-Dock. Bay 327 C2	.10	.25
○ Boosted TIE Cannon U1	.40	1.00		○ Death Star-Dock. Bay 327 C2	.10	.25
○ Boring Conversation R1	2.50	5.00		○ Death Star-Lvl 4 Military U1	.40	1.00
○ BoShek U1	.40	1.00		○ Death Star-Trash Comp. U1	.40	1.00
○ C-3PO R1	12.50	25.00		○ Death Star-War Room U2	.40	1.00
○ Caller U2	.40	1.00		○ Demotion R2	2.50	5.00

Jabba's Palace card No. 76 (Topps)

Shadows of the Empire card No. 20 (Topps)

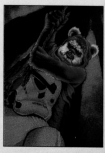

Indigenous Rebe[cut] & Affiliates No. 1 (Topps)

○ Devastator R1	6.00	12.00
○ Dice Ibegon R2	2.50	5.00
○ Disarmed R1	2.50	5.00
○ Disarmed R1	2.50	5.00
○ Djas Puhr R2	2.50	5.00
○ Don't Get Cocky R1	2.50	5.00
○ Don't Understand Our C1	.10	.25
○ Dr. Evazan R2	2.50	5.00
○ Droid Detector C2	.10	.25
○ Droid Shutdown C2	.10	.25
○ DS-61-2 U1	.40	1.00
○ DS-61-3 R1	6.00	12.00
○ Dutch R1	4.00	8.00
○ EG-6 U2	.40	1.00
○ Electrobinoculars C2	.10	.25
○ Elis Helrot U2	.40	1.00
○ Ellorrs Madek C2	.10	.25
○ Emergency Deployment U1	.40	1.00
○ Escape Pod U2	.40	1.00
○ Evacuate U2	.40	1.00
○ Expand the Empire R1	2.50	5.00
○ Eyes in the Dark U1	.40	1.00
○ Fear Will Keep Them R2	2.50	5.00
○ Feltipern Trevagg U1	.40	1.00
○ Figrin D'an U2	.40	1.00
○ Friendly Fire C2	.10	.25
○ Full Scale Alert U2	.40	1.00
○ Full Throttle R2	2.50	5.00
○ Fusion Gen. Sup. Tanks C2	.10	.25
○ Fusion Gen. Sup. Tanks C2	.10	.25
○ Gaderffii Stick C2	.10	.25
○ Garindan R2	2.50	5.00
○ General Dodonna U1	.40	1.00
○ General Tagge R2	2.50	5.00
○ Gift of the Mentor R1	2.50	5.00
○ Gold 1 R2	2.50	5.00

○ Gold 5 R2	2.50	5.00
○ Grand Moff Tarkin R1	12.50	25.00
○ Gravel Storm U2	.40	1.00
○ Han Seeker R2	2.50	5.00
○ Han Solo R1	20.00	40.00
○ Han's Back U2	.40	1.00
○ Han's Dice C2	.10	.25
○ Han's Blaster Pistol R2	2.50	5.00
○ Hear Me Baby, Hold Tog. C2	.10	.25
○ Help Me Obi-Wan Kenobi R1	2.50	5.00
○ How Did We Get Into This U2	.40	1.00
○ Hydroponics Station U2	.40	1.00
○ Hyper Escape C2	.10	.25
○ I Find Your Lack of Faith R 1	2.50	5.00
○ I Have You Now R2	2.50	5.00
○ I've Got a Bad Feeling C2	.10	.25
○ I've Got a Problem Here C2	.10	.25
○ I've Lost Artoo U1	.40	1.00
○ Imperial Barrier C2	.10	.25
○ Imperial Blaster C2	.10	.25
○ Imperial Code Cylinder C2	.10	.25
○ Imperial Pilot C2	.10	.25
○ Imperial Reinforcements C1	.10	.25
○ Imperial Trooper Guard C1	.10	.25
○ Imperial-Class Star Dest. U1	.40	1.00
○ Into the Garbage Chute R2	2.50	5.00
○ Ion Cannon U1	.40	1.00
○ It Could Be Worse C2	.10	.25
○ It's Worse C2	.10	.25
○ Jawa C2	.10	.25
○ Jawa C2	.10	.25
○ Jawa Pack U1	.40	1.00
○ Jawa Siesta U1	.40	1.00
○ Jedi Lightsaber U1	.40	1.00
○ Jedi Presence R1	2.50	5.00
○ Jek Porkins U1	.40	1.00

**Boba Fett card
No. 2 (Topps)**

○ Juri Juice R2	2.50	5.00		○ Macroscan C2	.10	.25
○ K'lor'slug R1	2.50	5.00		○ Mantellian Savrip R2	2.50	5.00
○ Kabe U1	.40	1.00		○ Millenium Falcon R1	20.00	40.00
○ Kal'Falnl C'ndros R1	4.00	8.00		○ Molator R1	2.50	5.00
○ Kessel U2	.40	1.00		○ Momaw Nadon U2	.40	1.00
○ Kessel U2	.40	1.00		○ Moment of Triumph R2	2.50	5.00
○ Kessel Run R2	2.50	5.00		○ Move Along R1	2.50	5.00
○ Ket Maliss C2	.10	.25		○ MSE-6 Mouse Droid U1	.40	1.00
○ Kintan Strider C1	.10	.25		○ Myo R2	2.50	5.00
○ Kitik Keed'kak R1	2.50	5.00		○ Nabrun Leids U2	.40	1.00
○ Krayt Dragon Howl R1	2.50	5.00		○ Narrow Escape C2	.10	.25
○ Labria R2	2.50	5.00		○ Nevar Yalnal R2	2.50	5.00
○ Laser Projector U2	.40	1.00		○ Nightfall U1	.40	1.00
○ Lateral Damage R2	2.50	5.00		○ Noble Sacrifice R2	2.50	5.00
○ Leesub Sirin R2	2.50	5.00		○ Obi-Wan Kenobi R1	20.00	40.00
○ Leia Organa R1	20.00	40.00		○ Obi-Wan's Cape R1	2.50	5.00
○ Leia's Back U2	.40	1.00		○ Obi-Wan's Lightsaber R1	4.00	8.00
○ Leia's Sporting Blaster U1	.40	1.00		○ Observation Holocam U2	.40	1.00
○ Lieutenant Tanbris U2	.40	1.00		○ Old Ben C2	.10	.25
○ Lift Tube C2	.10	.25		○ Ommni Box C2	.10	.25
○ Lift Tube C2	.10	.25		○ On The Edge R2	2.50	5.00
○ Light Repeating Blaster R1	2.50	5.00		○ Organa's Ceremonial R1	2.50	5.00
○ Lightsaber Proficiency R1	2.50	5.00		○ Our Most Desperate Hour R1	2.50	5.00
○ Limited Resources U2	.40	1.00		○ Out of Nowhere U2	.40	1.00
○ LIN-V8K C1	.10	.25		○ Overload C2	.10	.25
○ LIN-V8M C1	.10	.25		○ Owen Lars U1	.40	1.00
○ Local Trouble R1	2.50	5.00		○ Panic U1	.40	1.00
○ Lone Pilot R2	2.50	5.00		○ Physical Choke R1	2.50	5.00
○ Lone Warrior R2	2.50	5.00		○ Plastoid Armor U2	.40	1.00
○ Look Sir, Droids R1	2.50	5.00		○ Ponda Baba U1	.40	1.00
○ Luke Seeker R2	2.50	5.00		○ Pops U1	.40	1.00
○ Luke Skywalker R1	20.00	40.00		○ Precise Attack C2	.10	.25
○ LUKE! LUUUKE! U1	.40	1.00		○ Presence of the Force R1	5.00	10.00
○ Luke's Back U2	.40	1.00		○ Prophetess U1	.40	1.00
○ Luke's X-34 Landspeeder U1	.40	1.00		○ Proton Torpedoes C2	.10	.25
○ M'iiyoom Onith U2	.40	1.00		○ Quad Laser Cannon U1	.40	1.00

Droids birthday
trading card
(Topps)

Star Wars Finest
trading card
(Topps)

○ R1-G4 C2	.10	.25
○ R2-X2 C2	.10	.25
○ R4-E1 C2	.10	.25
○ R4-M9 C2	.10	.25
○ Radar Scanner C2	.10	.25
○ Reactor Terminal U2	.40	1.00
○ Rebel Barrier C2	.10	.25
○ Rebel Guard C2	.10	.25
○ Rebel Pilot C2	.10	.25
○ Rebel Planners R2	2.50	5.00
○ Rebel Reinforcements C1	.10	.25
○ Rebel Trooper C3	.10	.25
○ Red 1 U1	.40	1.00
○ Red 3 R2	2.50	5.00
○ Red Leader R1	4.00	8.00
○ Restraining Bolt C2	.10	.25
○ Restraining Bolt C2	.10	.25
○ Restricted Deployment U1	.40	1.00
○ Return of a Jedi U2	.40	1.00
○ Revolution R1	4.00	8.00
○ Rycar Ryjerd U1	.40	1.00
○ Sai'torr Kai Fas C2	.10	.25
○ Sandcrawler R2	2.50	5.00
○ Sandcrawler R2	2.50	5.00
○ Scanning Crew C2	.10	.25
○ Scomp Link Access C2	.10	.25
○ Send a Detachment Down R 1	2.50	5.00
○ Sense U1	.40	1.00
○ Sense U1	.40	1.00
○ Set for Stun C2	.10	.25
○ Shistavanen Wolfman C2	.10	.25
○ Skywalkers R1	2.50	5.00
○ Solo Han R2	2.50	5.00
○ SoroSuub V-35 Landsp. C2	.10	.25
○ Spaceport Speeders U2	.40	1.00
○ Special Modifications U1	.40	1.00

○ Stormtroopr C3	.10	.25
○ Stormtrooper Backpack C2	.10	.25
○ Stormtrooper Utility Belt C2	.10	.25
○ Sunsdown U1	.40	1.00
○ Surprise Assault C1	.10	.25
○ Tactical Re-Call R2	2.50	5.00
○ Tagge Seeker R2	2.50	5.00
○ Takeel C2	.10	.25
○ Tallon Roll C2	.10	.25
○ Talz C2	.10	.25
○ Targeting Computer U1	.40	1.00
○ Tarkin Seeker R2	2.50	5.00
○ Tatooine C2	.10	.25
○ Tatooine C2	.10	.25
○ Tatooine Utility Belt C2	.10	.25
○ Tatooine-Cantina R2	2.50	5.00
○ Tatooine-Cantina R2	2.50	5.00
○ Tatooine-Docking Bay 94 C2	.10	.25
○ Tatooine-Docking Bay 94 C2	.10	.25
○ Tatooine-Dune Sea C1	.10	.25
○ Tatooine-Jawa Camp C1	.10	.25
○ Tatooine-Jawa Camp C1	.10	.25
○ Tatooine-Jund. Wastes C1	.10	.25
○ Tatooine-Lars' Farm C1	.10	.25
○ Tatooine-Lars' Farm U2	.40	1.00
○ Tatooine-Mos Eisley C1	.10	.25
○ Tatooine-Mos Eisley U2	.40	1.00
○ Tatooine-Obi-Wan's Hut R1	2.50	5.00
○ Thank the Maker R2	2.50	5.00
○ The Bith Shuffle C2	.10	.25
○ The Circle is Now Comp. R1	4.00	8.00
○ The Empire's Back U1	.40	1.00
○ The Force is Strong With R2	2.50	5.00
○ This is All Your Fault U1	.40	1.00
○ TIE Advanced x1 U2	.40	1.00
○ TIE Fighter C2	.10	.25

Galaxy trading card (Topps)

Return of the Jedi Widevision trading card (Topps)

○ TIE Scout C2	.10	.25
○ Timer Mine C2	.10	.25
○ Timer Mine C2	.10	.25
○ Tonnika Sisters R1	2.50	5.00
○ Traffic Control U2	.40	1.00
○ Trinto Duaba U1	.40	1.00
○ Trooper Charge U2	.40	1.00
○ Turbolaser Battery R2	2.50	5.00
○ Tusken Breath Mask U1	.40	1.00
○ Tusken Raider C2	.10	.25
○ Tusken Scavengers C2	.10	.25
○ Ubrikkian 9000-Z001 C2	.10	.25
○ Utinni! R1	2.50	5.00
○ Utinni! R1	2.50	5.00
○ Vader's Custom TIE R1	10.00	20.00
○ Vader's Eye R1	2.50	5.00
○ Vader's Lightsaber R1	7.50	15.00
○ Vaporator C2	.10	.25
○ Warrior's Courage R2	2.50	5.00
○ We're All Gonna Be A Lot R1	2.50	5.00
○ We're Doomed C2	.10	.25
○ WED-9-M1 Bantha R2	2.50	5.00
○ WED15-1662 Treadwell R2	2.50	5.00
○ Wioslea U1	.40	1.00
○ Wrong Turn U1	.40	1.00
○ Wuher U2	.40	1.00
○ X-wing C2	.10	.25
○ X-wing C2	.10	.25
○ Yavin 4 C2	.10	.25
○ Yavin 4 C2	.10	.25
○ Yavin 4-Docking Bay C2	.10	.25
○ Yavin 4-Docking Bay C2	.10	.25
○ Yavin 4-Jungle C1	.10	.25
○ Yavin 4-Jungle U2	.40	1.00
○ Yavin 4-Mass. Throne U2	2.50	5.00
○ Yavin 4-Mass. War Room R1	2.50	5.00

○ Yavin Sentry U2	.40	1.00
○ Yerka Mig U1	.40	1.00
○ You Overestimate Their C1	.10	.25
○ Your Eyes Can Deceive U1	.40	1.00
○ Your Powers Are Weak R1	2.50	5.00

Star Wars Unlimited

○ Complete set (324)	400.00	600.00
○ Common card (1-324)	.10	.25
○ 2X-3KPR U1	.40	1.00
○ 5D6-RA-7 R1	2.00	4.00
○ A Disturbnce in the Force U1	.40	1.00
○ A Few Maneuvers C2	.10	.25
○ A Tremor in the Force U1	.40	1.00
○ Admiral Motti R2	2.00	4.00
○ Affect Mind R1	2.00	4.00
○ Alderaan R1	2.00	4.00
○ Alderaan U2	.40	1.00
○ Alter U1	.40	1.00
○ Alter U1	.40	1.00
○ Assault Rifle R2	2.00	4.00
○ Baniss Keeg C2	.10	.25
○ Bantha U2	.40	1.00
○ Beggar R1	2.00	4.00
○ Beru Lars U2	.40	1.00
○ Beru Stew U2	.40	1.00
○ Biggs Darklighter R2	2.00	4.00
○ Black 2 R1	3.00	6.00
○ Black 3 U1	.40	1.00
○ Blast Door Controls U2	.40	1.00
○ Blaster C2	.10	.25
○ Blaster Rack U1	.40	1.00
○ Blaster Rifle C1	.10	.25
○ Blaster Rifle C2	.10	.25
○ Blaster Scope U1	.40	1.00
○ Boosted TIE Cannon U1	.40	1.00
○ Boring Conversation R1	2.00	4.00

Star Wars Vehicles trading card (Topps)

Chewbacca button (Star Novelties)

Trilogy button

○ BoShek U1	.40	1.00
○ C-3PO R1	10.00	20.00
○ Caller U2	.40	1.00
○ Caller U2	.40	1.00
○ Cantina Brawl R1	2.00	4.00
○ Charming to the Last R2	2.00	4.00
○ Chief Bast U1	.40	1.00
○ Collateral Damage C2	.10	.25
○ Collision C2	.10	.25
○ Colonel Wullf Yularen U1	.40	1.00
○ Combined Attack C2	.10	.25
○ Comlink C1	.10	.25
○ Commander Praji U2	.40	1.00
○ Corelian Corvette U2	.40	1.00
○ Counter Assault C1	.10	.25
○ Crash Site Memorial U1	.40	1.00
○ CZ-3 C1	.10	.25
○ Dantooine U1	.40	1.00
○ Dantooine U1	.40	1.00
○ Dark Collaboration R1	2.00	4.00
○ Dark Hours U2	.40	1.00
○ Dark Jedi Lightsaber U1	.40	1.00
○ Dark Jedi Presence R1	2.00	4.00
○ Dark Maneuvers C2	.10	.25
○ Darth Vader R1	20.00	40.00
○ Dathcha U1	.40	1.00
○ Dead Jawa C2	.10	.25
○ Death Star Plans R1	2.00	4.00
○ Death Star Sentry U1	.40	1.00
○ Death Star Trooper C2	.10	.25
○ Death Star-Central Core U2	.40	1.00
○ Death Star-Det. Block C1	.10	.25
○ Death Star-Det. Block U2	.10	.25
○ Death Star-Dock.Bay 327 C2	.10	.25
○ Death Star-Dock.Bay 327 C2	.10	.25
○ Death Star-Level 4 Mil. U1	.40	1.00

○ Death Star-Trash Comp. U1	.40	1.00
○ Death Star-War Room U2	.40	1.00
○ Demotion R2	2.00	4.00
○ Devastator R1	5.00	10.00
○ Dice Ibegon R2	2.00	4.00
○ Disarmed R1	2.00	4.00
○ Disarmed R1	2.00	4.00
○ Djas Puhr R2	2.00	4.00
○ Don't Get Cocky R1	2.00	4.00
○ Don't Understand Our C1	.10	.25
○ Dr. Evazan R2	2.00	4.00
○ Droid Detector C2	.10	.25
○ Droid Shutdown C2	.10	.25
○ DS-61-2 U1	.40	1.00
○ DS-61-3 R1	2.00	4.00
○ Dutch R1	3.00	6.00
○ EG-6 U2	.40	1.00
○ Electrobinoculars C2	.10	.25
○ Elis Helrot U2	.40	1.00
○ Ellorrs Madek C2	.10	.25
○ Emergency Deployment U1	.40	1.00
○ Escape Pod U2	.40	1.00
○ Evacuate U2	.40	1.00
○ Expand the Empire R1	2.00	4.00
○ Eyes in the Dark U1	.40	1.00
○ Fear Will Keep Them R2	2.00	4.00
○ Feltipern Trevagg U1	.40	1.00
○ Figrin D'an U2	.40	1.00
○ Friendly Fire C2	.10	.25
○ Full Scale Alert U2	.40	1.00
○ Full Throttle R2	2.00	4.00
○ Fusion Gen. Sup. Tanks C2	.10	.25
○ Fusion Gen. Sup. Tanks C2	.10	.25
○ Gaderffii Stick C2	.10	.25
○ Garindan R2	2.00	4.00
○ General Dodonna U1	.40	1.00

Darth Vader ceramic figurine

○ General Tagge R2	2.00	4.00	
○ Gift of the Mentor R1	2.00	4.00	
○ Gold 1 R2	2.00	4.00	
○ Gold 5 R2	2.00	4.00	
○ Grand Moff Tarkin R1	6.00	12.00	
○ Gravel Storm U2	.40	1.00	
○ Han Seeker R2	2.00	4.00	
○ Han Solo R1	12.50	25.00	
○ Han's Back U2	.40	1.00	
○ Han's Dice C2	.10	.25	
○ Han's Blaster Pistol R2	2.00	4.00	
○ Hear Me Baby, Hold Tog. C2	.10	.25	
○ Help Me Obi-Wan Kenobi R1	2.00	4.00	
○ How Did We Get Into This U2	.40	1.00	
○ Hydroponics Station U2	.40	1.00	
○ Hyper Escape C2	.10	.25	
○ I Find Your Lack of Faith R1	2.00	4.00	
○ I Have You Now R2	2.00	4.00	
○ I've Got a Bad Feeling C2	.10	.25	
○ I've Got a Problem Here C2	.10	.25	
○ I've Lost Artoo U1	.40	1.00	
○ Imperial Barrier C2	.10	.25	
○ Imperial Blaster C2	.10	.25	
○ Imperial Code Cylinder C2	.10	.25	
○ Imperial Pilot C2	.10	.25	
○ Imperial Reinforcements C1	.10	.25	
○ Imperial Trooper Guard C1	.10	.25	
○ Imperial-Class Star Dest. U1	.40	1.00	
○ Into the Garbage Chute R2	2.00	4.00	
○ Ion Cannon U1	.40	1.00	
○ It Could Be Worse C2	.10	.25	
○ It's Worse C2	.10	.25	
○ Jawa C2	.10	.25	
○ Jawa C2	.10	.25	
○ Jawa Pack U1	.40	1.00	
○ Jawa Siesta U1	.40	1.00	

○ Jedi Lightsaber U1	.40	1.00	
○ Jedi Presence R1	2.00	4.00	
○ Jek Porkins U1	.40	1.00	
○ Juri Juice R2	2.00	4.00	
○ K'lor'slug R1	2.00	4.00	
○ Kabe U1	.40	1.00	
○ Kal'Falnl C'ndros R1	2.00	4.00	
○ Kessel U2	.40	1.00	
○ Kessel U2	.40	1.00	
○ Kessel Run R2	2.00	4.00	
○ Ket Maliss C2	.10	.25	
○ Kintan Strider C1	.10	.25	
○ Kitik Keed'kak R1	2.00	4.00	
○ Krayt Dragon Howl R1	2.00	4.00	
○ Labria R2	2.00	4.00	
○ Laser Projector U2	.40	1.00	
○ Lateral Damage R2	2.00	4.00	
○ Leesub Sirin R2	2.00	4.00	
○ Leia Organa R1	12.50	25.00	
○ Leia's Back U2	.40	1.00	
○ Leia's Sporting Blaster U1	.40	1.00	
○ Lieutenant Tanbris U2	.40	1.00	
○ Lift Tube C2	.10	.25	
○ Lift Tube C2	.10	.25	
○ Light Repeating Blaster R1	2.00	4.00	
○ Lightsaber Proficiency R1	2.00	4.00	
○ Limited Resources U2	.40	1.00	
○ LIN-V8K C1	.10	.25	
○ LIN-V8M C1	.10	.25	
○ Local Trouble R1	2.00	4.00	
○ Lone Pilot R2	2.00	4.00	
○ Lone Warrior R2	2.00	4.00	
○ Look Sir, Droids R1	2.00	4.00	
○ Luke Seeker R2	2.00	4.00	
○ Luke Skywalker R1	12.50	25.00	
○ LUKE! LUUUKE! U1	.40	1.00	

Klaatu ceramic figurine

Darth Vader mask (Don Post)

Darth Vader plastic mask (Ben Cooper)

○ Luke's Back U2	.40	1.00
○ Luke's X-34 Landspeeder U1	.40	1.00
○ M'iiyoom Onith U2	.40	1.00
○ Macroscan C2	.10	.25
○ Mantellian Savrip R2	2.00	4.00
○ Millenium Falcon R1	12.50	25.00
○ Molator R1	2.00	4.00
○ Momaw Nadon U2	.40	1.00
○ Moment of Triumph R2	2.00	4.00
○ Move Along R1	2.00	4.00
○ MSE-6 Mouse Droid U1	.40	1.00
○ Myo R2	2.00	4.00
○ Nabrun Leids U2	.40	1.00
○ Narrow Escape C2	.10	.25
○ Nevar Yalnal R2	2.00	4.00
○ Nightfall U1	.40	1.00
○ Noble Sacrifice R2	2.00	4.00
○ Obi-Wan Kenobi R1	15.00	30.00
○ Obi-Wan's Cape R1	2.00	4.00
○ Obi-Wan's Lightsaber R1	4.00	8.00
○ Observation Holocam U2	.40	1.00
○ Old Ben C2	.10	.25
○ Ommni Box C2	.10	.25
○ On The Edge R2	2.00	4.00
○ Organa's Ceremonial R1	2.00	4.00
○ Our Most Desperate Hour R1	2.00	4.00
○ Out of Nowhere U2	.40	1.00
○ Overload C2	.10	.25
○ Owen Lars U1	.40	1.00
○ Panic U1	.40	1.00
○ Physical Choke R1	2.00	4.00
○ Plastoid Armor U2	.40	1.00
○ Ponda Baba U1	.40	1.00
○ Pops U1	.40	1.00
○ Precise Attack C2	.10	.25
○ Presence of the Force R1	2.00	4.00

**Return of the
Jedi glass
(Burger King)**

**The Empire Strikes
Back glass
(Burger King)**

○ Prophetess U1	.40	1.00
○ Proton Torpedoes C2	.10	.25
○ Quad Laser Cannon U1	.40	1.00
○ R1-G4 C2	.10	.25
○ R2-X2 C2	.10	.25
○ R4-E1 C2	.10	.25
○ R4-M9 C2	.10	.25
○ Radar Scanner C2	.10	.25
○ Reactor Terminal U2	.40	1.00
○ Rebel Barrier C2	.10	.25
○ Rebel Guard C2	.10	.25
○ Rebel Pilot C2	.10	.25
○ Rebel Planners R2	2.00	4.00
○ Rebel Reinforcements C1	.10	.25
○ Rebel Trooper C3	.10	.25
○ Red 1 U1	.40	1.00
○ Red 3 R2	2.00	4.00
○ Red Leader R1	3.00	6.00
○ Restraining Bolt C2	.10	.25
○ Restraining Bolt C2	.10	.25
○ Restricted Deployment U1	.40	1.00
○ Return of a Jedi U2	.40	1.00
○ Revolution R1	3.00	6.00
○ Rycar Ryjerd U1	.40	1.00
○ Sai'torr Kai Fas C2	.10	.25
○ Sandcrawler R2	2.00	4.00
○ Sandcrawler R2	2.00	4.00
○ Scanning Crew C2	.10	.25
○ Scomp Link Access C2	.10	.25
○ Send a Detachment Down R1	2.00	4.00
○ Sense U1	.40	1.00
○ Sense U1	.40	1.00
○ Set for Stun C2	.10	.25
○ Shistavanen Wolfman C2	.10	.25
○ Skywalkers R1	2.00	4.00
○ Solo Han R2	2.00	4.00

○ SoroSuub V-35 Landsp. C2	.10	.25	○ This is All Your Fault U1	.40	1.00	
○ Spaceport Speeders U2	.40	1.00	○ TIE Advanced x1 U2	.40	1.00	
○ Special Modifications U1	.40	1.00	○ TIE Fighter C2	.10	.25	
○ Stormtrooper C3	.10	.25	○ TIE Scout C2	.10	.25	
○ Stormtrooper Backpack C2	.10	.25	○ Timer Mine C2	.10	.25	
○ Stormtrooper Utility Belt C2	.10	.25	○ Timer Mine C2	.10	.25	
○ Sunsdown U1	.40	1.00	○ Tonnika Sisters R1	2.00	4.00	
○ Surprise Assault C1	.10	.25	○ Traffic Control U2	.40	1.00	
○ Tactical Re-Call R2	2.00	4.00	○ Trinto Duaba U1	.40	1.00	
○ Tagge Seeker R2	2.00	4.00	○ Trooper Charge U2	.40	1.00	
○ Takeel C2	.10	.25	○ Turbolaser Battery R2	2.00	4.00	
○ Tallon Roll C2	.10	.25	○ Tusken Breath Mask U1	.40	1.00	
○ Talz C2	.10	.25	○ Tusken Raider C2	.10	.25	
○ Targeting Computer U1	.40	1.00	○ Tusken Scavengers C2	.10	.25	
○ Tarkin Seeker R2	2.00	4.00	○ Ubrikkian 9000-Z001 C2	.10	.25	
○ Tatooine C2	.10	.25	○ Utinni! R1	2.00	4.00	
○ Tatooine C2	.10	.25	○ Utinni! R1	2.00	4.00	
○ Tatooine Utility Belt C2	.10	.25	○ Vader's Custom TIE R1	5.00	10.00	
○ Tatooine-Cantina R2	2.00	4.00	○ Vader's Eye R1	2.00	4.00	
○ Tatooine-Cantina R2	2.00	4.00	○ Vader's Lightsaber R1	5.00	10.00	
○ Tatooine-Docking Bay 94 C2	.10	.25	○ Vaporator C2	.10	.25	
○ Tatooine-Docking Bay 94 C2	.10	.25	○ Warrior's Courage R2	2.00	4.00	
○ Tatooine-Dune Sea C1	.10	.25	○ We're All Gonna Be A Lot R1	2.00	4.00	
○ Tatooine-Jawa Camp C1	.10	.25	○ We're Doomed C2	.10	.25	
○ Tatooine-Jawa Camp C1	.10	.25	○ WED-9-M1 Bantha R2	2.00	4.00	
○ Tatooine-Jund. Wastes C1	.10	.25	○ WED15-1662 Treadwell R2	2.00	4.00	
○ Tatooine-Lars' Farm C1	.10	.25	○ Wioslea U1	.40	1.00	
○ Tatooine-Lars' Farm U2	.10	.25	○ Wrong Turn U1	.40	1.00	
○ Tatooine-Mos Eisley C1	.10	.25	○ Wuher U2	.40	1.00	
○ Tatooine-Mos Eisley U2	.40	1.00	○ X-wing C2	.10	.25	
○ Tatooine-Obi-Wan's Hut R1	2.00	4.00	○ X-wing C2	.10	.25	
○ Thank the Maker R2	2.00	4.00	○ Yavin 4 C2	.10	.25	
○ The Bith Shuffle C2	.10	.25	○ Yavin 4 C2	.10	.25	
○ The Circle is Now Comp. R1	2.00	4.00	○ Yavin 4-Docking Bay C2	.10	.25	
○ The Empire's Back U1	.40	1.00	○ Yavin 4-Docking Bay C2	.10	.25	
○ The Force is Strong With R2	2.00	4.00	○ Yavin 4-Jungle C1	.10	.25	

**Star Wars Trilogy
THX VHS**

**C-3PO
Pez dispenser**

**Chewbacca
Pez dispenser**

○ Yavin 4-Jungle U2	.40	1.00
○ Yavin 4-Mass. Throne U2	.40	1.00
○ Yavin 4-Mass. War Room R1	2.00	4.00
○ Yavin Sentry U2	.40	1.00
○ Yerka Mig U1	.40	1.00
○ You Overestimate Their C1	.10	.25
○ Your Eyes Can Deceive U1	.40	1.00
○ Your Powers Are Weak R1	2.00	4.00

Chess sets

DANBURY MINT

○ Darth Vader Chess

○ Wicket Chess

○ Stormtrooper

○ R2-D2

Electronic

Palitoy (England)

○ Destroy the Death Star Game

Kenner

○ Electronic Laser Battle

○ Electronic Battle Command

Micro Games of America

○ Star Wars, Gold Package

○ Star Wars

○ The Empire Strikes Back

○ Return of the Jedi

○ Star Wars with Darth Vader medallion

Jigsaw Puzzles

Kenner

○ Han Solo and Chewbacca in black box

○ Victory Celebration with sticker
   and two extra characters on box

○ Entering Mos Eisley

○ Luke Skywalker

**Stormtrooper
Pez dispenser**

○ Space Battle

○ R2-D2 and C-3PO

○ Han Solo and Chewie

○ Luke and Leia

○ Ben and Darth

○ Trapped in Trash

○ Luke meets R2-D2

○ X-wing fighter

○ Victory celebration

○ Sand People

○ Stormtroopers

○ Cantina Band

○ Selling of the Droids

○ Bantha

○ Jawas capture R2-D2

○ Aboard the Falcon

○ Corridor of Lights

Craft Master

○ Battle on Endor

○ Ewok Leaders

○ B-Wings Attack

○ Friends of Jabba

○ Jabba the Hutt

○ Death Star

○ Side open boxes

○ Friends of Jabba

○ Jabba the Hutt

○ Death Star

○ Ewoks

○ Fishing Hole

○ Afternoon Swim

○ Ewok Nature Lesson

Milton Bradley

○ Star Wars

○ The Empire Strikes Back

○ Return of the Jedi

○ 3-D Millennium Falcon

**Darth Vader
Pez dispenser**

**Yoda
Pez dispenser**

Frame tray puzzles

- ○ Gamorrean Guard
- ○ Princess Leia
- ○ Darth Vader
- ○ Wicket
- ○ Ewoks hang gliding
- ○ Wicket and R2-D2
- ○ Ewok Village
- ○ Kneesaa and Baga

AUSTRALIA

- ○ Wicket frame tray puzzle
- ○ Gamorrean Guard frame tray puzzle
- ○ Darth Vader frame tray puzzle
- ○ Princess Leia and Wicket frame tray puzzle

ENGLAND

- ○ Style A with Death Star
- ○ Jabba the Hutt boxed puzzle
- ○ Luke Skywalker boxed puzzle
- ○ Heroes boxed puzzle
- ○ Darth Vader boxed puzzle

Milton Bradley

- ○ Star Wars 60-piece boxed
- ○ Return of the Jedi 60-piece boxed
- ○ Star Wars 100-piece boxed

FRANCE

- ○ Entree Dans La Villy

GREECE

- ○ Heroes
- ○ Han Solo
- ○ Admiral Ackbar
- ○ Max Rebo Band
- ○ Luke Skywalker and Darth Vader
- ○ Sail Barge
- ○ Emperor's Arrival

Applause

- ○ Star Wars puzzle cube

Match blocks

- ○ Return of the Jedi
- ○ Ewoks

Role-playing games

West End Games

- ○ Movie Trilogy Sourcebook hardcover
- ○ Riders of the Mealstrom
- ○ Mission to Lianna
- ○ Miniatures Battles Starter Set boxed set
- ○ Bounty Hunters
- ○ Imperial Sourcebook hardcover 2nd Edition
- ○ Planets Collection
- ○ Platt's Starport Guide
- ○ Rebel SpecForce Handbook
- ○ Kathol Rift
- ○ Thrawn Trilogy Sourcebook softcover
- ○ Platts Smugglers Guide
- ○ Stock Ships
- ○ Player's Guide to Tapani
- ○ Fantastic Technology Tech Gear
- ○ Introductory Adventure Game
- ○ The Roleplaying Game hardcover book
- ○ The Roleplaying Game hardcover 2nd Edition

**Stormtrooper
Pizza Hut box**

Sourcebooks

- ○ The Star Wars Sourcebook hardcover
- ○ The Star Wars Sourcebook hardcover 2nd Edition
- ○ The Imperial Soucrebook hardcover
- ○ The Imperial Sourcebook softcover
- ○ The Rebel Alliance Sourcebook hardcover
- ○ The Rebel Alliance Sourcebook hardcover 2nd Edition
- ○ Heir to the Empire Sourcebook hardcover
- ○ Heir to the Empire Sourcebook softcover

**R2-D2
Pizza Hut box**

- ○ Dark Force Rising Sourcebook hardcover
- ○ The Last Command Sourcebook hardcover
- ○ Han Solo Corporate Sector Sourcebook
- ○ Shadows of the Empire Sourcebook

Early Adventures

- ○ Strike Force Shantipole
- ○ Battle for the Golden Sun
- ○ Starfall
- ○ Otherspace
- ○ Otherspace II
- ○ Scavenger Hunt
- ○ Riders of the Maelstrom
- ○ Black Ice

Escape from the Death Star board game (Kenner)

Later Adventures

- ○ Classic Campaigns
- ○ Classic Adventures
- ○ Flashpoint Brak Sector
- ○ Alliance Inteligence Reports
- ○ Craken's Rebel Operatives
- ○ Platt's Starport Guide
- ○ Goroth Slave of the Empire
- ○ Twin Stars of Kira
- ○ Supernova
- ○ Death in the Undercity
- ○ Planet of the Mists
- ○ Isis Cordinates
- ○ The Abduction
- ○ Mission to Lianna
- ○ Scoundrel's Luck
- ○ Jedi's Honor

Guide Books

- ○ Galaxy Guide #1-#12
- ○ Galaxy Guide #1-#12 2nd Edition
- ○ Planets Collection
- ○ Planets of the Galaxy Volume #1-#3
- ○ Minatures Battles

Monopoly, Classic Trilogy Edition board game (Parker Brothers)

- ○ Miniatures Battles 2nd Edition
- ○ Miniatures Battle Companion
- ○ Death Star Technical Companion
- ○ Death Star Technical Companion 2nd edition
- ○ Wanted by Craken

Supplements

- ○ Light Saber dueling pack
- ○ Starfighter battle book
- ○ Campaign pack
- ○ Gamemaster kit
- ○ Gamemaster handbook

West End Games
- ○ Adventure Journals #1-#15
- ○ Platt's Smuggler's Guide

Video games

PARKER BROTHERS
- ○ Star Wars: Jedi Arena
- ○ The Empire Strikes Back
- ○ Return of the Jedi: Death Star Battle

NINTENDO
- ○ Star Wars
- ○ The Empire Strikes Back
- ⊗ Super Star Wars
- ⊗ Super The Empire Strikes Back
- ○ Star Wars Gameboy
- ○ Star Wars Game Gear

PC games

- ○ X-wing Collector's CD-ROM MAC
- ○ Star Wars Chess
- ○ Dark Forces MAC CD
- ○ Dark Forces IBM CD
- ○ Dark Forces Preview Disc
- ○ X-wing
- ○ Imperial Pursuit
- ○ B-Wing

Hoth Ice Planet Adventure board game (Kenner)

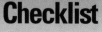

○ Rebel Assault MAC CD
○ Rebel Assault IBM CD
○ Rebel Assault II MAC CD
○ Rebel Assault II IBM CD
○ Lucasarts Macintosh Archives Volume I
○ TIE Fighter Collector's IBM CD
○ X-wing Collector's Mac CD
○ X-wing Collector's IBM CD

JEWELRY

Key chains

○ Placo products
○ Han Solo in Carbonite (FAO Schwartz Exclusive)

Bracelets

○ R2-D2, C-3PO and Darth Vader

Key chains

○ Star Wars pen light, silver
○ Star Wars pen light, blue

A.H. Prismatic
○ R2-D2 and C-3PO
○ X-wing, hologram
○ Millennium Falcon, hologram
○ Darth Vader, hologram
○ B-Wing
○ Millennium Falcon
○ TIE Interceptor and X-wing
○ Millennium Falcon and Star Wars Logo
○ Darth Vader
○ Imperial Star Destroyer
○ X-wing
○ TIE Fighter
○ AT-AT and Snowspeeder

Adam Joseph
○ Darth Vader
○ R2-D2
○ Wicket
○ Kneesaa

Hollywood Pins
○ New Republic
○ Millennium Flacon
○ Darth Vader
○ Yoda
○ Don't Underestimate the Poweer of the Dark Side
○ R2-D2
○ Rebel Forces Antique Gold

Rawcliffe
○ R2-D2
○ Snowspeeder
○ Rebel Logo
○ Imperial Symbol
○ Return of the Jedi logo
○ The Empire Strikes Back logo
○ Star Wars logo
○ Shuttle Tyderium
○ TIE Fighter
○ AT-AT
○ AT-ST
○ Blaster Rifle
○ Blaster Pistol
○ Darth Vader
○ Yoda
○ Obi-Wan Kenobi
○ Shadows of the Empire

Placo Products
○ Luke Skywalker
○ C-3PO
○ Darth Vader
○ R2-D2

Necklaces

Factors
○ R2-D2
○ Chewbacca

QVC
○ C-3PO

Battle at the Sarlaac Pit board game (Parker Brothers)

Wicket the Ewok Food-Gathering Game (Parker Brothers)

Adam Joseph
- ⃝ Imperial Guard
- ⃝ Wicket
- ⃝ Darth Vader
- ⃝ R2-D2
- ⃝ Return of the Jedi
- ⃝ C-3PO Bust
- ⃝ Salacious Crumb

Factors
- ⃝ C-3PO
- ⃝ Darth Vader

Howard Eldon
- ⃝ Darth Vader

Pins

- ⃝ C-3PO, die cut
- ⃝ R2-D2, die cut

A.H. Prismatic
- ⃝ B-Wing
- ⃝ Millennium Falcon
- ⃝ TIE Interceptor and X-wing
- ⃝ Millennium Falcon and Star Wars Logo
- ⃝ Darth Vader
- ⃝ Imperial Star Destroyer
- ⃝ X-wing
- ⃝ TIE Fighter
- ⃝ AT-AT and Snowspeeder
- ⃝ Darth Vader
- ⃝ R2-D2 and C-3PO
- ⃝ X-wing
- ⃝ Millennium Falcon

Adam Joseph
- ⃝ Royal Guard
- ⃝ Wicket
- ⃝ C-3PO bust
- ⃝ Yoda
- ⃝ Salacious Crumb
- ⃝ R2-D2
- ⃝ X-wing Fighter logo

Two-Player Collectible Card Game, Blizzard 2 (Decipher)

Two-Player Collectible Card Game, Chewbacca (Decipher)

- ⃝ Return of the Jedi logo
- ⃝ The Force
- ⃝ May The Force Be With You
- ⃝ Star Wars logo
- ⃝ Wicket , plastic
- ⃝ Kneesaa, plastic

Howard Eldon
- ⃝ The Empire Strikes Back Logo
- ⃝ Darth Vader
- ⃝ R2-D2
- ⃝ C-3PO

HOLLYWOOD PINS
- ⃝ Crossed Light Sabers
- ⃝ Ben Kenobi
- ⃝ Yoda
- ⃝ Imperial Emblem
- ⃝ Max Rebo Band
- ⃝ AT-AT
- ⃝ Princess Leia
- ⃝ Millennium Falcon
- ⃝ Darth Vader head
- ⃝ X-wing Pewter
- ⃝ X-wing Fighter
- ⃝ TIE Fighter
- ⃝ Darth Vader
- ⃝ Jabba the Hutt
- ⃝ New Rebellion logo large
- ⃝ New Alliance logo small
- ⃝ New Alliance logo gold small
- ⃝ New Alliance logo red and gold small
- ⃝ C-3PO
- ⃝ Emperor
- ⃝ Stormtrooper
- ⃝ Chewbacca
- ⃝ New Alliance logo gold large
- ⃝ Luke on Taun-Taun
- ⃝ Boba Fett
- ⃝ Ewok
- ⃝ Imperial Guard

Two-Player Collectible Card Game, C-3PO (Decipher)

- ○ Star Wars Theme
- ○ Lando Calrissian
- ○ Return of the Jedi theme
- ○ Darth Vader "Don't underestimate the Force"
- ○ Darth Vader mask
- ○ TIE Fighter Round
- ○ X-wing Round
- ○ R2-D2
- ○ Gamorrean Guard
- ○ Star Wars Rebel Forces

BELGIUM
- ○ Star Wars

GERMANY
- ○ Jedi Convention '94

Rings

WEINGEROFF
- ○ R2-D2
- ○ C-3PO
- ○ Chewbacca
- ○ Darth Vader
- ○ Stormtrooper
- ○ X-wing

WALLACE BERRIE
- ○ Darth Vader
- ○ X-wing
- ○ May the Force Be With You
- ○ R2-D2
- ○ C-3PO
- ○ Yoda

UNLICENSED
- ○ TIE Fighter, plastic
- ○ X-wing, plastic

Scatter pins / tie tacks

- ○ R2-D2, C-3PO and Darth Vader

Stickpins

- ○ R2-D2
- ○ C-3PO
- ○ Darth Vader

KITCHEN ITEMS

Tumblers

Deka Plastic
- ○ The Empire Strikes Back 17 oz. tumbler

Bowls

- ○ Star Wars soup bowl
- ○ Star Wars insulated bowl
- ○ Star Wars cereal bowl
- ○ The Empire Strikes Back cereal bowl
- ○ Return of the Jedi soup bowl
- ○ Return of the Jedi cereal bowl

Cake pans / kits / accessories

WILTON ENTERPRISES
- ○ Darth Vader cake pan
- ○ R2-D2 cake pan
- ○ R2-D2 cake decorating kit
- ○ Darth Vader cake decorating kit
- ○ C-3PO cake pan
- ○ Darth Vader cake pan
- ○ Boba Fett cake pan
- ○ R2-D2 and C-3PO cake put-ons
- ○ Darth Vader and Stormtrooper cake toppers
- ○ Chewbacca candle
- ○ Darth Vader candle
- ○ R2-D2 candle

Candy molds

- ○ C-3PO sucker mold
- ○ R2-D2 candy mold

CHINA
- ○ Plate, Bowl and mug set

Cups / mugs

- ○ Star Wars mug
- ○ Yoda mug
- ○ Darth Vader mug
- ○ Good Guys mug

Two-Player Collectible Card Game, Darth Vader with Lightsaber (Decipher)

Two-Player Collectible Card Game, Leia Organa (Decipher)

Two-Player Collectible Card Game, Luke Skywalker (Decipher)

- ○ Luke Skywalker mug
- ○ Princess Leia mug

Dinner ware sets

- ○ Ewok Dinner Set

Paper cups

American Can Company/James River-Dixie

- ○ Star Wars Fun Cup Assortment
- ○ The Empire Strikes Back boxes
- ○ Yoda
- ○ X-wing in swamp
- ○ Luke on Tauntaun
- ○ Twin Pod Cloud Car
- ○ AT-ATs
- ○ Millennium Falcon
- ○ Darth Vader

OTHER

- ○ Floral Dixie Cup with TESB cards offered, small box
- ○ Floral Dixie Cup with TESB cards offered, large box
- ○ Star Wars boxes
- ○ R2-D2 and C-3PO
- ○ Ben Kenobi
- ○ Princess Leia
- ○ Luke Skywalker
- ○ Stormtrooper
- ○ Space Ships
- ○ Darth Vader
- ○ The Empire Strikes Back boxes
- ○ Yoda
- ○ X-wing on Dagobah
- ○ Luke on Taun-Taun
- ○ Cloud City
- ○ Millennium Falcon
- ○ Star Destroyer
- ○ Darth Vader
- ○ Return of the Jedi boxes
- ○ Luke Skywalker
- ○ Jabba the Hutt

Two-Player Collectible Card Game, Milennium Falcon (Decipher)

- ○ Darth Vader
- ○ Star Wars Saga boxes
- ○ R2-D2 and C-3PO
- ○ Han and Leia
- ○ Darth Vader
- ○ Luke and Yoda
- ○ Premiums/Promotions
- ○ Rebel Collector's set
- ○ Empire Collector's set with poster
- ○ Set of 24 cards
- ○ The Empire Strikes Back placemat det

Pitchers

Star Wars
- ○ The Empire Strikes Back
- ○ Return of the Jedi

Plates

- ○ Star Wars compartment plate
- ○ The Empire Strikes Back compartment plate
- ○ Return of the Jedi compartment plate

Tableware

TUMBLERS
- ○ Star Wars 11 oz
- ○ Star Wars 17 oz
- ○ The Empire Strikes Back 6 oz
- ○ The Empire Strikes Back 17 oz
- ○ Return of the Jedi 6 oz
- ○ Return of the Jedi 11 oz
- ○ Return of the Jedi 17 oz

Model Kits / Rockets

Structors
- ○ AT-ST
- ○ Boba Fett's Slave 1
- ○ Speeder Bike
- ○ ROTJ Snap X-wing
- ○ ROTJ Snap TIE Interceptor
- ○ ROTJ Snap A-Wing
- ○ ROTJ Snap B-Wing
- ○ ROTJ Snap AT-ST

Two-Player Collectible Card Game, Obi-Wan Kenobi (Decipher)

○ Luke Skywalker's X-wing Fighter Large box

○ Luke Skywalker's X-wing Fighter Small box

○ X-wing, ROTJ

○ X-wing, ROTJ, Snap

○ X-wing, ROTJ-MPC/Ertl logo

○ X-wing, ROTJ, Snap-MPC/Ertl logo

○ X-wing Fighter-AMT/Ertl logo

○ X-wing Fighter Small-AMT/Ertl logo

○ Limited Edition Gold X-wing-AMT/Ertl logo

○ X-wing Fighter Flight Display-AMT/Ertl logo

○ Darth Vader TIE Fighter, large box

○ Darth Vader TIE Fighter, small box

○ Darth Vader TIE Fighter-MPC/Ertl logo

○ Darth Vader TIE Fighter-AMT/Ertl logo

○ TIE Fighter Flight Display-AMT/Ertl logo

○ Darth Vader

○ Darth Vader-MPC/Ertl logo

○ Darth Vader Figure-AMT/Ertl logo

○ Darth Vader Bust

○ R2-D2 Large box

○ 2-D2 Small box

○ R2-D2, ROTJ

○ C-3PO Large box

○ C-3PO Small box

○ C-3PO, ROTJ

○ Darth Vader Van

○ Luke Skywalker Van

○ R2-D2 Van

○ Han Solo's Millennium Falcon Lights

○ Millennium Falcon No Lights

○ Millennium Falcon-MPC/Ertl logo

○ Millennium Falcon-AMT/Ertl logo

○ Millennium Falcon Cutaway-AMT/Ertl logo

○ AT-AT

○ AT-AT, ROTJ

○ AT-AT-MPC/Ertl logo

○ AT-AT-AMT/Ertl logo

○ Boba Fett's Slave-1

Two-Player
Collectible Card
Game, R2-D2
(Decipher)

○ Star Destroyer

○ Star Destroyer-MPC/Ertl logo

○ Star Destroyer-AMT/Ertl logo

○ Star Destroyer with Fiber Optics-AMT/Ertl logo

○ Luke Skywalker's Snowspeeder

○ Luke Skywalker's Snowspeeder-MPC/Ertl logo

○ Luke Skywalker's Snowspeeder-AMT/Ertl logo

○ Battle on Ice Planet Hoth

○ Battle on Hoth Action Scene-AMT/Ertl logo

○ Encounter with Yoda

○ Encounter with yoda Action Scene-AMT/Ertl logo

○ Encounter with Yoda, Mailer box

○ Rebel Base

○ Rebel Base, Mailer box

○ Rebel Base-MPC/Ertl logo

○ Rebel Base-AMT/Ertl logo

○ Speeder Bike

○ Speeder Bike-MPC/Ertl logo

○ TIE Interceptor

○ TIE Interceptor-MPC/Ertl logo

○ TIE Interceptor-AMT/Ertl logo

○ Limited Edition Gold TIE Interceptor-AMT/Ertl logo

○ A-Wing

○ A-Wing-MPC/Ertl logo

○ B-Wing

○ Limited Edition Gold B-Wing-AMT/Ertl logo

○ Shuttle Tyderium

○ Shuttle Tyderium-MPC/Ertl logo

○ Shuttle Tyderium-AMT/Ertl logo

○ Jabba's Throne Room

○ Jabba's throne Room-AMT/Ertl logo

○ Y-Wing Fighter

○ Y-Wing Fighter

○ AT-ST

○ AT-ST-MPC/Ertl logo

○ AT-ST-AMT/Ertl logo

○ Three-Piece Gift Set-MPC/Ertl logo

Two-Player
Collectible Card
Game, Wedge
Antilles
(Decipher)

STRUCTORS

- ○ C-3PO
- ○ AT-AT
- ○ AT-ST

Mirra-Kits

- ○ Y-Wing
- ○ X-wing
- ○ TIE Interceptor
- ○ Shuttle Tyderium
- ○ AT-ST
- ○ Speeder Bike

Screamin' 1/4 Scale

- ○ Darth Vader
- ○ C-3PO
- ○ Yoda
- ○ Han Solo
- ○ Stormtrooper
- ○ Chewbacca
- ○ Boba Fett
- ○ Tusken Raider
- ○ Luke Skywalker

Screamin / Kaiyodo 1/6 Scale

- ○ Darth Vader
- ○ C-3PO
- ○ Han Solo
- ○ Stormtrooper
- ○ Boba Fett

Polydata (Canada)

- ○ Luke Skywalker
- ○ Ben Kenobi
- ○ Tusken Raider
- ○ Princess Leia
- ○ Luke Skywalker
- ○ Darth Vader
- ○ Han Solo
- ○ Xizor
- ○ Emperor Palpatine

Two-Player
Collectible Card
Game, Attack
Run
(Decipher)

Two-Player
Collectible Card
Game, General
Tagge
(Decipher)

MODEL ROCKETRY

- ○ X-wing ROTJ
- ○ Star Destroyer
- ○ Speeder Bike
- ○ Proton Torpedo
- ○ TIE Fighter
- ○ X-wing
- ○ Maxi Brute X-wing
- ○ R2-D2

MUSIC / OTHER RECORDINGS

Carrying cases

- ○ Return of the Jedi Tape Tote

Star Wars-related

- ○ Original Soundtrack LP
- ○ Original Soundtrack eight-track
- ○ Original Soundtrack cassette
- ○ Original Soundtrack CD6
- ○ The Story of Star Wars LP
- ○ The Story of Star Wars eight-track
- ○ The Story of Star Wars cassette
- ○ The Story of Star Wars LP-sized cassette
- ○ The Story of Star Wars CD
- ○ Star Wars radio show cassette
- ○ Themes from Star Wars LP
- ○ CE3K and Star Wars LP
- ○ Something Out There LP
- ○ Star Trek, with Star Wars LP
- ○ Time Warp LP
- ○ Christmas in the Stars LP
- ○ Zubin Mehta Conducts Star Wars LP
- ○ Zubin Mehta Conducts Star Wars promo
- ○ Galactic Funk LP
- ○ Music from Star Wars LP
- ○ Music from Star Wars eight-track
- ○ Star Wars: A Stereo Odyssey LP
- ○ Spaced Out Disco LP

Two-Player
Collectible Card
Game, Captain
Piett
(Decipher)

- ○ Music from Other Galaxies LP
- ○ A New Hope (Walt Disney Records)
- ○ Disco Dancin' eight-track
- ○ Jefferson Starship, gold eight-track
- ○ Star Power eight-track
- ○ Star Wars Special Edition Soundtrack CD
- ○ Star Wars reel-to-reel5
- ○ Star Wars 45 Main Title and Cantina Band

GERMAN
- ○ Star Wars Soundtrack LP
- ○ Star Wars promo

MEXICO
- ○ Story of Star Wars cassette

The Empire Strikes Back-related

- ○ TESB Original Soundtrack LP
- ○ TESB Original Soundtrack cassette
- ○ TESB Original Soundtrack CD
- ○ Adventures of Luke Skywalker LP
- ○ Empire Jazz LP
- ○ Boris Midney LP
- ○ Boris Midney promo
- ○ The Story of The Empire Strikes Back LP
- ○ The Story of The Empire Strikes Back cassette
- ○ The Story of The Empire Strikes Back CD
- ○ Irwin Strikes Back LP
- ○ The Empire Strikes Back Radio Show cassette
- ○ TESB 45 The Imperial March and The Battle in the Snow

Return of the Jedi-related

- ○ ROTJ Original Soundtrack LP
- ○ ROTJ Original Soundtrack cassette
- ○ ROTJ Original Soundtrack CD
- ○ The Story of Return of the Jedi LP
- ○ The Story of Return of the Jedi cassette
- ○ The Story of Return of the Jedi CD
- ○ Ewok Celebration LP
- ○ Pops in Space LP
- ○ Out of this World LP
- ○ Return of the Jedi Radio Show cassette

FRANCE
- ○ Story of Return of the Jedi CD

Compilations

- ○ Sci-Fi Greatest Hits Vol. 1 LP
- ○ Sci-Fi Greatest Hits Vol. 2 LP
- ○ Sci-Fi Greatest Hits Vol. 3 LP
- ○ Not of this Earth LP
- ○ The Best of Meco CD
- ○ John Williams Conducts John Williams CD
- ○ The Star Wars Trilogy cassette

Two-Player Collectible Card Game, Target The Main Generator (Decipher)

Star Wars saga — general

- ○ Trilogy "Story Of ..." pack cassette
- ○ Droid World cassette
- ○ Droid World LP 7-inch
- ○ Planet of the Hoojibs cassette
- ○ Planet of the Hoojibs LP 7-inch
- ○ Ewoks Join the Fight cassette
- ○ Ewoks Join the Fight LP 7-inch
- ○ Ewok Adventure cassette
- ○ Ewok Adventure LP 7-inch
- ○ Adventures in Colors and Shapes cassette
- ○ Adventures in Colors and Shapes LP 7-inch
- ○ Adventures in ABCs cassette
- ○ Adventures in ABCs LP 7-inch

Other Star Wars Saga-related cassettes

- ○ The Mixed Up Droid
- ○ Heir to the Empire
- ○ Dark Force Rising
- ○ The Truce at Bakura
- ○ Jedi Search
- ○ Krytos Trap
- ○ Shield of Lies
- ○ Wedge's Gamble
- ○ Rogue Squadron
- ○ Before the Storm
- ○ The New Rebellion
- ○ Assault on Selonia

Electronic Laser Battle game (Kenner)

- ○ Dark Saber
- ○ Showdown at Centerpoint
- ○ Dark Apprentice
- ○ Champions of the Force
- ○ Shadows of the Empire
- ○ Children of the Jedi
- ○ Ambush at Corelia
- ○ The Hutt Gambit
- ○ Paradise Snare
- ○ New Rebellion
- ○ Tyrant's Nest
- ○ The Bacta War
- ○ Jedi Academy Omnibus
- ○ Dark Empire
- ○ Dark Empire II
- ○ Tales of the Jedi
- ○ Dark Lords of the Sith

**Jigsaw puzzle
(Kenner)**

Sheet music

- ○ Main title
- ○ Star Wars music book
- ○ Princess Leia's theme
- ○ Cantina Band
- ○ Star Wars Deluxe Souvenir Folio of Music Selections
- ○ The Empire Strikes Back music book
- ○ The Imperial March
- ○ Yoda's Theme
- ○ Return of the Jedi music book

**Jigsaw puzzle
(Kenner)**

PARTY ITEMS

Bags or boxes

Quela, S.A. (Mexico)
- ○ Party box (flat)
- ○ Party bags
- ○ Invitations
- ○ Party blowers
- ○ Paper plates
- ○ Paper cups
- ○ Napkins
- ○ Party hats

Party bags

Por Quela S.A. (Mexico)
- ○ Star Wars bags

Gift bags

DRAWING BOARD
- ○ Return of the Jedi
- ○ Ewok Party Bags

HALLMARK
- ○ Party Bags

Balloons

DRAWING BOARD
- ○ Return of the Jedi
- ○ Return of the Jedi punch balloons
- ○ Ewoks

UNKNOWN
- ○ Foil balloon

Banners

DRAWING BOARD
- ○ The Empire Strikes Back birthday banner

HALLMARK
- ○ Star Wars
- ○ Blowouts

DRAWING BOARD
- ○ The Empire Strikes Back
- ○ Return of the Jedi, red header
- ○ Return of the Jedi, black header

HALLMARK
- ○ Star Wars

Centerpieces

DRAWING BOARD
- ○ The Empire Strikes Back
- ○ Return of the Jedi
- ○ Ewoks

HALLMARK
- ○ Star Wars

Paper cups

- ○ The Empire Strikes Back
- ○ Return of the Jedi
- ○ Ewoks

**Jigsaw puzzle
(Kenner)**

Party Games

HALLMARK

Star Wars

Gift cards / tags

DRAWING BOARD

- ◯ R2-D2 Thank You cards
- ◯ X-wing gift tag
- ◯ R2-D2 and C-3PO Gift Tag
- ◯ R2-D2 and C-3PO self-adhesive pack of five
- ◯ Luke, Han and Leia gift tag
- ◯ R2-D2 package decoration
- ◯ Cloud City gift tag
- ◯ Yoda package decoration
- ◯ Dog Fight gift tag
- ◯ Return of the Jedi

Gift wrap

DRAWING BOARD

- ◯ Ewok wrap and trim
- ◯ Return of the Jedi wrap and trim
- ◯ Dog Fight gift wrap, flat
- ◯ Dog Fight gift wrap, roll
- ◯ Characters gift wrap, flat
- ◯ Characters gift wrap, roll
- ◯ Happy Birthday gift wrap, flat
- ◯ Happy Birthday gift wrap, roll
- ◯ Battle Scene gift wrap, flat
- ◯ Battle Scene gift wrap, roll
- ◯ Cloud City gift wrap, flat
- ◯ Return of the Jedi gift wrap, roll
- ◯ Ewoks gift wrap, flat
- ◯ Ewoks gift wrap, roll
- ◯ Droids Roll

Hats

DRAWING BOARD

- ◯ The Empire Strikes Back
- ◯ Return of the Jedi
- ◯ Ewoks

Dark Forces computer game (Lucas Arts)

Invitations

DRAWING BOARD

- ◯ R2-D2
- ◯ R2-D2 and C-3PO
- ◯ Cloud City
- ◯ Heroes and Villians
- ◯ Return of the Jedi
- ◯ Ewoks

HALLMARK

- ◯ Star Wars

AUSTRALIA

- ◯ Darth Vader
- ◯ Biker Scout

Name badges

- ◯ Darth Vader
- ◯ Star Wars

Napkins

DRAWING BOARD

- ◯ Star Wars, beverage
- ◯ Star Wars, luncheon
- ◯ The Empire Strikes Back, beverage
- ◯ The Empire Strikes Back, luncheon
- ◯ Return of the Jedi, beverage
- ◯ Return of the Jedi, luncheon
- ◯ Ewoks, beverage
- ◯ Ewoks, luncheon

Place cards

DRAWING BOARD

- ◯ R2-D2 and C-3PO

Place mats

DRAWING BOARD

- ◯ Star Wars
- ◯ The Empire Strikes Back, boxed set of four

Checklist

Rebel Assault computer game (Lucas Arts)

SIGMA

- ○ R2-D2 and C-3PO
- ○ Boba Fett and Chewbacca
- ○ Luke Skywalker and Yoda
- ○ Darth Vader and Leia

ROY LEE CIN (AUSTRALIA)

- ○ Han and Chewbacca
- ○ Darth Vader
- ○ Luke and Leia

Paper plates

DRAWING BOARD

- ○ Star Wars, luncheon
- ○ Star Wars, dinner
- ○ The Empire Strikes Back, luncheon
- ○ The Empire Strikes Back, dinner
- ○ Return of the Jedi, luncheon
- ○ Return of the Jedi, dinner
- ○ Ewoks, luncheon
- ○ Ewoks, dinner

Table covers

DRAWING BOARD

- ○ The Empire Strikes Back
- ○ Return of the Jedi
- ○ Ewoks

HALLMARK

- ○ Star Wars

Wall decorations

HALLMARK

- ○ Star Wars

PEWTER

Miniatures

- ○ Admiral Ackbar
- ○ Ben Kenobi
- ○ Bib Fortuna

- ○ Boba Fett
- ○ Chewbacca
- ○ Darth Vader
- ○ Emperor
- ○ Gamorrean Guard
- ○ Han Solo
- ○ Luke Skywalker
- ○ Princess Leia
- ○ R2-D2
- ○ Stormtrooper
- ○ Wicket
- ○ Yoda
- ○ Shuttle Tyderium
- ○ X-wing, Small
- ○ TIE Fighter
- ○ Y-Wing
- ○ Snowspeeder
- ○ A-Wing
- ○ B-Wing
- ○ Imperial Star Destroyer
- ○ X-wing, Large
- ○ Millennium Falcon
- ○ Darth Vader's TIE Fighter
- ○ Millennium Falcon (Small)

Heritage or Star Trek Galore 1977 (Unlicensed)

- ○ Bantha, no saddle
- ○ Bantha, with saddle
- ○ Tusken with gadderfi
- ○ Tusken with gun
- ○ Luke Skywalker
- ○ Princess Leia
- ○ Jawa
- ○ Darth Vader
- ○ Snitch (Garindan Long snoot)
- ○ Chewbacca

Rebel Assault II computer game (Lucas Arts)

Role-Playing game

POSTERS / PRESS KITS

Theatrical posters

United States
- ○ Star Wars Mylar Advance
- ○ Star Wars First Advance
- ○ Star Wars Teaser B
- ○ Star Wars A Sheet
- ○ Star Wars A Sheet Record poster
- ○ Star Wars Style C
- ○ Star Wars Style D
- ○ Star Wars 1979 Reissue
- ○ Star Wars 1981 Reissue
- ○ The Empire Strikes Back advance
- ○ The Empire Strikes Back Style A
- ○ The Empire Strikes Back Style B
- ○ The Empire Strikes Back 1981 Reissue
- ○ The Empire Strikes Back 1982 Reissue
- ○ Revenge of the Jedi advance
- ○ Return of the Jedi Style A
- ○ Return of the Jedi Style B
- ○ Star Wars: Episode I Version A

England
- ○ England Star Wars Special Edition quad poster
- ○ England TESB Special Edition quad poster
- ○ England ROTJ Special Edition quad poster

Germany
- ○ German Special Edition advance poster
- ○ German Star Wars Special Edition poster
- ○ German TESB Special Edition poster
- ○ German ROTJ Special Edition poster

Japan
- ○ 1/2 sheet
- ○ George Lucas Super Live Adventure poster
- ○ The Empire Strikes Back
- ○ The Empire Strikes Back advance

Premiums

Kenner
- ○ Star Wars is Forever

Tickets

England
- ○ Special Edition

Mexico
- ○ Special Edition

Credit sheets
- ○ Return of the Jedi

Commercial posters

AMERICAN CAN COMPANY (DIXIE CUPS)
- ○ Luke
- ○ Vader

AMERICAN LIBRARY ASSOCIATION
- ○ Read

Bantam Books
- ○ Heir to the Empire
- ○ Glove of Darth Vader
- ○ Truce at Bakura

BING HARRIS (AUSTRALIA)
- ○ Advertising banner

BLOCKBUSTER VIDEO
- ○ Lithograph from THX trilogy
- ○ Lithograph from Special Edition

Burger Chef
- ○ Luke Skywalker
- ○ C-3PO
- ○ Darth Vader
- Chewbacca

Coca-Cola Burger King
- ○ Borris Vealejo
- ○ Coming to a theater near you
- ○ Luke

Millenium Falcon ornament (Hallmark)

C-3PO ring (Weingeroff)

- R2-D2
- Darth Vader
- Chewbacca

CBS FOX VIDEO
- TXH trilogy poster, 1995
- Lithograph Sun Coast Motion Pictures stores
- THX Video
- SW video

Coca Cola
- HI-C two-sided poster

CONCERT
- R2-D2 and C-3PO with instruments

DARK HORSE COMICS
- Special Edition Comics "on sale here" (two-sided)

DECIPHER
- Dagobah Checklist (two-sided)
- A New Hope
- A New Hope 2
- "Do or do not"

DRAWING BOARD GREETING CARDS
- Star Wars display
- TESB display
- ROTJ display

Factors
Hildebrandt
- R2-D2 and C-3PO
- Darth Vader
- X-wings with three circles
- Cantina
- Boba Fett
- Yoda
- Darth Vader
- Droids

**Darth Vader ring
(Weingeroff)**

**R2-D2 ring
(Weingeroff)**

Factors / Weekly Reader Books
- TESB poster

- FAN CLUB INC.
- Inside 1995
- Lucasfilm
- Special Edition
- Millenium Falcon

Highbridge
- Radio Show reprint

Kenner
- Action figures poster
- ROTJ sweepstakes
- 1984 poster

KENNER / GENERAL ELECTRIC
- Star Wars: The Movie

Killian Enterprises
- Poster checklist
- Star Wars 15-year poster
- TESB 10-year poster
- ROTJ 10-year poster
- ROTJ gold mylar 10-year
- Heir to the Empire print

KMET
- B&W concert poster

LIPTON TEA
- Luke Skywalker
- Darth Vader

LUCASARTS
- TIE Fighter

MARVEL COMICS
- ROTJ Super Special

MELANIE TAYLOR KENT
- Star Wars

MGM/UA
- Ewok Battle for Endor
- Ewok Adventure

**Chewbacca candle
(Wilton)**

MIND'S EYE PRESS
○ John Alvin First Ten Years

NATIONAL GEOGRAPHIC WORLD
○ TESB poster

NATIONAL PUBLIC RADIO
○ Star Wars Radio Show
○ The Empire Strikes Back Radio Show

NEW FRONTIERS
○ TESB by Michael David Ward, limited signed

Official Star Wars Fan Club
○ Star Wars
○ TESB
○ ROTJ

Oral B
○ Return of the Jedi two-sided

PARKER BROTHERS
○ Death Star Battle
○ Jedi Arena
○ TESB

Portal Publications
○ Star Wars Style C
○ Star Wars Style D
○ Space Battle
○ Ewoks Montage
○ Return of the Jedi Style A reprint
○ "All I Need to Know ..."
○ Star Wars battle scene

Proctor and Gamble
1978
○ Darth Vader and Ben Kenobi
○ Droids
○ Heroes

1980
○ Droids
○ Princess Leia and Han Solo
○ Luke Skywalker
○ Darth Vader

1983
○ Lando Calrissian
○ Luke Skywalker
○ R2-D2 and Ewoks
○ Princess Leia

ROLLING THUNDER
○ Dark Empire
○ Dewback Patrol
○ Ben Kenobi
○ Dark Empire II
○ Smugglers' Moon
○ Shadows of the Empire Print

RSO RECORDS
○ Trilogy soundtracks

Sales Corporation
○ Star Wars Style D
○ Darth Vader Montage
○ Darth Vader door poster
○ ROTJ Style A
○ Space Battle
○ ROTJ Style B
○ TESB advance
○ Heroes in the Forest
○ Star Wars Style D
○ Mini posters
○ Darth Vader
○ Ewoks
○ Jabba and Friends
○ Revenge artwork
○ ROTJ collage
○ ROTJ Style A
○ ROTJ Style B
○ Shuttle Landing
○ Space Battle
○ Speeder Bike

Star Tours
○ Hoth
○ Dagobah

**R2-D2 candle
(Wilton)**

Dixie cups

○ Tatooine

○ Endor

○ Yavin

○ Ultimate Adventure

TOPPS

○ ROTJ stickers sold here

○ TESB press sheet

○ SW Movie giant pin-up

○ TESB Movie giant pin-up

○ Star Wars Galaxy sold here

○ Star Wars Galaxy II sold here

○ Galaxy Magazine posters #1-#9

○ Galaxy II cards sold here

20TH CENTURY FOX RECORDS

○ Story of Star Wars LP poster

○ Star Wars soundtrack poster

U.S. DEPARTMENT OF HEALTH

○ Immunization

Weekly Reader

○ Ewoks

Western Graphics

○ Yoda

○ Star Wars

○ Darth Vader

○ Stormtrooper

○ Darth Vade

○ Yoda poster

○ Death Star Trench (1996)

England

○ Imperial Invasion (1995 video promotional tour)

Germany

○ German Special Edition video poster

Press material

○ Ten-Year Convention

GERMAN

○ Poster sheet set of 8

Lobby cards

STAR WARS

○ Stormtrooper

○ Darth Vader's entrance

○ Selling of R2-D2

○ Dewback

○ Photobusta Set

○ Tusken Raider 16 x 20

○ Trash Compactor 16 x 20

○ The Leap 16 x 20

○ Final Ceremony

○ The Empire Strikes Back

○ Return of the Jedi

○ Rebel Base

THE EMPIRE STRIKES BACK

○ Luke on Wampa

○ Hoth scanner

○ Luke vs. Vader

○ Luke on Dagobah

○ Return of the Jedi 16 x 20 Lobby Cards

○ Star Destroyer

○ Strike Team on Endor

○ Luke Skywalker and Darth Vader

○ R2-D2 and C-3PO

○ Cockpit of Shutle Tyderium

○ Luke and Leia on Sail Barge

○ Lando Calrissian

○ Luke Skywalker

○ Han Solo

○ Princess Leia in Slave Outfit

○ C-3PO, Chewbacca and Princess Leia

○ Caravan of Courage

Germany

○ German Special Edition lobby card set

TIE Fighter model (Structors)

Return of the Jedi music carrying case

Ewoks Join the Fight cassette

Press kits

Star Wars

○ The Empire Strikes Back
○ Return of the Jedi
○ Star Wars Holiday Special
○ Ewoks
○ Caravan of Courage
○ 10-year convention

Planet of the Hoojibs record

Press books

Star Wars

○ The Empire Strikes Back
○ Return of the Jedi
○ SW SE
○ TESB SE
○ ROTJ SE

Programs

Droid World record

Star Wars

○ The Empire Strikes Back Collector's Edition
○ Return of the Jedi Collector's Edition

JAPAN

○ Star Wars
○ The Empire Strikes Back
○ Return of the Jedi

Credit sheets

Star Wars

○ The Empire Strikes Back
○ Return of the Jedi

Other press material

○ 1982 20th Century Fox Summer Book
○ Performances folder
○ 1977 20th Century Fox Yearbok
○ Premier by Memorial Hospital
○ Return of the Jedi marketing guide

○ Revenge of the Jedi two-page fold-out
○ Revenge of the Jedi four-page fold-Out
○ Return of the Jedi production notes
○ CBS THX Fox Video press book
○ Topps Press Kit for Galaxy II
○ JVC press kit for Star Wars, Nintendo

SHOW SOUVENIRS

Badges, metal

GEORGE LUCAS SUPER LIVE ADVENTURE

○ 2 1/4-inch button

Cups, containers

GEORGE LUCAS SUPER LIVE ADVENTURE

○ Small plastic mug

Electronics, electric

GEORGE LUCAS SUPER LIVE ADVENTURE

○ Head of Darth Vader swivel light

Pennants

GEORGE LUCAS SUPER LIVE ADVENTURE

○ Die-cut with movie characters

TENTH ANNIVERSARY CONVENTION

○ Star Wars pennant

Stationery

SAN FRANCISCO EXHIBIT

○ Black pen

T-Shirts

TENTH ANNIVERSARY CONVENTION

○ Ten-Year Convention T-shirt
○ Ten-Year Convention T-shirt, Starlog

SAN DIEGO COMIC CONVENTION

○ 1995 Comic Con T-shirt

Star Wars Official Soundtrack LP

Other

TENTH ANNIVERSARY CONVENTION
- ○ Star Wars magnetic pad
- ○ Star Wars Ten-Year cap

SPORTS / OUTDOOR ACTIVITY

Balls
UNICE (SPAIN)
- ○ Star Wars ball

Gym sets
- ○ Speeder Bike swing attachment

Kites
- ○ Star Wars kite (1995)
- ○ Activity Pack (1995)
- ○ Darth Vader kite
- ○ Darth Vader figural
- ○ Luke Skywalker figural
- ○ Wicket figural
- ○ Star Wars box kite
- ○ Ewok kite
- ○ Speeder Bike kite
- ○ Star Wars montage 42-inch Delta Wing kite
- ○ Star Wars 64-inch kite
- ○ Droids 80-inch kite

Skates / skateboards
- ○ Darth Vader roller skates
- ○ Ewok roller skates

Other
- ○ *Worlds Apart Limited (England)*
- ○ Star Wars yo-yo

STAMPS, STICKERS AND DECALS

Sticker albums

Panini (Belgium)
- ○ 100 count display box

The Empire Strikes Back Official Soundtrack LP

Star Wars Main Title 45 rpm record

Pacosa Dos Internacional (Mexico)
- ○ Set of 187 stickers (1977)

Dynamics
- ○ Set of 168 stickers
- ○ Single stickers
- ○ Chase sticker singles

OTHER
- ○ Judge Dredd comic book poly-bagged with ROTJ sticker album
- ○ Return of the Jedi stickers

ITALY
- ○ Star Wars Album with stickers

SPAIN
- ○ The Empire Strikes Back sticker album

Topps/Panini
- ○ ROTJ Album

Panini (England)
- ○ ROTJ Album

Dynamics (Mexico)
- ○ Special Edition Sticker Album

Panini (Puerto Rico)
- ○ Box for sticker packs

Decals

- ○ Industrial Light and Magic 1-inch sticker
- ○ Industrial Light and Magic 3-inch sticker
- ○ First Ten Years Sticker
- ○ Darth Vader Holographic
- ○ West End Games
- ○ I support the Rebel Alliance Sticker
- ○ Early Bird stickers
- ○ Bounty Hunters
- ○ Yoda
- ○ Image Marketing static cling
- ○ Darth Vader
- ○ R2-D2 and C-3PO
- ○ Yoda
- ○ Millennium Falcon

A.H. Prismatic

- ◯ B-Wing
- ◯ Millennium Falcon
- ◯ TIE Interceptor and X-wing
- ◯ Millennium Falcon and Star Wars Logo
- ◯ Darth Vader
- ◯ Imperial Star Destroyer
- ◯ X-wing
- ◯ TIE Fighter
- ◯ AT-AT and Snowspeeder
- ◯ R2-D2 and C-3PO, Hologram
- ◯ Millennium Falcon, Hologram
- ◯ Darth Vader, Hologram
- ◯ X-wing, Hologram
- ◯ Sheet of 9 stickers

AUSTRALIA

- ◯ Clothing Tag, Kortex 1983

JAPAN

- ◯ Sticker Sheet with 21 small stickers
- ◯ Sticker Sheet with three Stickers

STAMPS

- ◯ Star Wars Stamp Kit
- ◯ Sports Stamps Collectors Association
- ◯ First Day Stamp boxed set
- ◯ Star Wars Gold Stamp wallet
- ◯ The Empire Strikes Back Gold Stamp wallet
- ◯ Return of the Jedi Gold Stamp sallet

Other stickers

Merlin (England)
- ◯ Sticker sheet

Skybox/Fleer
- ◯ Sticker book pack

Drawing Board Greeting Cards Company
- ◯ Bad Guys Perk Up stickers
- ◯ Good Guys 3-D Perk Up stickers
- ◯ Bad Guys 3-D Perk Up stikcers

- ◯ Return of the Jedi Perk Up Stickers
- ◯ Return of the Jedi 3-D Perk Up stickers
- ◯ Ewok Perk Up stickers
- ◯ Ewok 3-D Perk Up stickers
- ◯ Return of the Jedi Prismatic stickers

Topps
- ◯ The Empire Strikes Back puffy stickers

Hallmark
- ◯ Sticker sheet

FUN PRODUCTS (ENGLAND)
- ◯ Admiral Ackbar
- ◯ Baby Ewok
- ◯ C-3PO
- ◯ Chewbacca
- ◯ Darth Vader
- ◯ Gamorrean Guard
- ◯ Imperial Shuttle
- ◯ Jabba the Hutt
- ◯ Klaatu
- ◯ Paploo
- ◯ R2-D2
- ◯ Klaatu, vacuformed sticker

GERMANY
- ◯ Return of the Jedi Sticker Sheet #1
- ◯ Return of the Jedi Sticker Sheet #2
- ◯ Return of the Jedi Sticker Sheet #3
- ◯ Return of the Jedi Sticker Sheet #4

SCHOOL SUPPLIES

Postcards

Mexico
- ◯ TESB Special Edition poster postcard

Binders

Mead Corp Ring
- ◯ Han and Chewbacca

The Story of Star Wars LP

Official Star Wars soundtrack 8-track

Stuart Hall Poly
- ◯ Darth and Stormtroopers
- ◯ Luke on Dagobah
- ◯ Yoda
- ◯ R2-D2 and C-3PO
- ◯ Five photos

Folders / portfolios / file boxes

Mead Star Wars
- ◯ Leia/Luke
- ◯ Darth Vader/Stormtroopers
- ◯ Droids at Ceremony
- ◯ Ben/Stromtroopers
- ◯ Luke, Han, Chewbacca
- ◯ Spaceships

Stuart Hall The Empire Strikes Back
- ◯ Darth Vader and Stormtroopers
- ◯ Yoda
- ◯ Luke on Dagobah
- ◯ R2-D2 and C-3PO
- ◯ Five Photos

Memo pads / books

Stuart Hall
- ◯ Boba Fett
- ◯ Yoda
- ◯ Luke
- ◯ Aliens
- ◯ R2-D2 and C-3PO
- ◯ Darth Vader and Stormtroopers

Spiral notebooks

Mead Star Wars
- ◯ 60 sheets 10 1/2 x 8, 89¢ printed on back
- ◯ Darth Vader
- ◯ Stormtroopers
- ◯ Chewbacca and Han
- ◯ R2-D2 and C-3PO
- ◯ Heroes

- ◯ Spaceships

Stuart Hall The Empire Strikes Back
- ◯ 50 sheets 10 1/2 x 8
- ◯ Heroes on Hoth
- ◯ Yoda
- ◯ Boba Fett
- ◯ Spaceships
- ◯ Vader in freeze chamber

Address books
- ◯ Star Wars address book

Binders / rings

Mead, 1977
- ◯ Han and Chewbacca
- ◯ Heroes
- ◯ R2-D2 and C-3PO
- ◯ Darth Vader

Stuart Hall Polybinders, 1980
- ◯ Darth Vader
- ◯ Luke on Dagobah
- ◯ Creatures

England
- ◯ Star Wars with X-wing

Book covers

- ◯ Return of the Jedi book cover

Cork boards

- ◯ Yoda
- ◯ Jabba the Hutt
- ◯ Max Rebo Band

**The Imperial
March 45 rpm**

- ○ Lightsaber duel
- ○ Endor

Envelopes

England
- ○ Star Wars envelopes

Erasers

- ○ Darth Vader
- ○ Yoda
- ○ Jabba the Hutt
- ○ R2-D2
- ○ Wicket
- ○ Gamorrean Guard
- ○ Admiral Ackbar
- ○ Max Rebo
- ○ Baby Ewoks
- ○ Bob Fortuna
- ○ Imperial Guard
- ○ Return of the Jedi pack of three
- ○ Return of the Jedi pencil sharpener and eraser

Australia
- ○ Glow in the Dark eraser

England
- ○ Return of the Jedi perfumed erasers
- ○ Chewbacca
- ○ Wicket
- ○ R2-D2 and C-3PO
- ○ Han Solo
- ○ Darth Vader
- ○ Gamorrean Guard
- ○ Return of the Jedi record eraser

Folders, portfolios, file boxes

STAR WARS MEAD, 1977
- ○ R2-D2 and C-3PO on Tatooine portfolio
- ○ Space Ships portfolio
- ○ Luke Skywalker and Princess Leia

- ○ Darth Vader
- ○ R2-D2 and C-3PO at Ceremony
- ○ Ben Kenobi
- ○ Luke, Han, and Chewbacca

THE EMPIRE STRIKES BACK STUART HALL, 1980
- ○ Darth Vader
- ○ Yoda
- ○ Luke Skywalker
- ○ R2-D2 and C-3PO
- ○ Creatures

RETURN OF THE JEDI STUART HALL, 1983
- ○ Max Rebo Band
- ○ Wicket, R2-D2 and C-3PO
- ○ Luke Skywalker and Darth Vader
- ○ Jabba the Hutt
- ○ Speederbikes
- ○ Spaceships

Glue / tape

- ○ Return of the Jedi glue, blue
- ○ Return of the Jedi tape dispensor

Greeting cards

Valentine
- ○ Return of the Jedi Soft box

Paper Magic Group
- ○ Box of 30 Valentines
- ○ Box of 30 foil Valentines

Drawing Board
- ○ Star Wars blue border
- ○ C-3PO
- ○ Darth Vader
- ○ Chewbacca
- ○ Millennium Falcon
- ○ C-3PO
- ○ Ben Kenobi
- ○ Spaceships

Kenny Baker autograph

- Luke and C-3PO
- R2-D2 and C-3PO
- Luke
- R2-D2
- Darth Vader
- Trash compactor
- R2-D2 and C-3PO
- C-3PO
- Chewbacca
- Halloween Cards
- Luke
- Leia
- Spaceships
- Millennium Falcon
- Luke, Han, Chewbacca
- Darth Vader
- C-3PO
- Chewbacca
- Ben Kenobi
- Die-cut cards
- Ben Kenobi
- R2-D2
- R2-D2 and C-3PO
- Luke, Han and Leia
- Stormtrooper
- C-3PO
- Darth Vader
- Chewbacca
- Christmas
- Droids
- Ben Kenobi
- Chewbacca
- Luke, Han, and Chewbacca
- Valentines
- Ewoks Valentines, soft box
- Return of the Jedi Valentines, soft box
- Halloween

- Luke firing
- Princess Leia
- Dog fight
- Millennium Falcon
- Luke, Han, and Chewbacca
- Darth Vader
- C-3PO
- Chewbacca
- Ben Kenobi
- Star Wars die-cut
- Ben Kenobi
- Droids
- Luke, Leia, and Han
- C-3PO
- Darth Vader
- The Empire Strikes Back die-cut
- Yoda
- The Empire Strikes Back game vards
- Leia, Han, and Chewbacca
- Darth Vader
- Yoda
- Return of the Jedi
- Darth Vader and Guards
- Leia and Mogaar
- Luke and Leia
- C-3PO and Ewoks
- Max Rebo Band
- Ewoks
- Darth Vader
- Wicket and R2-D2
- Ewok with flowers
- Ewoks Birthday

Carrie Fisher autograph

Maria De'Aragon autograph

- ○ Archery Practice
- ○ Swimming Hole
- ○ Baby Ewoks
- ○ Fishing Hole
- ○ Hang Gliding
- ○ Making Music
- ○ Nature Lesson
- ○ Kneesaa and Baga

Portal Publications
- ○ Star Wars

THE PAPER GROUP
- ○ Box of 30 Valentines

HALLMARK, 1995
- ○ Card #1205
- ○ Card #5113
- ○ Card #1326
- ○ Card #1179
- ○ Card #1194
- ○ Card #7820
- ○ Card #1191
- ○ Card #7823

Markers
Stuart Hall
- ○ Return of the Jedi Markers
- ○ Darth Vader Purple Marker

Memo pads / books

STUART HALL
- ○ A-d
- ○ R2-D2 and C-3PO
- ○ Darth Vader

MEED
- ○ The Force Neat Book

England
- ○ Han Solo
- ○ R2-D2 and C-3PO

David Prowse autograph

- ○ Princess Leia
- ○ Darth Vader
- ○ Luke Skywalker

Spiral notebooks

MEAD STAR WARS
- ○ 10 1/2-inch by 8-inch 60 sheets
- ○ Darth Vader
- ○ Stormtroopers
- ○ Han and Chewbacca
- ○ R2-D2 and C-3PO
- ○ Heroes
- ○ Spaceships

11-inch by 8 1/2-inch 60 sheets
- ○ Darth Vader
- ○ Stormtrooper
- ○ Han and Chewbacca
- ○ R2-D2 and C-3PO
- ○ Heroes
- ○ Spaceships
- ○ 1997, The Force

STUART HALL THE EMPIRE STRIKES BACK
11-inch by 8 1/2-inch 84 sheets
- ○ Darth Vader silhouette
- ○ Chewbacca
- ○ Han, Leia and Luke on Hoth
- ○ Yoda
- ○ Boba Fett
- ○ Star Destroyer
- ○ Vader in Freeze Chamber
- ○ Characters
- ○ Montage #1 Creatures
- ○ Montage #2 Heroes and Villians

11-inch by 8 1/2-inch 46 sheets
- ○ Vader silhouette
- ○ Chewbacca
- ○ Han, Leia and Luke on Hoth
- ○ Yoda

C-3PO/ R2-D2 bank (Thinkway Toys)

- ○ Boba Fett
- ○ Star Destroyer
- ○ Vader in Freeze Chamber
- ○ Characters

10 1/2-inch by 8-inch 50 sheets
- ○ Vader silhouette
- ○ Chewbacca
- ○ Han, Leia and Luke on Hoth
- ○ Yoda
- ○ Boba Fett
- ○ Star Destroyer
- ○ Vader in Freeze Chamber
- ○ Characters

11-inch by 8 1/2-inch 170 sheets
- ○ Luke

STUART HALL RETURN OF THE JEDI
11-inch by 8 1/2-inch
- ○ Max Rebo Band
- ○ Wicket, R2-D2 and C-3PO
- ○ Luke and Vader
- ○ Jabba the Hutt
- ○ Speeder Bikes
- ○ Spaceships

10 1/2-inch by 8-inch
- ○ Max Rebo Band
- ○ Wicket, R2-D2 and C-3PO
- ○ Luke and Vader
- ○ Jabba the Hutt
- ○ Speeder Bikes
- ○ Spaceships

ANTIOCH
- ○ Mini notebook

ENGLAND
- ○ Luke and Leia
- ○ R2-D2 notepad
- ○ C-3PO notepad
- ○ Chewbacca notepad

Behind the Magic CD ROM (Lucas Arts)

Dark Forces PC game manual

Note cards

- ○ Droids note cards
- ○ Hildebrandt note cards
- ○ Assorted notes
- ○ R2-D2 foldover notes

Notepads

Drawing Board
- ○ Wookie doodle pad
- ○ Official Duty Roster
- ○ Ewoks notepad

Stuart Hall
- ○ R2-D2 and C-3PO tablet
- ○ Ships tablet
- ○ Creatures tablet
- ○ Darth Vader Learn to Letter and Write
- ○ Boba Fett Learn to Letter and Write
- ○ Luke Skywalker Learn to Letter and Write
- ○ Return of the Jedi Pencil tablet
- ○ Return of the Jedi doodle pad
- ○ Return of the Jedi scribble pad
- ○ Return of the Jedi Learn to Letter

ENGLAND
- ○ Rebel Jotter

JAPAN
- ○ Stormtrooper in Desert

Paper

- ○ Return of the Jedi construction paper

Han Solo / Chewbacca mouse pad

Pencil / pencil tops

○ X-wing pencil topper (Unlicensed)

○ Star Wars Streamer pencil (Fantasma)

○ Return of the Jedi Darth Vader character pencil

○ Return of the Jedi C-3PO character pencil

○ Return of the Jedi Pop-A-Point pencil

○ Return of the Jedi pencil with Darth Vader topper

○ Return of the Jedi pencil with C-3PO opper

○ Return of the Jedi pencil with Wicket t opper

Stuart Hall Pencil Toppers 1983

○ C-3PO

○ Wicket

○ Star Wars pencil (Fantasma)

Fan Club

○ The Empire Strikes Back pencil, blue

○ The Empire Strikes Back pencil, red

ENGLAND

○ Darth Vader pencil topper

○ Luke Skywalker pencil topper

○ Chewbacca pencil topper

○ Han Solo

MEXICO

○ Darth Vader pencil topper (Unlicensed)

SWITZERLAND

○ Star War pencil

Pencil cases

Stuart Hall

○ Return of the Jedi pencil bag

Metal Box Company

○ Chewbacca pencil tin

○ Yoda pencil tin

○ Darth Vader pencil tin

○ R2-D2 and C-3PO pencil tin

Yoda mousepad

A.H. PRISMATIC

○ TIE Interceptor

○ X-wing

○ AT-AT

○ Millennium Falcon, hologram

○ R2-D2 and C-3PO, hologram

○ Darth Vader, hologram

○ X-wing, hologram

○ B-Wing

○ Millennium Falcon

○ TIE Fighter

○ Millennium Falcon and logo

○ Darth Vader

○ Star Destroyer

○ X-wing

○ TIE Fighter

○ AT-AT

Helix Vinyl Zippered Bags (England)

○ Stormtrooper

○ R2-D2

○ C-3PO

○ Darth Vader

Computer wrist rest

Pens

○ Art of Star Wars exhibit pen, red

○ Art of Star Wars exhibit pen, black

○ Star Wars pen (Fantasma)

○ Return of the Jedi blue ink pens

Postcards

Drawing Board

○ Star Wars postcards

○ The Empire Stikes Back set of six Postcards

Fantasma

○ Star Wars postcard

Classico

○ Star Wars postcards

Topps

○ German Topps Special
   Edition magazine postcard

A. H. Prismatic

○ Darth Vader

○ Millennium Falcon in Asteroids

○ Millennium Falcon and TIE Fighters

○ ○ X-wings and Death Star

Gian Speeder and Theed play set (Galoob)

Rulers

○ Return of the Jedi ruler

ENGLAND

○ Return of the Jedi ruler

Scissors

○ Return of the Jedi scissors

○ Return of the Jedi scissors

School sets

○ Return of the Jedi school set

ENGLAND

▪ Pencil Top Gift Set

▪ Pencil Top Gift Set

▪ Pencil Top Gift Set

▪ Return of the Jedi Stationery Gift Set

▪ Return of the Jedi Stationery Gift Set

▪ Star Wars Math set

Scrapbooks / photo albums

○ Star Wars Collector's Album (Antioch)

Sharpeners / accessories

○ R2-D2 pencil sharpener

○ Darth Vader pencil sharpener

○ Darth Vader crayon holder

○ R2-D2 compass

○ Ewok magnifying glass

○ Return of the Jedi foil reinforcements

AUSTRALIA

○ R2-D2 sharpener and Jabba eraser

ENGLAND

○ Return of the Jedi pencil sharpener, blue

○ Return of the Jedi pencil sharpener, red

○ Luke and Leia sharpener

○ R2-D2 and C-3PO sharpener

○ Darth Vader and Stormtroopers sharpener

Stationery

○ R2-D2 stationery

ENGLAND

○ Droids writing pad

ISRAEL

○ Return of the Jedi R2-D2 and C-3PO on Tatooine

○ Return of the Jedi R2-D2 and C-3PO on Endor

JAPAN

○ Star Wars lap pack

Stencils

JAPAN

○ #1 yellow, red or blue

○ #2 red

○ #3 red or blue

○ #4 red

○ #5 red or blue

○ #6 red

**Episode I poster
(Star Wars Fan Club)**

Wallet cards

Antioch
- ⭕ Millennium Falcon
- ⭕ Boba Fett
- ⭕ Luke Skywalker
- ⭕ AT-AT
- ⭕ TIE Fighter
- ⭕ X-wing

Star Tours

Postcard
- ⭕ Endor postcard
- ⭕ Bespin postcard
- ⭕ Tatooine postcard
- ⭕ Fat pen, black
- ⭕ Fat pen, white
- ⭕ Pen set
- ⭕ Pencil, gold foil
- ⭕ Pencil, silver foil
- ⭕ Pencil, gold lined
- ⭕ Pencil, silver lined
- ⭕ Pencil, silver speckled

STORE DISPLAYS

Smiths (Holland)
- ⭕ Shelf talker
- ⭕ Header card

Confection Concepts International (New Zealand)
- ⭕ Chocolate Bar display for cards

Pepsi
- ⭕ Pizza Hut flyer
- ⭕ Pizza Hut poster
- ⭕ Pizza Hut Family Feast mobile

Gamesa
- ⭕ Large Darth Vader bust 2-sided
- ⭕ Hanging display 2-sided

Mervyn's Department Store
- ⭕ Darth Vader display

Pepsi (England)
- ⭕ Cardboard two-sided hanging display header

Gamesa (Mexico)
- ⭕ Header display

Pepsi
- ⭕ Trim (per section)
- ⭕ Poster pole sign
- ⭕ Poster pole sign Exclusively Vons
- ⭕ R2-D2 pole sign
- ⭕ Boba Fett plastic "wobbler"
- ⭕ Darth Vader static sign
- ⭕ C-3PO Die-cut shelf talker
- ⭕ Poster offer shelf talker

Pepsi Mexico
- ⭕ Hanging mobile

Sabritas (Mexico)
- ⭕ Display strip

Sonrics (Mexico)
- ⭕ Candy triangular display
- ⭕ Gum Card strip display

Books

A.H. Prismatic
- ⭕ Counter Top Bookmark display

Bantam
- ⭕ C-3PO Stand Up for Book Dump

Buttons

Adam Joseph
- ⭕ Display box for Return of the Jedi Photo buttons

Costumes

Don Post Studios
- ⭕ Blue, black and white header for masks, 1982

Film / video / slides

CBS Fox Video
- ⭕ THX Video dump display

STAP with Battle Droid toy (Kenner)

Wicket night light

Yoda, Darth Vader and C-3PO night lights

○ Special Edition dump display

○ TESB Reservation Form countertop display

○ THX video display box (Germany)5

Food

Coca-Cola

○ Darth Vader display

Natural balance

○ R2-D2 Vitamin display

Pepperidge Farm

○ Cookies floor display

Games

○ Parker Brothers Play for the Power full display box

○ Booster Pack Display box, Decipher

○ Starter Deck Display box, Decipher

○ Rebel Assault II display from England

Jewelry

○ Hollywood Pins countertop display

○ Scatter Pins display, full

Posters

○ Sales Corporation poster header display

○ Kenner poster shelf display

Stickers

○ Topps ROTJ sticker album display box

○ Topps ROTJ stickers display box

Toiletries

○ Bubble Bath Refueling Station counter display

Wall Decorations

○ Chromart countertop display, blue

○ Chromart countertop display, black

○ Zanart large floor display

Other

○ Small Applause Display card 2-sided

○ Large Applause Display card 2-sided

TOYS

KENNER
1978 STAR WARS 12-BACKS

○ Ben Kenobi-white hair	15.00	250.00
○ Ben Kenobi-grey hair	15.00	250.00
○ C-3PO	15.00	150.00
○ Chewbacca	10.00	225.00
○ Darth Vader	12.00	250.00
○ Death Squad Commander	12.00	225.00
○ Han Solo-large head	30.00	700.00
○ Han Solo-small head	40.00	600.00
○ Jawa	15.00	250.00
○ Jawa-plastic cape	300.00	3200.00
○ Luke Skywalker	30.00	350.00
○ Princess Leia	40.00	300.00
○ R2-D2	15.00	150.00
○ Sand People	15.00	250.00
○ Stormtrooper	15.00	225.00

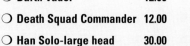

Star Wars metal lunchbox

1978 Star Wars 20/21-backs

○ Ben Kenobi-grey hair	15.00	125.00
○ Ben Kenobi-white hair	15.00	125.00
○ Boba Fett	40.00	1300.00
○ C-3PO	15.00	100.00
○ Chewbacca	10.00	125.00
○ Darth Vader	12.00	125.00
○ Death Squad Commander	12.00	100.00

Time magazine, May 1980

○ Death Star Droid	10.00	150.00		○ Boba Fett	40.00	375.00
○ Greedo	10.00	150.00		○ Bossk	8.00	100.00
○ Hammerhead	8.00	150.00		○ C-3PO	15.00	125.00
○ Han Solo-large head	30.00	475.00		○ C-3PO-remov.limbs	10.00	60.00
○ Jawa	15.00	100.00		○ Chewbacca	10.00	125.00
○ Luke Skywalker	30.00	300.00		○ Cloud Car Pilot	20.00	60.00
○ Luke Skywalker-X-wing	12.00	150.00		○ Darth Vader	12.00	80.00
○ Princess Leia	40.00	325.00		○ Death Squad Commander	12.00	100.00
○ Power Droid	10.00	125.00		○ Death Star Droid	10.00	125.00
○ R2-D2	15.00	125.00		○ Dengar	10.00	50.00
○ R5-D4	10.00	100.00		○ FX-7	10.00	50.00
○ Sand People	15.00	100.00		○ Greedo	10.00	125.00
○ Snaggletooth-red	8.00	150.00		○ Hammerhead	8.00	125.00
○ Snaggletooth-blue	175.00			○ Han Solo-bespin	15.00	125.00
○ Stormtrooper	15.00	150.00		○ Han Solo-hoth gear	15.00	90.00
○ Walrusman	10.00	125.00		○ Han Solo-large head	30.00	250.00
				○ Han Solo-small head	40.00	300.00

3-2-1 Contact magazine, Aug. 1980

1979-80 Star Wars 12-inch Dolls

○ Ben Kenobi	200.00	425.00		○ IG-88	15.00	120.00
○ Boba Fett	250.00	600.00		○ Imperial Commander	10.00	60.00
○ C-3PO	50.00	150.00		○ Imperial Stormtrooper	10.00	60.00
○ Chewbacca	75.00	150.00		○ Jawa	15.00	100.00
○ Darth Vader	75.00	150.00		○ Lando Calrissian	10.00	80.00
○ Han Solo	250.00	500.00		○ Lando Calrissian w/o teeth	10.00	80.00
○ IG-88	400.00	1100.00		○ Leia Bespin-front/crew	20.00	200.00
○ Jawa	100.00	250.00		○ Leia Bespin-front/turtle	20.00	200.00
○ Luke Skywalker	150.00	325.00		○ Leia Bespin-profile/crew	20.00	150.00
○ Princess Leia	125.00	250.00		○ Leia Bespin-profile/turtle	20.00	150.00
○ R2-D2	75.00	150.00		○ Lobot	10.00	40.00
○ Stormtrooper	150.00	325.00		○ Luke Bespin-looking/blonde	20.00	200.00

Fantastic Films magazine, Oct. 1980

1980 SW: Empire Strikes Back

○ 2-1B	12.00	75.00		○ Luke Bespin-looking/brown	20.00	200.00
○ 4-LOM	15.00	175.00		○ Luke Bespin-walking/blonde	20.00	150.00
○ AT-AT Commander	10.00	50.00		○ Luke Bespin-walking.brown	20.00	150.00
○ AT-AT Driver	10.00	75.00		○ Luke Skywalker-brown hair	30.00	200.00
○ Ben Kenobi-grey hair	15.00	125.00		○ Luke Skywalker-hoth gear	10.00	100.00
○ Ben Kenobi-white hair	15.00	125.00		○ Luke Skywalker-X Wing	12.00	100.00
○ Bespin guard-black	10.00	50.00		○ Power Droid	10.00	100.00
○ Bespin guard-white	10.00	50.00				

Nintendo Power magazine, Nov. 1992

○ Princess Leia	40.00	300.00
○ Princess Leia-hoth gear	20.00	125.00
○ R2-D2	15.00	75.00
○ R2-D2 w/sensorscope	10.00	60.00
○ R5-D4	10.00	100.00
○ Rebel Commander	8.00	50.00
○ Rebel Soldier-hoth gear	8.00	50.00
○ Sand People	15.00	100.00
○ Snaggletooth-red	8.00	125.00
○ Stormtrooper	15.00	100.00
○ TIE-Fighter Pilot	15.00	100.00
○ Ugnaught	8.00	50.00
○ Walrusman	10.00	125.00
○ Yoda w/orange snake	25.00	100.00
○ Zuckuss	8.00	100.00

1980 SW: Empire Strikes Back Micro Set

○ Bespin Control Room	20.00	50.00
○ Bespin Freeze Chamber	40.00	100.00
○ Bespin Gantry	20.00	50.00
○ Bespin World	90.00	200.00
○ Death Star Compactor	30.00	80.00
○ Death Star Escape	30.00	80.00
○ Death Star World	75.00	150.00
○ Hoth Generator Attack	20.00	50.00
○ Hoth Ion Cannon	20.00	50.00
○ Hoth Turret Defense	20.00	50.00
○ Hoth Wompa Cave	15.00	40.00
○ Hoth World	75.00	150.00
○ Imperial TIE Fighter	40.00	100.00
○ Millenium Falcon	200.00	400.00
○ Snowspeeder	100.00	225.00
○ X-wing	40.00	100.00

1980 SW: Empire Strikes Back Mini Rigs

○ CAP-2	10.00	30.00
○ INT-4	10.00	30.00
○ MLC-3	10.00	30.00

○ MTV-7	10.00	30.00
○ PDT-8	10.00	30.00

1983 SW: Return of the Jedi

○ 2-1B	12.00	75.00
○ 4-LOM	15.00	40.00
○ 8D8	10.00	40.00
○ Admiral Ackbar	8.00	40.00
○ AT-AT Commander	10.00	40.00
○ AT-AT Driver	10.00	50.00
○ AT-ST Driver	8.00	40.00
○ B-Wing Pilot	8.00	40.00
○ Ben Kenobi-blue saber	15.00	50.00
○ Ben Kenobi-grey hair	15.00	50.00
○ Ben Kenobi-white hair	15.00	50.00
○ Bespin Guard-black	10.00	50.00
○ Bespin Guard-white	10.00	30.00
○ Bib Fortuna	8.00	40.00
○ Biker Scout	12.00	50.00
○ Boba Fett	30.00	300.00
○ Bossk	8.00	70.00
○ C-3PO-remov.limbs	10.00	40.00
○ Chewbacca	10.00	60.00
○ Chief Chirpa	10.00	40.00
○ Cloud Car Pilot	15.00	50.00
○ Darth Vader	12.00	60.00
○ Death Squad Commander	12.00	60.00
○ Death Star Droid	10.00	80.00
○ Dengar	10.00	40.00
○ Emperor	8.00	40.00
○ Emperors Royal Guard	10.00	60.00

**Rolling Stone
magazine,
Aug. 1977**

**Sci-Fi Universe
magazine,
July 1994**

○ FX-7	10.00	50.00
○ Gamorrean Guard	8.00	40.00
○ General Madine	8.00	40.00
○ Greedo	10.00	60.00
○ Hammerhead	8.00	80.00
○ Han Solo-bespin	15.00	100.00
○ Han Solo-death star corridor		200.00
○ Han Solo-hoth gear	15.00	100.00
○ Han Solo-large head	30.00	200.00
○ Han Solo-trench coat	10.00	50.00
○ IG-88	15.00	80.00
○ Imperial Commander	10.00	40.00
○ Imperial Stormtrooper	10.00	50.00
○ Jawa	15.00	50.00
○ Klaatu	10.00	30.00
○ Klaatu-skiff	10.00	30.00
○ Lando Calrissian	10.00	50.00
○ Lando Calrissian-skiff	20.00	50.00
○ Leia Bespin-front/crew	20.00	125.00
○ Leis Bespin-front/turtle	20.00	125.00
○ Lobot	10.00	40.00
○ Logray	10.00	40.00
○ Luke Bespin-looking/blonde	20.00	175.00
○ Luke Bespin-looking/brown	20.00	125.00
○ Luke Skywalker	30.00	200.00
○ Luke Skywalker-gunner card	30.00	200.00
○ Luke Skywalker-hoth gear	10.00	50.00
○ Luke Skywalker-Jedi/blue	60.00	200.00
○ Luke Skywalker-Jedi/green	50.00	100.00
○ Luke Skywalker-X Wing	12.00	60.00
○ Lumat	20.00	50.00
○ Nien Numb	8.00	40.00
○ Nikto	8.00	40.00
○ Paploo	20.00	50.00
○ Power Droid	10.00	50.00
○ Princess Leia	40.00	500.00

○ Princess Leia-hoth gear	20.00	125.00
○ Princess Leia-poncho	20.00	75.00
○ Princess Leia-Boussh	20.00	60.00
○ Prune Face	8.00	40.00
○ R2-D2-sensorscope	10.00	50.00
○ R5-D4	10.00	50.00
○ Rancor Keeper	8.00	40.00
○ Rebel Commander	8.00	40.00
○ Rebel Commando	8.00	40.00
○ Rebel Soldier-hoth gear	8.00	40.00
○ Ree-Yees	8.00	40.00
○ Sand People	15.00	80.00
○ Snaggletooth-red	8.00	50.00
○ Squid Head	10.00	40.00
○ Stormtrooper	15.00	60.00
○ Sy and band	60.00	200.00
○ Teebo	12.00	50.00
○ TIE-Fighter Pilot	15.00	75.00
○ Ugnaught	8.00	40.00
○ Walrusman	10.00	60.00
○ Weequay	25.00	30.00
○ Wicket	20.00	60.00
○ Yoda-brown snake	30.00	100.00
○ Zuckuss	12.00	50.00

1983-84 SW: Return of the Jedi Mini Rigs

○ AST-5	6.00	15.00
○ CAP-2	8.00	20.00
○ Desert Sail Skiff	6.00	15.00
○ Endor Forest Ranger	6.00	15.00
○ INT-4	8.00	20.00
○ ISP-6	10.00	30.00
○ MLC-3	8.00	20.00
○ MTV-7	10.00	30.00
○ PDT-8	8.00	20.00

1985 SW: Droids Cartoon

○ A-Wing Fighter	200.00	600.00

Time magazine Feb. 1997

Vanity Fair magazine, Feb. 1999

Ewok magnets

○ A-Wing Pilot	80.00	250.00
○ ATL Interceptor	20.00	50.00
○ Boba Fett	400.00	1200.00
○ C-3PO	50.00	125.00
○ Jann Tosh	10.00	30.00
○ Jord Dusat	10.00	30.00
○ Kea Moll	10.00	30.00
○ Kez-Iban	10.00	30.00
○ Lightsaber	50.00	125.00
○ R2-D2	40.00	100.00
○ Sidegunner	25.00	60.00
○ Sise Fromm	40.00	100.00
○ Thall Joben	10.00	30.00
○ Tig Fromm	30.00	80.00
○ Uncle Gundy	8.00	25.00

1985 SW: Ewoks Cartoons

○ Dulok Scout	12.00	30.00
○ Dulok Shaman	12.00	30.00
○ King Gorneesh	12.00	30.00
○ Lady Gorneesh	12.00	30.00
○ Logray	12.00	30.00
○ Wicket	15.00	40.00

1985 SW: Power of the Force

○ A-Wing Pilot	40.00	125.00
○ Amanaman	125.00	250.00
○ Anakin Skywalker	30.00	2500.00
○ AT-ST Driver	8.00	60.00
○ B-Wing Pilot	8.00	40.00
○ Barada	50.00	125.00
○ Ben Kenobi-blue saber	15.00	125.00
○ Biker Scout	12.00	100.00
○ C-3PO-remov.limbs	10.00	80.00
○ Chewbacca	10.00	100.00
○ Darth Vader	12.00	125.00
○ Emperor	8.00	75.00
○ EV-9D9	75.00	150.00

○ Gamorrean Guard	8.00	250.00
○ Han Solo-carbonite	100.00	250.00
○ Han Solo-trench coat	10.00	400.00
○ Imperial Dignitary	30.00	100.00
○ Imperial Gunner	75.00	150.00
○ Jawa	15.00	100.00
○ Lando Calrissian	10.00	125.00
○ Luke Skywalker-poncho	50.00	125.00
○ Luke Skywalker-stormtrooper		
	150.00	400.00
○ Luke Skywalker-X Wing	12.00	150.00
○ Lumat	20.00	60.00
○ Nikto	15.00	600.00
○ Paploo	20.00	50.00
○ Princess Leia-poncho	20.00	120.00
○ R2-D2-saber	75.00	175.00
○ Romba	20.00	60.00
○ Stormtrooper	15.00	225.00
○ Teebo	12.00	125.00
○ Warok	20.00	75.00
○ Wicket	15.00	200.00
○ Yak Face	175.00	2000.00
○ Yoda-brown snake	30.00	600.00

1978-85 Star Wars Accessories

○ A-Wing Fighter	150.00	500.00
○ AT-AT (ESB)	125.00	400.00
○ AT-AT (ROTJ)	125.00	200.00
○ B-Wing Fighter (ROTJ)	100.00	200.00
○ Biker Scout Laser		
Pist. (ROTJ)	20.00	100.00

Mini-action figure storage case (Kenner)

Return of the Jedi trash can

○ C-3PO Case (ROTJ)	15.00	40.00	○ Laser Rifle Case (ROTJ)	15.00	50.00	
○ Cantina Cafè (SW)	75.00	150.00	○ Millenium Falcon (ESB)	75.00	250.00	
○ Chewbacca Strap (ROTJ)	5.00	20.00	○ Millenium Falcon (ROTJ)	75.00	200.00	
○ Cloud Car (ESB)	30.00	125.00	○ Millenium Falcon (SW)	75.00	400.00	
○ Cloud City (ESB)	150.00	400.00	○ Mini Action Figure Case (ESB)	20.00	25.00	
○ Dagobah (ESB)	30.00	100.00	○ Mini Action Figure Case (SW)	20.00	50.00	
○ Darth Vader Case (ESB)	10.00	30.00	○ Patrol Dewback (ESB)	20.00	250.00	
○ Darth Vader Case (ROTJ)	10.00	30.00	○ Patrol Dewback (SW)	20.00	100.00	
○ Death Star (SW)	100.00	300.00	○ Radio Controlled R2-D2 (SW)	75.00	150.00	
○ Droid Factory (ESB)	75.00	200.00	○ Rancor Monster (ROTJ)	50.00	80.00	
○ Droid Factory (SW)	75.00	200.00	○ Rebel Comm.Center (ESB)	80.00	200.00	
○ Ewok Assault Catapult (ROTJ)	12.00	40.00	○ Rebel Transport (ESB)	50.00	125.00	
○ Ewok Battle Wagon (ROTJ)	50.00	150.00	○ Sand Skimmer (POTF)	40.00	100.00	
○ Ewok Glider (ROTJ)	12.00	40.00	○ Scout Walker (ESB)	20.00	125.00	
○ Ewok Village (ROTJ)	80.00	150.00	○ Scout Walker (ROTJ)	20.00	100.00	
○ Hoth Wampa (ESB)	25.00	80.00	○ Security Scout Vehicle (POTF)	60.00	100.00	
○ Ice Planet Hoth (ESB)	60.00	200.00	○ Slave 1 (ESB)	50.00	200.00	
○ Imperial Attack Base (ESB)	30.00	100.00	○ Snowspeeder (ESB)	40.00	100.00	
○ Imperial Cruiser (ESB)	40.00	100.00	○ Sonic Land Speeder-JCP (SW)	150.00	400.00	
○ Imperial Shuttle (ROTJ)	225.00	400.00	○ Speeder Bike (ROTJ)	15.00	40.00	
○ Imperial Sniper Vehicle (POTF)	40.00	80.00	○ Star Destroyer (ESB)	50.00	150.00	
○ Imperial Transport (ESB)	40.00	125.00	○ Tatooine Skiff (POTF)	400.00	700.00	
○ Imperial Transport (SW)	40.00	125.00	○ Tauntaun (ESB)	25.00	80.00	
○ Jabba Dungeon (ROTJ)	50.00	150.00	○ Tauntaun-split belly (ESB)	40.00	125.00	
○ Jabba Dungeon (POTF)	200.00	350.00	○ TIE-Fighter (ESB)	40.00	250.00	
○ Jabba Playset (ROTJ)	40.00	125.00	○ TIE-Fighter (SW)	40.00	200.00	
○ Jawa Sandcrawler (ESB)	200.00	500.00	○ TIE-Fighter Battle Dam. (ROTJ)	40.00	100.00	
○ Jawa Sandcrawler (SW)	200.00	300.00	○ TIE-Interceptor (ROTJ)	75.00	150.00	
○ Jedi Vinyl Case (ROTJ)	15.00	100.00	○ Turret and Probot (ESB)	50.00	150.00	
○ Land of the Jawas (ESB)	75.00	250.00	○ Vader Head Case (ROTJ)	15.00	50.00	
○ Land of the Jawas (SW)	75.00	150.00	○ Vader's TIE-Fighter (SW)	60.00	150.00	
○ Landspeeder (SW)	20.00	80.00	○ X-wing Battle Damage (ESB)	40.00	150.00	
○ Laser Pistol (ESB)	20.00	100.00	○ X-wing Battle Damage (ROTJ)	40.00	90.00	
○ Laser Pistol (ROTJ)	20.00	80.00	○ X-wing Fighter (ESB)	40.00	250.00	
○ Laser Rifle (ESB)	75.00	250.00	○ X-wing Fighter (SW)	40.00	150.00	
○ Laser Rifle (SW)	40.00	100.00	○ Y-Wing Fighter (ROTJ)	60.00	200.00	

Ewok Centerpiece (Drawing Boar

Star Wars giftwrap (Drawing Boar

Return of the Jedi lunch napkins (Drawing Boar

1995 SW: Power of the Force

○ Ben Kenobi-Half Shot Lg.Saber	20.00	50.00
○ Ben Kenobi-Full Shot Lg.Saber	20.00	50.00
○ Ben Kenobi-Full Shot Sh.Saber	4.00	10.00
○ Chewbacca	4.00	10.00
○ C-3PO	4.00	10.00
○ Darth Vader-Lg.Saber	12.00	30.00
○ Darth Vader-Sh.Saber	4.00	10.00
○ Darth Vader-Sh.Sbr./Long Pack	8.00	20.00
○ Han Solo	4.00	10.00
○ Luke Skywalker-Lg.Saber	15.00	40.00
○ Luke Skywalker-Sh.Saber	6.00	15.00
○ Princess Leia-2 bands	6.00	15.00
○ Princess Leia-3 bands	8.00	20.00
○ R2-D2	4.00	10.00
○ Stormtrooper	5.00	12.00

1995-98 SW: Power of the Force Accessories

○ A-Wing Fighter	10.00	25.00
○ Air Speeder	8.00	20.00
○ C-3PO Talking Case	8.00	20.00
○ Chewbacca Bowcaster	8.00	20.00
○ Cloud Car	8.00	25.00
○ Cruise Missile	6.00	15.00
○ Darth Vader TIE Fighter	12.00	30.00
○ Darth Vader Lightsaber	8.00	20.00
○ Dash Rendar Outrider	20.00	50.00
○ Death Star Playset	8.00	25.00
○ Detention Cell Block	8.00	20.00
○ Electronic AT-AT	40.00	110.00
○ Endor Playset	8.00	20.00
○ Han's Blaster Pistol	8.00	20.00
○ Heavy Blaster	8.00	20.00
○ Hoth Playset	8.00	20.00
○ Imperial AT-ST	30.00	60.00
○ Imperial Speeder Bike	8.00	20.00
○ Landspeeder	4.00	10.00

○ Laser Blaster	8.00	20.00
○ Luke on Speeder Bike	6.00	15.00
○ Luke on Speeder Bike- no gloves	8.00	20.00
○ Luke's Lightsaber	12.00	30.00
○ Luke's Utility Belt	8.00	20.00
○ Millenium Falcon	25.00	60.00
○ Rebel Snowspeeder	8.00	20.00
○ Remote R2-D2	8.00	20.00
○ Slave 1	8.00	20.00
○ Star Destroyer	8.00	30.00
○ Swoop	8.00	20.00
○ T-16	8.00	20.00
○ TIE Fighter	10.00	25.00
○ X-wing Fighter	10.00	30.00
○ X-wing Simulator	8.00	20.00

1996 SW: Power of the Force

○ Boba Fett-Circle on Hand	4.00	12.00
○ Boba Fett-Half Circle on Hand	15.00	70.00
○ Boba Fett Full circ.on one hand	15.00	100.00
○ Chewbacca	4.00	10.00
○ Dash Rendar	2.00	6.00
○ Death Star Gunner-Green	4.00	10.00
○ Death Star Gunner-Red	8.00	20.00
○ Greedo-Green	2.00	8.00
○ Greedo-Red	8.00	20.00
○ Hammerhead-Green	2.00	8.00
○ Hammerhead-Red	8.00	20.00

Immunizations poster

Darth Vader Coca-Cola poster

○ Han Solo-Carbonite	2.00	6.00
○ Han Solo-Carbon.& Freeze Ch.	5.00	12.00
○ Han Solo-Hoth Open Hand	8.00	20.00
○ Han Solo-Hoth Closed Hand	4.00	10.00
○ Jawas-Red	8.00	20.00
○ Jawas-Green	3.00	8.00
○ Lando Calrissian	4.00	12.00
○ L.Skywalker-Dag. Lg.Saber	10.00	25.00
○ L.Skywalker-Dag. Sh.Saber	4.00	12.00
○ L.Skywalker-Dag.Sh.Sbr.Lg.pack	6.00	15.00
○ L.Skywalker-Jedi Brown Vest	25.00	60.00
○ L.Skywalker-Jedi Black Vest	3.00	8.00
○ L.Skywalker-Imperial Guard	2.00	6.00
○ L.Skywalker-Stormtr.-Red	8.00	20.00
○ L.Skywalker-Stormtr.-Green	4.00	10.00
○ L.Sky.-X-wing Lg.Saber	10.00	25.00
○ L.Sky.-X-wing Sh.Saber	4.00	10.00
○ L.Sky.-X-wing Sh.Saber Lg.Pack	10.00	25.00
○ Prince Xizor	2.00	6.00
○ Princess Leia-Boussh	2.00	6.00
○ R5-D4-Red	8.00	20.00
○ R5-D4-Green/Str.Latch	8.00	20.00
○ R5-D4-Green/Hook Latch	2.00	6.00
○ Sandtrooper	4.00	10.00
○ Tatooine Stormtrooper	8.00	20.00
○ TIE Fighter w/o Sticker	2.00	6.00
○ TIE Fighter w/ Sticker	10.00	25.00
○ Tusk Raider-Closed/Green	12.00	30.00
○ Tusk Raider-Open/Green	2.00	6.00
○ Tusk Raider-Closed/Red	8.00	20.00
○ Tusk Raider-Open/Red	10.00	30.00
○ Yoda	4.00	10.00

1996-97 SW: Power of the Force 2-Packs and 3-Packs

○ Ben/Darth/Luke	15.00	40.00
○ Boba Fett/IG-88	15.00	40.00
○ Chewbacca/Han/Lando	15.00	40.00

○ C-3PO/R2-D2/Stormtrooper	15.00	40.00
○ Luke/Tusk.Raider/B.Kenobi	15.00	40.00
○ Luke/Lando/TIE Fighter	15.00	40.00
○ Luke/AT-ST Driver/Leia	15.00	40.00
○ Xizor/Darth Vader	15.00	40.00

1996-97 SW: Power of the Force 12-inch Figures

○ Admiral Ackbar	15.00	30.00
○ AT-AT Driver-ESB	20.00	40.00
○ Ben Kenobi-dk.blue insert	30.00	60.00
○ Ben Kenobi-lt.blue/gold	20.00	50.00
○ Ben Kenobi-lt.blue/silver	20.00	45.00
○ Boba Fett	30.00	60.00
○ Ceremonial Luke-NH	20.00	40.00
○ Chewbacca	30.00	75.00
○ C-3PO	15.00	30.00
○ Darth Vader	20.00	40.00
○ Grand Moff Tarkin-NH	15.00	30.00
○ Greedo-NH	15.00	30.00
○ Han Solo-dk.blue insert	20.00	40.00
○ Han Solo-lt.blue insert	10.00	20.00
○ Han Solo Hoth-ESB	15.00	30.00
○ Jawa	10.00	20.00
○ Lando Calrissian	15.00	30.00
○ Luke Skywalker	20.00	40.00
○ Luke Skywalker Bespin	20.00	40.00
○ Luke Skywalker Hoth-ESB	15.00	35.00
○ Luke Skywalker X-wing	15.00	35.00
○ Princess Leia	15.00	35.00
○ R2-D2	10.00	20.00
○ Sandtrooper-NH	15.00	30.00
○ Snowtrooper-ESB	20.00	40.00
○ Stormtrooper	15.00	30.00
○ Tie-Fighter Pilot	15.00	30.00
○ Tusken Raider w/Blaster	15.00	35.00
○ Tusk.Raider w/Gaderffi		
Sticker	15.00	35.00
○ Yoda	10.00	20.00

Star Wars radio drama poster

The Empire Strikes Back radio drama poster

"All I Need To Know" poster (Portal)

1996-97 SW: Power of the Force Deluxe Packs

○ Boba Fett	4.00	10.00
○ Crowd Control Stormtrooper	4.00	10.00
○ Crowd Ctl.Strmtrpr.w/Sticker	20.00	50.00
○ Han Solo w/Smuggler Flight	4.00	10.00
○ Hoth Rebel Soldier	4.00	10.00
○ Imperial Probe Droid-Orange	8.00	20.00
○ Imperial Probe Droid-Green	4.00	10.00
○ Luke w/Desert Skiff	4.00	10.00
○ Snowtrooper	4.00	10.00

1997 Star Wars Cinema Scenes

○ Death Star Escape-TRU	6.00	15.00
○ Cantina Show Down	6.00	15.00
○ Jedi Final Dual (.00)	6.00	15.00
○ Jedi Final Dual (.01)	6.00	15.00
○ Purchase of Droids	6.00	15.00

1997 SW: Power of the Force

○ 2-1B	2.00	6.00
○ 4-LOM	2.00	6.00
○ Admiral Ackbar	2.00	6.00
○ ASP-7	2.00	6.00
○ AT-ST Driver	2.00	6.00
○ Bib Fortuna	2.00	6.00
○ Bossk	2.00	6.00
○ Dengar	2.00	6.00
○ Emperor Palatine	2.00	6.00
○ Emperors Royal Guard	2.00	6.00
○ EV-9D9	2.00	6.00
○ Gamorrean Guard	2.00	6.00
○ Garindan	2.00	6.00
○ Grand Tarkin	2.00	6.00
○ Han Solo Bepsin	2.00	6.00
○ Han Solo-endor gear/blue	2.00	6.00
○ Han Solo-endor gear/brown	2.00	15.00
○ Hoth Rebel Soldier	2.00	6.00
○ Hoth Rebel Soldier II	2.00	10.00

○ Hoth Snowtrooper	2.00	6.00
○ Lando Calrissian	2.00	6.00
○ Luke Skywalker Ceremonial	2.00	6.00
○ Luke Skywalker-hoth gear	2.00	6.00
○ Luke Skywalker-hoth gear II	2.00	10.00
○ Malakili	2.00	6.00
○ Nien Numb	2.00	6.00
○ Ponda Baba	2.00	6.00
○ Princess Leia	2.00	10.00
○ Rebel Fleet Trooper	2.00	6.00
○ Rebel Fleet Trooper II	2.00	20.00
○ Saelt-Marae	2.00	6.00
○ Weequay	2.00	6.00

1997 SW: Power of the Force Electronic Power FX

○ Ben Kenobi	3.00	8.00
○ Darth Vader	3.00	8.00
○ Emperor (.00)	4.00	10.00
○ Emperor (.01)	3.00	8.00
○ Luke Skywalker	3.00	8.00
○ R2-D2	4.00	10.00

1997-98 SW: Power of the Force Beast Assortment

○ Han Solo/Jabba (.00)	20.00	40.00
○ Han Solo/Jabba (.01)	10.00	20.00
○ Jawa/Ronto	10.00	20.00
○ Sandtrooper/Dewback	10.00	20.00
○ Tauntaun w/Luke	10.00	20.00

Star Wars commercial poster (Portal)

Return of the Jedi reprint (Portal)

1997-98 SW: Power of the Force Exclusives/Mail-Ins

○ AT-AT Driver 12-inch	30.00	80.00
○ B'Omarr Monk-MI	12.50	25.00
○ Cantina Band Member-MI	15.00	30.00
○ Darth Vader w/Obi Wan	50.00	100.00
○ Doikk Na'ts	20.00	40.00
○ Elect.Ben/D.Vader 12-inch	50.00	100.00
○ Figin D'an	30.00	60.00
○ Grand Moff w/Gunner 12-inch	65.00	125.00
○ Greedo 12-inch	30.00	60.00
○ Han Solo Stormtrooper-MI	15.00	30.00
○ Han Solo/Tauntaun 12-inch	50.00	125.00
○ Ickabel	20.00	40.00
○ Luke Theatre Edition-MI	40.00	100.00
○ Luke w/Bib Fortuna 12-inch	60.00	150.00
○ Luke w/Han Strmtrpr. 12-inch	65.00	125.00
○ Luke w/Wampa 12-inch	65.00	125.00
○ Nalan	20.00	40.00
○ Oola w/Salacious Crumb	20.00	40.00
○ Sandtrooper 12-inch-Diam.	30.00	75.00
○ Spirit of Obi Wan Kenobi-MI	10.00	15.00
○ Tech	20.00	40.00
○ Tedn	20.00	40.00

1998 SW: Power of the Force

○ Ben Kenobi (.00)	2.00	15.00
○ Ben Kenobi (.01)	2.00	6.00
○ Biggs Darklighter (.00)	5.00	12.00
○ Captain Piett (.00)	3.00	8.00
○ Darth Vader Rem.helmet (.00)	5.00	12.00
○ Endor Rebel Soldier (.00)	2.00	15.00
○ Endor Rebel Soldier (.01)	2.00	6.00
○ Han Solo Bespin (.00)	2.00	30.00
○ Han Solo Bespin (.01)	2.00	6.00
○ Han Solo Carbonite (.00)	2.00	15.00
○ Han Solo Carbonite (.01)	2.00	6.00
○ Han Solo Endor (.00)	2.00	15.00

○ Han Solo Endor (.01)	2.00	6.00
○ Hoth Rebel Soldier (.00)	2.00	15.00
○ Hoth Rebel Soldier (.01)	2.00	6.00
○ Ishi Tibb (.00)	5.00	12.00
○ Lak Sivrak (.00)	5.00	12.00
○ Lando Calrissian (.00)	2.00	15.00
○ Lando Calrissian (.01)	2.00	6.00
○ Lando Calrissian Skiff (.00)	2.00	15.00
○ Lando Calrissian Skiff (.01)	2.00	6.00
○ Leia Ewok Gear (.00)	2.00	15.00
○ Leia Ewok Gear (.01)	2.00	6.00
○ Leia Jabbas prisoner (.00)	2.00	15.00
○ Leia Jabbas prisoner (.01)	2.00	6.00
○ L.Skywalker Bespin (.00)	2.00	30.00
○ L.Skywalker Bespin (.01)	2.00	15.00
○ L.Skywalker Stormtrooper (.00)	2.00	15.00
○ L.Skywalker Stormtrooper (.01)	2.00	3.00
○ Rebel Fleet Trooper (.00)	2.00	15.00
○ Rebel Fleet Trooper (.01)	2.00	6.00
○ Zuckuss (.00)	2.00	15.00

The Empire Strikes Back lobby card

1998 Star Wars Complete Galaxy

○ Dagobah w/Yoda	10.00	20.00
○ Death Star w/Darth Vader	10.00	20.00
○ Ewok w/Glider	10.00	20.00
○ Luke	10.00	20.00

1998 Star Wars Epic Force

○ Boba Fett	6.00	15.00
○ C-3PO	6.00	15.00
○ Chewbacca	6.00	15.00
○ Darth Vader	6.00	15.00
○ Luke Skywalker	6.00	15.00
○ Obi-Wan Kenobi	6.00	15.00

The Empire Strikes Back lobby card

○ Princess Leia	6.00	15.00	
○ Stormtrooper	6.00	15.00	

1998 Star Wars Millenium Mint

○ Bespin Han Solo	6.00	15.00
○ Chewbacca	6.00	15.00
○ Endor Leia		
○ Endor Luke		
○ Snowtrooper	6.00	15.00

1998 Star Wars: Princess Leia Collection

○ Leia/Luke (.00)	6.00	20.00
○ Leia/Luke (.01)	6.00	15.00
○ Leia/Han (.00)	6.00	20.00
○ Leia/Han (.01)	6.00	15.00
○ Leia/Wicket (.00)	6.00	20.00
○ Leia/Wicket (.01)	6.00	15.00
○ Leia/R2-D2 (.00)	6.00	20.00
○ Leia/R2-D2 (.01)	6.00	15.00

1998 Star Wars Episode 1

○ STAP w/Battle Driod	10.00	20.00
○ Mace Windu MI	15.00	30.00

1999 Star Wars Expanded Universe

○ Clone Emperor Palpatine	5.00	12.00
○ Dark Trooper	5.00	12.00
○ Grand Admiral Thrawn	5.00	12.00
○ Imperial Sentinel	5.00	12.00
○ Kyle Katarn	5.00	12.00
○ Luke Skywalker	5.00	12.00
○ Mara Jade	5.00	12.00
○ Princess Leia	5.00	12.00
○ Spacetrooper	5.00	12.00

GALOOB

1995-97 Star Wars Action Fleet

○ AT-AT	4.00	10.00

○ AT-ST KB	6.00	15.00
○ A-Wing (Green)	4.00	10.00
○ A-Wing (Red)	4.00	10.00
○ Darth Vader TIE Fighter (Lg)	4.00	10.00
○ Darth Vader TIE Fighter (Sm)	4.00	10.00
○ Imperial Shuttle	4.00	10.00
○ Jawa Sandcrawler	5.00	12.00
○ Rancor Monster	4.00	10.00
○ Slave 1	5.00	12.00
○ Snowspeeder	4.00	10.00
○ TIE Bomber	4.00	10.00
○ TIE Interceptor	5.00	12.00
○ X-wing	6.00	15.00
○ Xizors Virago	4.00	10.00
○ Y-Wing	4.00	10.00

1995-97 Star Wars Action Fleet Playsets

○ Death Star	15.00	30.00
○ Hoth	15.00	30.00
○ Rebel Base	15.00	30.00

1995-97 Star Wars Battle Packs

○ Alien/Creatures	4.00	10.00
○ Galactic Empire	4.00	10.00
○ Imperial Hunters	4.00	10.00
○ Rebel Alliance	4.00	10.00

The Empire
Strikes Back
lobby card

The Empire
Strikes Back
lobby card

Return of the Jedi
program

⭕ Shadows of the Empire	4.00	10.00
⭕ Cantina	4.00	10.00
⭕ Desert Palace	4.00	10.00
⭕ Droid Escape	4.00	10.00
⭕ Dune Sea	4.00	10.00
⭕ Endor Ambassador	4.00	10.00
⭕ Mos Eisley	4.00	10.00

Other Toys

1993 Star Wars Bend Ems

⭕ Admiral Ackbar	4.00	10.00
⭕ Ben Kenobi	4.00	10.00
⭕ Bib Fortuna	10.00	25.00
⭕ Boba Fett	4.00	10.00
⭕ C-3PO	4.00	10.00
⭕ Chewbacca	4.00	10.00
⭕ Darth Vader	4.00	10.00
⭕ Emperor	4.00	10.00
⭕ Emperor's Royal Guard	4.00	10.00
⭕ Gamorrean Guard	4.00	10.00
⭕ Han Solo	4.00	10.00
⭕ Lando Calrissian	4.00	10.00
⭕ Luke Skywalker	4.00	10.00
⭕ Luke Skywalker Xwing Pilot	6.00	15.00
⭕ Princess Leia	6.00	15.00
⭕ R2-D2	4.00	10.00
⭕ Stormtrooper	4.00	10.00
⭕ Tusken Raider	4.00	10.00
⭕ Yoda	5.00	12.00
⭕ Wicket	4.00	10.00
⭕ 4-pack Gift Set	10.00	25.00
⭕ 6-pack Gift Set	12.50	30.00
⭕ 8-pack Gift Set	12.50	30.00
⭕ 10-pack Gift Set	15.00	40.00

Displays

⭕ Display from Early Bird kit

⭕ Action Display loose stickers not applied

⭕ Display Arena

⭕ Darth Vader Carrying Case 41-back

Pro-doh sets

⭕ Millennium Falcon Set

Wonderworld sets

⭕ Star Wars Space Battle Set

Playmates

PRESCHOOL

⭕ Ewok Fire Cart

⭕ Wicket Radio

⭕ Wicket Learning Phone

⭕ Wicket Clock

⭕ Ewok Woodland Wagon

Unlicensed

Spain

⭕ Star Wars Pistol

Fantasma

⭕ Laser Light Spinner

Worlds Apart Limited (England)

⭕ Star Wars Yoyo

KENNER

⭕ Yoda: The Jedi Master (magic 8-ball)

Puppets

⭕ Yoda hand puppet

Remote-controlled toys

⭕ Radio-controlled Sandcrawler

⭕ Super control R2-D2 (disc firing; from Japan)

The Empire Strikes Back theatrical poster "B" Sheet

The Empire Strikes Back theatrical poster "A" Sheet

Revenge of the Jedi theatrical advance poster

TRADING CARDS

TOPPS

1977 Star Wars

○ Complete set (330)	150.00	300.00
○ Comp. sticker set (55)	50.00	100.00
○ Comp.ser.1 set (66)	40.00	80.00
○ Comm.ser.1 card (1-66)	.50	1.25
○ Comp.ser.1 stick.set (11)	10.00	20.00
○ Comm.ser.1 stick.(1-11)	1.00	2.00
○ Comp.ser.2 set (66)	30.00	60.00
○ Common ser.2 (1-66)	.40	1.00
○ Comp.ser.2 stick.set (11)	10.00	20.00
○ Comm.ser.2.stick.(1-11)	1.00	2.00
○ Comp.ser.3 set (66)	30.00	60.00
○ Common ser.3 (1-66)	.40	1.00
○ Comp.ser.3 stick.set (11)	10.00	20.00
○ Comm.ser.3 stick.(1-11)	1.00	2.00
○ Comp.ser.4 set (66)	25.00	50.00
○ Common ser.4 (1-66)	.30	.75
○ Comp.ser.4 stick.set (11)	10.00	20.00
○ Comm.ser.4 stick.(1-11)	1.00	2.00
○ Comp.ser.5 set (66)	25.00	50.00
○ Common ser.5 (1-66)	.30	.75
○ Comp.ser.5 stick.set (11)	10.00	20.00
○ Comm.ser.5 stick.(1-11)	1.00	2.00

○ Luke Skywalker
○ C-3PO & R2-D2
○ The little droid R2-D2
○ Space pirate Han Solo
○ Princess Leia Organa
○ Ben Kenobi
○ The villainous Darth Vader
○ Grand Moff Tarkin
○ Rebels defend their ship
○ Princess Leia captured!
○ Artoo is imprisoned by the Jawas

○ The droids are reunited!
○ A sale on droids!
○ Luke checks out his new droid
○ R2-D2 is left behind
○ Jawas of Tatooine
○ Lord Vader threatens Princess Leia
○ R2-D2 is missing!
○ Searching for the little droid
○ Hunted by the Sandpeople!
○ The Tusken Raiders
○ Rescued by Ben Kenobi
○ C-3PO is injured
○ Stormtroopers seek the droids
○ Luke rushed to save his loved ones
○ A horrified Luke sees his family killed
○ Some repairs for C-3PO
○ Luke agrees to join Ben Kenobi
○ Stopped by Stormtroopers
○ Han in the Millennium falcom
○ Sighting the Death Star
○ Lord Vader's Guards
○ The droids in the control room
○ C-3PO diverts the guards
○ Luke and Han as stormtroopers
○ Blast of the laser rifle!
○ Cornered in the labyrinth
○ Luke and Han in the refuse room
○ Steel walls close in on out heroes!
○ Droids rescue their masters!

**Star Wars
commercial
poster**

Checklist

**Star Wars
theatrical
poster
Teaser "B"**

- Facing the deadly chasm
- Stromtroopers attack
- Luke prepares to swing across the chasm
- Han and Chewie shoot it out
- The light sabre
- A desperate moment for Ben
- Luke prepares for the battle
- R2-D2 is loaded aboard
- The rebels monitor the raid
- Rebel leaders wonder about their fate!
- C-3PO and Princess Leia
- Who will win the final Star War
- Battle in outer space
- The victors receive their reward
- Han, Chewie, and Luke
- A day of rejoicing
- Mark Hamill as Luke Skywalker
- Harrison Ford as Han Solo
- Alec Guinness as Ben Kenobi
- Peter Cushing as Grand Moff Tarkin
- Mark Hamill in control room
- Lord Vader's stormtroopers
- May the Force be with you
- Governor of Imperial Outlands
- Carrie Fisher and Mark Hamill
- Amazing robot-C-3Po
- C-3PO and Luke
- The Millennium Falcon
- Threepio's desert rek
- Special mission for R2-D2
- The incredible C-3PO
- Ben Kenobi rescues Luke
- The droids wait for Luke
- Luke Skywalker on Tatooine
- Darth Vader strangles a rebel
- R2-D2 on the rebel starship

- Waiting in the control room
- Droids to the rescue
- Preparing to board Solo's spaceship
- Where has R2-D2 gone?
- Weapons of the Death Star
- A daring rescue
- Aboard the Millennium Falcon
- Rebel pilot prepares for the raid
- Luke on the sand planet
- A mighty explosion
- The droids try to rescue Luke
- Stromtroopers guard Solo's ship
- The imprisoned Princess Leia
- Honoring the Victors
- Solo and Chewie prepare to leave Luke
- Advance of the Tusken Raider
- Stormtroopers blast the rebels
- Interrogated by Stormtroopers
- Sighting R2-D2
- The droids on Tatooine
- Meeting at the cantina
- C-3PO
- Ben with the light sabre
- Our heroes at the spaceport
- The Wookies Chewbacca
- Rebels prepare for the big fight
- Stormtroopers attack our heroes
- Luke's uncle and aunt
- Imperial soldiers burn through the starship
- A message from Princess Leia
- The Tusken Raider
- Princess Leia observes the battle
- Ben turns off the tractor beam
- Threepio fools the guards
- Chewie and Han Solo

Washington Post newspaper, May 18, 1980

R2-D2 eraser

- ○ Threatened by Sandpeople
- ○ Ben hides from Imperial stormtroopers
- ○ Planning to escape
- ○ Hiding in the Millennium Falcon
- ○ Honored for their heroism
- ○ Chewbacca posed as a prisoner
- ○ R2-D2 and C-3PO
- ○ Threepio, Ben and Luke
- ○ Luke destroys an Imperial ship
- ○ Han Solo and Chewbacca
- ○ The Millenium Falcon
- ○ Solo blasts a stormtrooper
- ○ Threepio searches for R2-D2
- ○ Luke in disguise
- ○ A quizzical Threepio
- ○ The Rebel fleet
- ○ Roar of the Wookie
- ○ May the Force be with you
- ○ Pursued by the Jawas
- ○ Spectacular battle
- ○ Lord Vader and a soldier
- ○ Ben and Luke w/C-3PO
- ○ Luke dreams of being a star pilot
- ○ Cantina troubles
- ○ Danger from all sides
- ○ Luke attacked by a strange creature
- ○ On the track of the droids
- ○ Han Solo
- ○ R2-D2-where are you?
- ○ Some quick thinking by Luke
- ○ Darth Vader inspects the throttled ship
- ○ Droids on the sand planet
- ○ Harrison Ford as Han Solo
- ○ Escape from the Death Star
- ○ Luke Skywalkers aunt preparing dinner
- ○ Bargaining with the Jawas

- ○ The fearsome stormtroopers
- ○ The evil Grand Moff Tarkin
- ○ Shootout at the Chasm
- ○ Planning an escape
- ○ Spirited Princess Leia
- ○ The fantastic droid Threepio
- ○ Princess Leia comforts Luke
- ○ The Escape Pod is jettisoned
- ○ R2-D2 is lifted aboard
- ○ Learn about the Force, Luke
- ○ Rebel victory
- ○ Luke Skywalker's home
- ○ Destroying a world
- ○ Preparing for the raid
- ○ Han Solo cornered by Greedo
- ○ Caught in the tractor beam
- ○ Tusken Raiders capture Luke
- ○ Escaping from stormtroopers
- ○ A close call for Luke and Leia
- ○ Surrounded by Lord Vader's soldiers
- ○ Hunting the fugitives
- ○ Meeting at the Death Star
- ○ Luke and the Princess trapped
- ○ The walls are moving
- ○ Droids in the escape pod
- ○ The stormtroopers
- ○ Solo aims for trouble
- ○ A closer look at a Jawa
- ○ Luke Skywalkers dream

Wicket eraser

- ○ Solo swings into action
- ○ The Star Warriors
- ○ Stormtroopers search the spaceport
- ○ Princess Leia honors the victors
- ○ Peter Cushing as Grand Moff Tarkin
- ○ Deadly blasters
- ○ Dave Prowse as Darth Vader
- ○ Luke and his uncle
- ○ Luke on Tatooine
- ○ The Jawas
- ○ Threepio and friend
- ○ Starship under fire
- ○ Mark Hamill as Like
- ○ Carrie Fisher as Princess Leia
- ○ Life on the desert world
- ○ Liberated Princess
- ○ Like's uncle buys Threepio
- ○ Stormtroopers attack
- ○ Alec Guinness as Ben Kenobi
- ○ Lord Darth Vader
- ○ Leia blasts a stormtrooper
- ○ Luke decides to leave Tatooine
- ○ The star warriors aim for action
- ○ C-3PO searches for his counterpart
- ○ Raid at Mos Eisley
- ○ Inquiring about Obi-Wan Kenobi
- ○ A band of Jawas
- ○ Stalking the corridors of the Death Star
- ○ Desperate moments for out heroes
- ○ Searching for the missing droid
- ○ C-3PO
- ○ Luke Skywalker on the desert planet
- ○ The Rebel Troops
- ○ Princess Leia blasts the enemy
- ○ A proud moment for Han and Luke
- ○ A stormtrooper is blasted

- ○ Monitoring the battle
- ○ Luke and Leia
- ○ Han bows out of the battle
- ○ Han and Leia quarrel
- ○ The Dark Lord of Sith
- ○ Luke Skywalker's home destroyed
- ○ The swing to freedom
- ○ Im going to regret this
- ○ Princess Leia
- ○ Evacuate? In our moment of triumph
- ○ Han Solo covers his friends
- ○ Luke's secret yen for action
- ○ Aunt Beru Lars
- ○ Portrait of a Princess
- ○ Instructing the Rebel pilots
- ○ R2-D2 is inspected by the Jawas
- ○ Grand Moff Tarkin
- ○ Guarding the Millennium Falcon
- ○ Discussing the Death Star's future
- ○ The Empire strikes back
- ○ Raiding the Rebel starship
- ○ Envisioning the Rebel's destruction
- ○ Luke Skywalker
- ○ Readying the Rebel Fleet
- ○ The deadly grip of Darth Vader
- ○ Uncle Owen Lars
- ○ The young star warrior
- ○ Artoo's desperate mission
- ○ The rebel fighter ships
- ○ Death Star shootout
- ○ Rebels in the trench
- ○ Waiting at Mos Eisley
- ○ Member of the evil Empire
- ○ Stormtrooper
- ○ Soldier of evil

- Luke suspects the worst about his family
- Ben Kenobi
- Luke and Ben on Tatooine
- An overjoyed Han Solo
- The honored heroes
- R2-D2
- Darth Vader
- Luke poses with his weapon
- The marvelous droid-C3PO
- A pair of Jawas
- Fighting impossible droids
- Challenging the evil Empire
- Han Solo
- Fury of the Tusken Raider
- Creature of Tatooine
- The courage of Luke Skywalker
- Star pilot Luke Skywalker
- Anxious moments for the Rebels
- Threepio and Leia monitor the battle
- Non-nonsense privateer Han Solo
- Ben prepares to turn off the tractor beam
- Droids on the run
- Luke Skywalker
- Do you think they'll melt us down, Artoo?
- Corridors of the Death Star
- This is all your fault, Artoo!
- Droids trick the Stormtrooper!
- Guarding the Millenium Falcon
- It's not wise to upset a Wookiee!
- Bizarre inhabitants of the cantina!
- A narrow escape!
- Awaiting the Imperial attack
- Remember Luke, The Force will be with you
- A monstrous thirst!
- Hurry up Luke, we're gonna have company
- The Cantina musicians
- Distracted by Solo's assault

- Spiffed up for the Awards Ceremony
- Cantina denizens!
- Han and Chewie ready for action!
- Blasting the enemy!
- The Rebel fighters take off!
- Chewie aims for danger!
- Lord Vader senses The Force
- The Stormtroopers assemble
- A friendly chat among alien friends!
- Droids make their way to the Escape Pod
- Han and the Rebel Pilots
- Artoo-Detoo is abducted by Jawas!
- Inside the Sandcrawler
- Chewie gets riled!
- Leia wishes Luke good luck!
- A crucial moment for Luke Skywalker
- Luke, the Star Warrior!
- Threepio and Artoo
- Various droids collected by the Jawas
- The Jawas ready their new merchandise
- Director George Lucas and "Greedo"
- Technicians ready C-3PO for the cameras
- A touch-up for Chewbacca
- Directing the Cantina creatures
- The birthday celebration for Sir Alec Guinness
- Filming the Awards Ceremony
- The model builders proudly display their work
- Using the "blue screen" process for X-wings
- The birth of a Droid
- Shooting in Tunisia
- Inside the Millenium Falcon
- Photographing the miniature explosions

Stamp Collecting Kit

- ○ Filming explosions on the Death Star
- ○ Make-up for the Bantha
- ○ Dave Prowse and Alec Guinness rehearse
- ○ Flight of the Falcon
- ○ George Lucas directs his counterpart
- ○ Constructing the Star Destroyer
- ○ Aboard the Millenium Falcon
- ○ Chewbacca takes a breather
- ○ The princess
- ○ Animating the chessboard
- ○ Filming the sandcrawler
- ○ X-wings positioned for the cameras
- ○ Sir Alec Guinness/George Lucas
- ○ Filming Luke and Threepio

1980 Star Wars: Empire Strikes Back

○ Complete set (352)	75.00	150.00
○ Comp. sticker set (88)	40.00	80.00
○ Comp.ser.1 set (132)	30.00	60.00
○ Common ser.1 (1-132)	.20	.50
○ Comp.ser.1 stick.set (33)	15.00	30.00
○ Comm.ser.1 stick.(1-33)	.40	1.00
○ Comp.ser.2 set (132)	25.00	50.00
○ Common ser.2 (1-132)	.20	.50
○ Comp.ser.2 stick.set (33)	15.00	30.00
○ Comm.ser.2 stick.(1-33)	.40	1.00
○ Comp.ser.3 set (88)	25.00	50.00
○ Common ser.3 (1-88)	.25	.60
○ Comp.ser.3 stick.set (22)	10.00	20.00
○ Comm.ser.3 stick.(1-22)	.40	1.00

1980 Star Wars: Empire Strikes Back Photo Cards

○ Complete set (30)	45.00	90.00
○ Common card (1-30)	1.50	3.00

1983 Star Wars: Return of the Jedi

○ Complete set (220)	20.00	50.00
○ Comp. sticker set (55)	10.00	20.00
○ Comp.ser. 1 set (132)	15.00	30.00
○ Common ser. 1 (1-132)	.15	.40

○ Comp.ser. 1 stick.set (33)	5.00	10.00
○ Comm.ser. 1 stick.(1-33)	.20	.50
○ Comp.ser. 2 set (88)	10.00	20.00
○ Common ser. 2 (1-88)	.12	.30
○ Comp.ser. 2 stick.set (22)	5.00	10.00
○ Comm.ser. 2 stick.(1-22)	.20	.50

1993-95 Star Wars Galaxy

○ Complete set (365)	35.00	70.00
○ Comp.ser. 1 set (140)	15.00	30.00
○ Common ser. 1 (1-140)	.10	.25
○ Comp.foil prism set (6)	30.00	60.00
○ Common foil prism (1-6)	5.00	10.00
○ Comp.ser. 2 set (135)	10.00	20.00
○ Common ser. 2 (141-275)	.08	.20
○ Comp.etched foil set (6)	30.00	60.00
○ Common etch.foil (1-6)	5.00	10.00
○ Comp.ser. 3 set (90)	10.00	20.00
○ Common ser. 3 (276-365)	.10	.25
○ Comp. 1st day issue (90)	40.00	80.00
○ Common 1st day (1-90)	.40	1.00
○ Comp.empire chr.set (6)	30.00	60.00
○ Common Empire Chr.(1-6)	5.00	10.00
○ Comp.etch.prism set (6)	30.00	60.00
○ Common etch.prism (1-6)	5.00	10.00
○ Comp.Lucas foil set (12)	3.00	6.00
○ Comm.Lucas foil (1-12)	.20	.50

1995 Star Wars: Empire Strikes Back — Widevision

○ Complete set (144)	30.00	60.00
○ Common card (1-144)	.25	.60
○ Comp.Finest set (10)	50.00	100.00
○ Common Finest (1-10)	5.00	10.00
○ Finest stated odds 1:12		
○ Comp.poster set (6)	30.00	60.00
○ Common poster (1-6)	5.00	10.00
○ Poster stated odds 1:24		

Return of the Jedi tin container

Princess Leia Pop-Up comb

1995 Star Wars: Master Visions

○ Complete set (36)	20.00	40.00
○ Common card (1-36)	.50	1.25

1995 Star Wars: Widevision

○ Complete set (120)	30.00	60.00
○ Common card (1-120)	.25	.60
○ Comp.Finest set (10)	75.00	150.00
○ Common Finest (1-10)	7.50	15.00
○ Finest stated odds 1:11		

1996 Star Wars Finest

○ Complete set (90)	40.00	80.00
○ Common card (1-90)	.40	1.00
○ Comp.embossed set (6)	30.00	60.00
○ Common emboss. (1-6)	5.00	10.00
○ Comp.matrix set (4)	20.00	40.00
○ Common matrix (1-4)	5.00	10.00
○ Comp.refr.set (90)	700.00	1200.00
○ Common refr. (1-90)	7.50	15.00

1996 Star Wars: Return of the Jedi — Widevision

○ Complete set (144)	30.00	60.00
○ Common card (1-144)	.20	.50
○ Comp.Finest set (10)	50.00	100.00
○ Common Finest (1-10)	5.00	10.00
○ Finest stated odds 1:12		
○ Comp.mini post.set (6)	30.00	60.00
○ Comm.mini post. (1-6)	5.00	10.00
○ 3-D motion card	25.00	50.00

1996 Star Wars: Shadows of the Empire

○ Complete set (90)	7.50	15.00
○ Common card (1-90)	.10	.25
○ Comp.foil set (6)	15.00	30.00
○ Common foil (1-6)	2.50	5.00
○ Comp.embossed set (4)	15.00	30.00
○ Common embossed (1-4)	4.00	8.00

1997 Star Wars Trilogy: Widevision

○ Complete set (72)	15.00	30.00
○ Common card (1-72)	.20	.50
○ Comp.hologr.set (2)	20.00	40.00
○ Common hologr. (1-2)	10.00	20.00
○ Comp.laser. set (6)	30.00	60.00
○ Common laser. (1-6)	5.00	10.00
3-D card	10.00	20.00

1997 Star Wars Trilogy: Widevision Retail

○ Complete set (72)	20.00	50.00
○ Common card (1-72)	.30	.75
○ Comp.laser. set (6)	30.00	60.00
○ Common laser. (1-6)	5.00	10.00

1997 Star Wars: Vehicles

○ Complete set (72)	10.00	20.00
○ Common card (1-72)	.12	.30
○ Comp.peelaway set (4)	30.00	60.00
○ Comm.peelaway (1-4)	7.50	15.00
○ Comp. 3-D set (2)	20.00	40.00
○ Common 3-D (1-2)	15.00	20.00

1997 Star Wars: Widevision 3-D

○ Complete set (63)	50.00	100.00
○ Common card (1-63)	1.00	2.00
○ 3-D Death Star card	12.50	25.00

GENERAL MILLS
1977 Star Wars

○ Complete set (16)	25.00	50.00
○ Common card (1-16)	2.00	4.00

Boba Fett action figure with backpack

Radio-controlled R2-D2 disc-firing toy (Japan)

Radio-controlled R2-D2 toy (Kenner)

1978 Star Wars

⭘ Complete set (16)	20.00	40.00
⭘ Common card (1-16)	1.50	3.00

BURGER KING

1980 Star Wars

⭘ Complete set (36)	15.00	30.00
⭘ Common card (1-36)	.40	1.00

BURGER KING / COCA-COLA

1980 Star Wars: The Empire Strikes Back

⭘ Complete set (48)	15.00	25.00
⭘ Common sticker (1-48)	.20	.50

KELLOGG'S

1984 Star Wars Stick'R Trading Cards

⭘ Complete set (10)	25.00	50.00
⭘ Common card (1-10)	2.50	5.00

METALLIC IMPRESSIONS

1994 Star Wars Empire Strikes Back

⭘ Complete set (20)	20.00	40.00
⭘ Common card (1-20)	1.00	2.00

1995 Star Wars: Dark Empire

⭘ Complete set (12)	15.00	30.00
⭘ Common card (1-12)	1.50	3.00

MERLIN

1997 Star Wars

⭘ Complete set (125)	15.00	30.00
⭘ Common card (1-125)	.10	.30

Wonder Bread

⭘ Set of 16 cards

Scanlens (Australia)

⭘ Star Wars Set

⭘ TESB Set

⭘ ROTJ Set

O-Pee-Chee (Canada)

⭘ Series 1 with camera offer

⭘ Series 1 with diary offer

Canada Games

⭘ Set of four POG checklist cards

Mexico

⭘ Card packs

⭘ Chupa Chups insert stickers set of 24

⭘ Gum Card foil pack

⭘ Set of 30 gum cards

Culturama De Centroamerica, S.A. (Costa Rica)

⭘ Star Wars Sticker Pack

F.K.S. (England)

⭘ The Empire Strikes Back Sticker Set (225)

Topps England

⭘ Set of 10 cards from candy heads

Greece

⭘ The Empire Strikes Back Card pack

⭘ Pack of TESB cards

Monty Gum (Holland)

⭘ Full box

⭘ ROTJ card set

Japan

⭘ Star Wars cards

Brazil

⭘ Set of 23 stickers from candy

Topps Ireland

⭘ Box first series

ScoreBoard

Millennium Falcon Gold Card

Milk caps / pogs

⭘ Darth Vader Cap (Unlicensed)

⭘ Chase Caps Set

⭘ Slammers, gold Set

⭘ Slammers, black set

⭘ Slammers, silver set

Yoda Magic 8-ball (Kenner)

WALL DECORATIONS

Zanart Chromarts
- ◯ Bounty Hunters Framed and Matted
    (Wal-Mart)

Tin Signs International
- ◯ Star Wars
- ◯ The Empire Strikes Back
- ◯ Return of the Jedi

Zanart Chromarts
- ◯ Dark Forces
- ◯ TIE Fighter
- ◯ Rebel Assault
- ◯ Defenders of the Empire
- ◯ Bounty Hunters
- ◯ The Empire Strikes Back
- ◯ Star Wars
- ◯ Return of the Jedi
- ◯ AT-ATs
- ◯ Darth Vader
- ◯ R2-D2 and C-3PO
- ◯ Space Battle
- ◯ Star Destroyer
- ◯ Millennium Falcon
- ◯ B-Wings
- ◯ Star Wars Trilogy Movie Cards

A. H. Prismatic
- ◯ Millennium Flacon Hologram
- ◯ Darth Vader Hologram
- ◯ Millennium Falcon
- ◯ R2-D2 and C-3PO
- ◯ X-wing

THX VIDEO LITHOGRAPHS
- ◯ With logos from Blockbuster Video
- ◯ Without logos

WATCHES / CLOCKS

Clocks

BRADLEY TIME
- ◯ Darth Vader Clock Radio
- ◯ C-3PO and R2-D2 Talking Alarm Clock

Lucasfilm/Star Wars Fan Club
- ◯ Space Battle Clock

NOVELTY ITEMS
- ◯ R2-D2 Radio Watch
- ◯ Ewok Radio Watch
- ◯ 3-Way Anywhere Clock
- ◯ Digital R2-D2 and C-3PO

Watches

TEXAS INSTRUMENTS
- ◯ Star Wars digital; logo in black on silver face
- ◯ Star Wars digital; blue face plate with gray band
- ◯ Star Wars digital; blue face plate with gray band; with decals

BRADLEY TIME
- ◯ Star Wars C-3PO and R2-D2
- ◯ Star Wars C-3PO and R2-D2 child's size
- ◯ Star Wars C-3PO and R2-D2 child's with bigger copyright
- ◯ Star Wars digital C-3PO and R2-D2
- ◯ Star Wars, digital C-3PO and R2-D2 box variation
- ◯ Star Wars Darth Vader
- ◯ Star Wars digital Darth Vader
- ◯ Star Wars Ewoks
- ◯ Star Wars two Ewoks

Darth Vader watch (Bradley)

Yoda watch (Bradley)

Star Wars black digital watch (Texas Instruments)

○ Star Wars Yoda

○ Star Wars Jabba the Hutt

Fantasma

○ Darth Vader, with leather case

○ Darth Vader

○ Millennium Falcon

A. H. Prismatic

○ Darth Vader Hologram

○ Star Wars THX from Lucasarts Company Store

DURACELL

○ Darth Vader watch from eight-pack
    of AA batteries

Hope Industries

○ R2-D2 carded watch

○ Boba Fett carded watch

MISC. / OTHER

Animation Art

Cericels

○ R2-D2 and C-3PO

○ Boba Fett

Banks

ROMAN CERAMICS

○ R2-D2

○ C-3PO

○ Darth Vader

Metal Box Company

○ Darth Vader combination

Thinkway Toys (talking)

○ C-3PO & R2-D2

○ Darth Vader

Sigma Ceramics

○ Chewbacca

○ Yoda

Adam Joseph

○ Darth Vader

○ Princess Kneesaa

AUSTRALIA

○ Darth Vader ceramic

Coins

Silver and gold

RARETIES MINT

○ R2-D2 and C-3PO (10th Anniversary
logo on reverse)5

Raraties Mint

○ Luke and Leia 1 oz. silver

Action figure coins

Kenner STAR WARS

○ Amanaman

○ Anakin Skywalker

○ AT-AT

○ AT-ST Driver

○ A-wing Pilot

○ Barada

○ Bib Fortuna

○ Biker Scout

○ Boba Fett

○ B-wing Pilot

○ Chewbacca

○ Chief Chirpa

○ Creatures

○ C-3PO

○ Darth Vader

○ Droids

○ Emperor

○ Emperor's Royal Guard

○ EV-9D9

○ FX-7

**Star Wars grey /
blue digital watch
(Texas Instruments)**

- Gamorrean Guard
- Greedo
- Han Solo carbon freeze
- Han Solo rebel
- Han Solo rebel fighter
- Han Solo rebel hero
- Hoth Stromtrooper
- Imperial Commander
- Imperial Dignitary
- Imperial Gunner
- Jawas
- Lando Calrissian, rebel general
- Lando Calrissian with Millennium Falcon
- Luke Skywalker, rebel leader
- Luke Skywalker on Tauntaun
- Luke Skywalker with landspeeder
- Luke Skywalker on speeder bike
- Luke Skywalker with X-wing
- Luke Skywalker, Jedi Knight
- Luke Skywalker on Dagobah
- Logray
- Lumat
- Millennium Falcon
- Obi-Wan Kenobi
- Paploo
- Princess Leia as Boushh
- Princess Leia, rebel leader
- Princess Leia with R2-D2
- Romba
- R2-D2
- Sail Skiff
- Sail Skiff without Star Wars logo
- Star Destroyer Commander
- Stormtrooper
- Teebo
- TIE Fighter Pilot

- Too-One Bee
- Tusken Raider
- Warok
- Wicket
- Yak Face
- Yoda
- Zuckuss

KENNER DROIDS
- Kra Moll
- Thall Joeben
- Jann Tosh
- A-wing Pilot
- C-3PO
- C-3PO, protocal droid
- Boba Fett
- Tig Fromm
- Jord Dusat
- Kez-Iban
- Sise Fromm
- R2-D2
- Uncle Gundy

KENNER EWOKS
- Dulok Scout
- King Gorneesh
- Dulok Shaman
- Logray
- Wicket
- Urgah Lady Gornesh

Computer-Related

Mousepads

- Rebel Assault
- Darth Vader
- Luke and Leia

○ Millennium Falcon

○ Yoda

PepsiCo/British Petroleum Gas Stations (Singapore)

○ C-3PO

○ Darth Vader

Programs

○ Star Wars Visual Clips

○ Star Wars Audio Clips

○ Behind the Magic

○ Star Wars Trilogy CD-ROM Entertainment Utility

Manuals

○ Dark Forces Official Player's Guide

Furniture

Night lights

○ C-3PO night-light

○ C-3PO Dimensional night-light

○ Wicket night-light

○ Kneesaa night-light

○ Yoda night-light

○ Darth Vader night-light

Household

Telemania

○ Light Saber Universal Remote Control

Christmas Ornaments

HALLMARK

○ X-wing, TIE Fighter and AT-AT

○ R2-D2 and C-3PO

○ Millennium Falcon

Doorsigns

○ C-3PO

Household products

○ R2-D2 Frisbee

○ C-3PO Frisbee

○ X-wing Frisbee

○ Darth Vader Frisbee

○ Hoth tissue box with Han Solo

○ Hoth tissue box

○ Dagobah tissue box

○ Dagobah tissue box with R2-D2

○ Bespin tissue box

○ Star Wars growth chart

○ Star Wars checks with leather checkbook

○ Star Wars checks with vinyl checkbook

Telephone / telephone cards

P&J PROMOTIONS (ENGLAND)

○ Star Wars #1 (crew in cockpit)

○ B-Wings

Luggage / Carryalls

Duffle bags

○ Yoda barrel bag, red

○ R2-D2 and C-3PO barrel bag

○ Wicket barrel bag, blue

○ Wicket barrel bag, red

Luggage

○ Return of the Jedi 3-piece Suitcase Set

Tote

○ R2-D2 and C-3PO

○ Darth Vader

○ Wicket, blue

○ Wicket, red

○ Wicket, tan

○ R2-D2 and C-3PO ditty bag

Knapsacks

○ Darth Vader knapsack

Star Tours

○ Black hand bag

Lunch boxes

○ Star Wars, metal

○ Star Wars, plastic

○ Star Wars thermos

○ TESB, metal

○ TESB, plastic

○ TESB thermos

○ ROTJ, metal

○ ROTJ, plastic

○ ROTJ thermos

○ Ewoks, plastic

○ Droids, plastic

Magazines

Licensed

○ Star Wars Galaxy Magazine #1-#2

○ Star Wars Galaxy Magazine #3 Deluxe

○ Star Wars Galaxy Magazine #4

○ Star Wars Galaxy Magazine #5 with "Deluxe" Sticker

○ Star Wars Galaxy Magazine #6-#13

Non-Licensed

○ Rolling Stone — August 1977

○ Pizzazz — October 1977

○ Time — May 1980

○ 3-2-1 Contact — August 1980

○ Questar — August 1980

○ Fantastic Films — October 1980

○ Life — June 1983

○ Moviegoer — June 1983

○ Prevue - July 1983

○ Enterprise Incidents Star Wars and Star Trek Blueprints

○ US — June 20, 1983

○ Nintendo Power — November 1992

○ Sci-Fi Universe — July 1994 (Premiere Issue)

○ Time — February 1997

○ Vanity Fair — February 1999, bagged (The Phantom Menace)

Magnets

A. H. Prismatic

○ B-Wing

○ Millennium Falcon

○ TIE Interceptor and X-wing

○ Millennium Falcon and Star Wars Logo

○ Darth Vader

○ Imperial Star Destroyer

○ X-wing

○ TIE Fighter

○ AT-AT and Snowspeeder

○ Darth Vader

○ R2-D2 and C-3PO

○ X-WIng

○ Millennium Falcon

Ata Boy

○ Darth Vader

○ Ben Kenobi

○ C-3PO

○ R2-D2

○ Luke Skywalker with Light Saber

○ Stormtroopers

○ Yoda

○ Darth Vader

○ Luke and Leia

○ Darth Vader

○ Han Solo

○ R2-D2 and C-3PO

- ○ Space Battle
- ○ Return of the Jedi one sheet
- ○ Luke and Yoda
- ○ Han and Chewbacca
- ○ Crew in Cockpit
- ○ TIE Interceptor
- ○ Millennium Falcon
- ○ Darth Vader
- ○ X-wing
- ○ Princess Leia and R2-D2
- ○ Han on Taun Taun
- ○ X-wings
- ○ Luke Skywalker
- ○ Han Solo
- ○ X-wing and Vader TIE
- ○ Millennium Falcon
- ○ B-Wings
- ○ Star Wars one-sheet
- ○ The Empire Strikes Back One sheet
- ○ Ben Kenobi
- ○ Luke on Tatooine
- ○ Han Solo in Cockpit
- ○ Ben Kenobi with Lightsaber
- ○ Luke on Tatooine
- ○ Dewback
- ○ Luke in garage
- ○ Luke and Leia
- ○ Luke, Han, and Leia

Adam Joseph
- ○ Return of the Jedi
- ○ Wicket and Kneesaa

Patches

- ○ Revenge of the Jedi logo
- ○ Star Wars logo
- ○ The Empire Strikes Back logo

- ○ Vader in flames
- ○ Yoda
- ○ Lucasfilm Fanclub
- ○ Lucasfilm Fanclub, grey

Plaques and Sculpture, Limited Editions

Willits Designs
- ○ Creatures Film Frame

Applause
- ○ Darth Vader Collectible Figurine
- ○ Luke Skywalker Collectible Figurine
- ○ Shadows of the Empire statue
- ○ Jabba the Hutt and Princess Leia statue
- ○ Bounty Hunters statuette

Icons
- ○ Luke Skywalker Light Saber
- ○ Darth Vader's Light Saber

Illusive Concepts
- ○ Admiral Ackbar maquette

ScoreBoard
- ○ R2-D2 and C-3PO Plaque

Printed Material

Kenner
- ○ Jawa/Sand People rebate form

Poster magazines

Paradise Press
- ○ Star Wars #1-#18
- ○ The Empire Strikes Back #1-#5
- ○ Return of the Jedi #1-#3
- ○ Compendium

Product catalogs

Kenner
- ○ 1997 in Product booklet

Merchandise catalogs

ATARI
- ○ Star Wars arcade game ad

CBS FOX VIDEO
- ○ 1995 press kit for video release
- ○ 1990 video flyer
- ○ Entertainment Guide 1984
- ○ The Empire Strikes Back Video reservation form
- ○ Gift Pack Card

CEDICO
- ○ 1996 Calendar cover page

CENTER FOR THE ARTS
- ○ The Art of Star Wars booklet

DARK HORSE COMICS
- ○ Dave Dorman comic booklet
- ○ Dark Horse comics checklist cards
- ○ Cam Kennedy comic booklet
- ○ Dark Empire II comic booklet
- ○ Shadows of the Empire comic booklet
- ○ Droids comic booklet
- ○ Heir to the Empire comic booklet

DECIPHER
- ○ 1997 two-sided flyer
- ○ Dagobah pamphlet

DEKA PLASTICS
- ○ TESB flyer

DELUXE
- ○ 1996 catalog

DRAWING BOARD
- ○ 1977 catalog
- ○ 1980 catalog

ESTES ROCKETS
- ○ 1978 catalog
- ○ 1980 catalog

FACTORS
- ○ 1981 catalog
- ○ Poster samples

FAN CLUBS INC. (FRANCE)
- ○ Postcard
- ○ Merchandise flyer

GALOOB
- ○ Action Fleet toy mooklet
- ○ Micro Machine booklet (Germany)
- ○ Toys R Us coupon flyer

HAMILTON COLLECTION
- ○ Star Wars porcelain cards flyer
- ○ Space vehicles plates flyer

HBO
- ○ Star Wars press book sheets
- ○ HBO Guide 1983

ICONS
- ○ 1997 packet

MAX
- ○ Special effects ticket

JVC
- ○ Star Wars Nintendo press kit

KELLOGGS
- ○ C-3PO's Coupon Page

KENNER
- ○ First booklet
- ○ Toy booklet
- ○ X-wing toy nook
- ○ X-wing book #2
- ○ Burger Chef booklet #1
- ○ Burger Chef booklet #2
- ○ Death Star Batle toy book

- ○ Sweepstakes form
- ○ Cash refund booklet
- ○ The Empire Strikes Back toy book
- ○ Luke and Yoda toy book
- ○ Luke and Yoda toy book #2
- ○ Star Wars Collections book
- ○ Return of the Jedi toy book
- ○ Jabba the Hutt toy book
- ○ Classic Line toy nooklet 1995
- ○ Classic Line toy nooklet 1997
- ○ Return of the Jedi toy flyer
- ○ Win the Speeder Bike form
- ○ PDT-8 Instructions
- ○ Jawa refund flyer
- ○ How do you do it questionnaire
- ○ Sand People refund flyer
- ○ Imperial Troop Transport instruction
- ○ Death Star Backdrop from Display Arena
- ○ Trash Compacter Backdrop from Display Arena
- ○ Get Star Wars Cash form
- ○ Micro Collection X-wing Instructions
- ○ CAP-2 Instruction
- ○ Y-Wing Sticket Sheet
- ○ ISP-6 Instructions
- ○ Jabba the Hutt Dungeon instructions
- ○ INT-4 Instructions
- ○ Tri Pod Laser Cannon instructions
- ○ TESB Final Scene Backdrop from Display Arena
- ○ Micro Collection TIE Fighter sticker sheet
- ○ Micro Collection Hoth Turret Defense instructions
- ○ Free poster entry form
- ○ Endor Forest Ranger instructions
- ○ TESB Sweepstakes entry form
- ○ Imperial Attack Base instructions
- ○ Vehicle maintenance instructions
- ○ Ewok Village instructions

- ○ Micro Collection Snowspeeder instructions
- ○ Radar Laser Cannon instructions
- ○ Micro Collection Bespin Freeze Chamber instructions
- ○ Slave-1 instructions
- ○ Scout Walker instructions
- ○ Movie View instructions
- ○ Micro Collection Death Star World instructions
- ○ Micro Collection Bespin World instructions
- ○ Micro Collection Hoth Ion Canon instructions
- ○ TIE Interceptor instructions
- ○ Light Saber instructions
- ○ Micro Collection Bespin Control Room instructions
- ○ Speeder Bike instructions
- ○ Survival Kit instructions
- ○ Turret and Probot instructions
- ○ We really do care flyer
- ○ Destroy the Death Star game instructions
- ○ Creature Cantina instructions
- ○ B-Wing instructions
- ○ Nien Nunb flyer
- ○ Star Wars case sticker sheets
- ○ MLC-3 instructions
- ○ CAP-2 sticker sheet
- ○ AT-AT instructions
- ○ C-3PO case sticker sheet
- ○ X-wing instructions
- ○ MTV-7 instructions
- ○ Micro Collection Bespin Gantry instructions
- ○ Star Wars case photo guide
- ○ Rebel Transport instructions
- ○ Millenium Falcon Star Wars instructions
- ○ Millenium Falcon ROTJ instructions
- ○ Dagobah instructions
- ○ Ewok Assault catapult instructions
- ○ Jabba the Hutt instructions

○ Darth Vader case instructions

○ Y-Wing instructions

LUCASFILM

○ Shadows of the Empire two-sided, two-tone flyer

○ 10-year Convention Licensee card

○ THX Festival booklet

MANTON CORK CORP.

○ TESB Flyer

METAL BOX COMPANY

○ Flyer #1

○ Flyer #2

MILTON BRADLEY (GERMANY)

○ Toy booklet

OMNI COSMETICS

○ 1981 catalog

ORVIL REDENBOCKERS

○ Popcorn coupon with Star Tours

RIDELL

○ 1997 two-page catalog

ROMAN CERAMICS

○ C-3PO cookie jar color photo

○ C-3PO cookie jar black and white photo

○ R2-D2 cookie jar color photo

○ R2-D2 cookie jar black and white photo

○ Color photo of banks photo

SIGMA CERAMICS

○ Book ends color photo

○ 1981 catalog

SPORT STAMPS COLLECTOR'S ASSOCIATION

○ Star Wars stamps booklet

STUART HALL

○ Character pencils header

○ TESB flyer

TOPPS

○ Galaxy 3 sales sheet

20TH CENTURY FOX RECORDS

○ T-shirt order form from Star Wars soundtrack

WEST END GAMES

○ Coming This Fall flyer

Newspapers

○ Star Wars Newspaper

○ Yuma Sun Newspaper Revenge of the Jedi

○ Herald Examiner June 13-19 1977, with SW novelization

○ The Washington Post May 18, 1980, review of TESB

Miscellaneous

○ Star Wars Spectacular

○ Press Pass for San Francisco Exhibit

○ San Francisco Exhibit brochure

○ The Empire Strikes Back Video reservation form

○ Millennium Falcon model flyer

○ Kenner Free Anakin Skywalker form

○ Kenner Jawa and Sand People rebate flyer

○ Return of the Jedi toy flyer

○ Revenge of the Jedi toy flyer

○ Win This Speeder Bike form

○ First Ten Years card

○ Jedi Adventure entry form

○ THX Film Fest invitation

○ Radio Program guide from Iowa, blue

○ Bounty Hunter capture log, palitoy

○ Sweepstakes entry form

○ Set of 12 Star Wars business cards (Unlicensed)

Kenner

◯ Kenner Star Wars Cash

◯ Star Wars Special Edition Sweepstakes entry form

◯ Kenner Jawa rebate form

England

◯ England Walker Crisps sweepstakes entry form

◯ England winner letter

Germany

◯ German Video booklet

◯ German Kenner toy booklet

Shopping Bags / Show Bags

◯ Children's World premiere Shopping Bag

JAPAN

◯ Return of the Jedi shopping bag

◯ R2-D2 AND C-3PO shopping bag

GERMAN

◯ Comic book two-sided bag

Standees

FACTORS

◯ C-3PO

◯ Chewbacca

SALES CORPORATION OF AMERICA

◯ Darth Vader and Royal Guards

◯ R2-D2 and C-3PO

◯ Wicket

ADVANCED GRAPHICS

◯ Jawa

◯ Boba Fett

◯ Yoda

◯ Chewbacca

◯ Luke Skywalker

◯ C-3PO

◯ R2-D2

◯ Princess Leia

◯ Han Solo

◯ Stormtrooper

◯ Han Solo in Carbonite

◯ Darth Vader

◯ Darth Vader #2

◯ Imperial Guard

STAR TOURS

◯ Launch Ticket, Jan. 8, 1987

◯ Wrist band

◯ Star Wars pistol

◯ Picture frame

◯ Plastic shopping bag

◯ Cast, Family, and Crew boarding pass

◯ Inagural Flight Folder

◯ Boarding pass

◯ Wrist band

◯ R2-D2 PVC

◯ Chewbacca PVC

◯ Darth Vader PVC

◯ Stormtrooper PVC

◯ C-3PO PVC

◯ Opening Day watch

◯ M & M candy box

◯ Robot claw

◯ Han Solo street sign

Tinware

Chelnco INDUSTRIES

◯ Three-inch Darth Vader tin

Metal Box Company

◯ Macro tins

◯ Luke Skywalker

◯ Character tin

Cheinco Industries

◯ ROTJ tray

Containers

- ○ Darth Vader tin
- ○ Jabba the Hutt tin
- ○ Return of the Jedi character tin
- ○ Return of the Jedi carry-all tin
- ○ Cookie tin
- ○ Ewok Carry all tin
- ○ Lando Calrissian macro tin
- ○ Probot macro tin
- ○ Character tin

Trays

- ○ Return of the Jedi tray
- ○ Eowk lap tray with legs

Waste baskets

- ○ Return of the Jedi

Wallpaper

- ○ Star Wars
- ○ Return of the Jedi
- ○ Return of the Jedi border
- ○ Imperial Blueprint blue
- ○ Rebel blueprint blue
- ○ Ewoks green wallpaper
- ○ Ewoks green border

Checklist

Steve Fritz, a regular contributor to *Beckett Sci-Fi Collector* magazine, has been collecting Star Wars-related memorabilia since 1977, the year "Star Wars" first dazzled moviegoers around the world.

Matt Brady, who saw "Star Wars" 13 times within two weeks of its opening (good thing it came out in the summer!), has been following and collecting Star Wars items for more than 20 years.

Designer: Don Brown.

Thanks to Kathy Flood, Kyle Hogue, James Holzhauer, Tom Holzhauer, Doug Kale, Rudy Klancnik, Angie Luker, Brian Semling, Bill Sutherland and The Remember When Shop in Dallas for allowing us to photograph portions of their Star Wars collections for this book.

Special thanks to Lance Worth, owner of Star Force Collectibles, for contributing to the checklist for this book. To order Star Wars-related merchandise, e-mail Lance at theswstore@aol.com, or visit his Web site at www.starwarsstore.com.

Replica of the mask worn by David Prowse in "The Empire Strikes Back."